MW01484143

Daily Reflections on Divine Mercy:

365 Days with Saint Faustina

Daily Reflections on Divine Mercy:

365 Days with Saint Faustina

By
John Paul Thomas

My Catholic Life! Inc.
www.myCatholic.Life
www.DivineMercy.Life

Copyright © 2016, My Catholic Life! Inc.

www.myCatholic.Life
www.DivineMercy.Life
All rights reserved.

Diary numbers referenced in each reflection are taken from:

Divine Mercy in My Soul: Diary of Saint Maria Faustina Kowalska, Marian Press, English Edition Copyright © 1987 Congregation of Marians of the Immaculate Conception, Eden Hill, Stockbridge, MA 01262, All rights reserved.

The reference number identified in each reflection of this book allows you to see the primary source that the author of this book took *inspiration* from for that day's reflection. Though the primary text of the *Diary* is never quoted, nor are the reflections exact representations of the primary text, they do provide the foundational basis for the spiritual message shared in each reflection.

Saint Maria Faustina Kowalska, pray for us.

ISBN-13: 978-1530594658
ISBN-10: 1530594650

DEDICATION

To our Blessed Mother, the great Mother of Mercy. May we all imitate her motherly love.

To Saint John Paul II, the great pope of Mercy. May his intercession and example open the floodgates of Mercy.

To Saint Faustina, the hidden instrument of Mercy. May your witness and hidden life shine forth as a font of Mercy for all.

BY

JOHN PAUL THOMAS

"John Paul Thomas" is the pen name this priest picked in honor of the Apostles Saints John and Thomas and the great evangelist Saint Paul. This name also evokes the memory of the great Pope Saint John Paul II.

John is the beloved Apostle who sought out a deeply personal and intimate relationship with his Savior. Hopefully the writings in this book point us all to a deeply personal and intimate relationship with our God. May John be a model of this intimacy and love.

Thomas is also a beloved Apostle and close friend of Jesus but is well known for his lack of faith in Jesus' resurrection. Though he ultimately entered into a profound faith crying out, "my Lord and my God," he is given to us as a model of our own weakness of faith. Thomas should inspire us to always return to faith when we realize we have doubted.

As a Pharisee, Paul severely persecuted the early Christian Church. However, after going through a powerful conversion, he went on to become the great evangelist to the gentiles, founding many new communities of believers and writing many letters contained in Sacred Scripture. His letters are deeply personal and reveal a shepherd's heart. He is a model for all as we seek to embrace our calling to spread the Gospel.

Table of Contents

Introduction

The world we find ourselves living in today is a world of increasing violence, chaos, despair and interior isolation. It's a world in which so many are connected through the means of modern communication, such as through the daily headlines and social media. As a result, we are increasingly aware of the countless problems and tragedies that so many people face each and every day. These tragedies are becoming a means of constant curiosity, satisfaction, and even obsession for so many.

As a result of being constantly bombarded with the sensational problems in our world, we are drawn in, daily, to the painful drama of a fallen world. We see sin and its consequences everywhere we look and it takes a toll on our souls.

So how do we deal with this constant awareness of the evils, sins and pain of so many people on such a regular basis? The only answer to that is what this book is all about: The Divine Mercy.

The Divine Mercy must become the lens through which we see all things. It must become the filter for everything we take in and everything we give out. The Divine Mercy is so deeply needed today and we can rest assured that He who is divine, desires to bestow this precious gift in abundance.

What is Mercy? More specifically, what is The Divine Mercy? The Divine Mercy is the grace and love of God alive in our lives. It's God acting in us, upon us, and through us. It's God taking control of our lives and teaching us how to think and how to act. It's God possessing us so that we do not become possessed by the craziness of the world we live in.

The Divine Mercy of God is like a fountain of endless water in the midst of a parched and arid desert. It's the source of refreshment and newness of life that we all seek, whether we realize it or not. It's the deepest longing of our hearts and the only thing that will ever satiate the longing we have.

The world we live in tries to satisfy and satiate us through constant stimulation, excitement, drama and intrigue. The world is constantly offering us a false sense of happiness and fulfillment. The first step to discovering The Divine Mercy of God is to see the world for what it is. To see the lies and deceptions all around us and to turn our eyes to this font of truth and grace that we were made for. We need to turn to The Divine Mercy.

As a fountain of grace, gushing forth in an arid place, The Divine Mercy of God comes from a hidden source, keeps going and never runs out, and produces all that we need to find satisfaction in life. It's like a vast ocean that we are called to plunge into and enter its depths. It's endless and all-consuming.

Jesus has always given us images to try to describe the love He has for us. He is the loving Father, waiting for His wayward son to return. He is the Good Shepherd who seeks out the one stray sheep. He is the Good Samaritan who cared for the foreigner in dire need.

Of course, these can never fully explain the depths of His Mercy and love. Each image brings its own meaning to each person based on one's own personal experience and history. One recent gift that God gave to us is Sister Maria Faustina Kowalska. She was born on August 25, 1905 in Kraków, Poland and died October 5, 1938 in the same city at the age of thirty-three. At the young age of twenty she entered the Congregation of the Sisters of Our Lady of Mercy in Warsaw and was later transferred to Płock and then to Vilnius. It was in Vilnius where she met her confessor, Father Michał Sopoćko who helped her immensely with many mystical graces she received from God. Sister Faustina was graced to receive daily private revelations from Jesus by which He revealed to her the abundance of His Divine Mercy.

At the direction of her superior and Fr. Sopoćko and Jesus Himself, she kept a diary of these mystical experiences which is known, today, as *Divine Mercy in My Soul: Diary of Saint Maria Faustina Kowalska.*

The goal of this present book is to walk through the pages of her *Diary*, reflecting upon its messages over the period of a year. The *Diary* is reflected upon in a way that the reader will be able to easily ponder the message of Divine Mercy as it was revealed to Sister Faustina by Jesus Himself.

On April 30, 2000, Pope John Paul II canonized Sister Faustina on Divine Mercy Sunday. With her canonization, the messages of Saint Faustina continue to spread to a world so desperately in need of God's abundant grace.

On December 8, 2015, Pope Francis began an Extraordinary Jubilee of Mercy for the Church and world. This book is a fruit of that Year of Mercy and was written during that Jubilee Year so as to help each person who reads its pages to enter more deeply into the Divine Mercy of God for years to come.

Structure of this Book

Divine Mercy in My Soul: Diary of Saint Maria Faustina Kowalska is soon to become a classic spiritual book that everyone is encouraged to read in their lifetime. However, many find this invitation intimidating, not just because of the width of her book, but because of the depth of its message on The Divine Mercy in each of Saint Faustina's notebook entries. This book, *Daily Reflections on Divine Mercy*, was written with the hope of guiding you through Saint Faustina's *Diary* and her six notebooks of reflections. It can be used on its own to help you pause and reflect on the beauty of Jesus' messages to her, or as a companion book, as you simultaneously read Saint Faustina's *Diary*.

Daily Reflections on Divine Mercy offers 365 daily teachings, reflections and prayers based upon the pages of Saint Faustina's *Diary*. The structured way to use this daily reflection book is to do just that…reflect upon one page each day. However, some may feel called to skip around a bit, read a few reflections at a time, or return to a particular reflection through which God spoke to you. Therefore, though this book was written with the intent of providing one reflection for each day of the year, the best way to use it is any way you feel called and the way that benefits your relationship with God the most.

The first paragraph for each day offers this author's insights to the words and teachings of Saint Faustina. The section of her *Diary* used for the day's teaching is marked so that the reader can also read her *Diary* first hand so as to see the primary source that the author of this book took *inspiration* from for that day's reflection. Though the primary text of the *Diary* is never quoted, nor are the reflections of this book exact representations of the *Diary*, they do provide the foundational basis for the spiritual message shared in each reflection.

The second paragraph for each day offers a short reflection put more as a question to the reader. It offers the same insight in a different format so as to enter more deeply into the message of the day.

Finally, each daily reflection ends with a prayer focused upon the message and reflection for that day. The reader is encouraged to pray this prayer several times. Ideally, it is prayed first thing in the morning, again during the day, and again at night as an examination on how well the daily message was received.

As you seek to survive the world we live in, allow these pages to be a font of Mercy for you from God. Allow God's Divine Mercy to penetrate your heart so that you will know the abundance of His love and be more prepared to share that love with others.

Lord, as I begin my journey into Your Divine Mercy, help my heart to be open to all that You wish to bestow. Help me to hear You speak to me, to meet You personally, and to allow You to enter fully into my life. May I learn to trust You in all things as I encounter Your Divine Mercy. Jesus, I trust in You.

Introduction for Priests

Priest of God, you are called to be a continual Incarnation of the Mercy of God. How do you do this? Is it sufficient to simply preach about Mercy and strive to be merciful in your actions? No, the Mercy that a priest is to offer the Church and world is much greater.

The foundational act of Mercy that you can offer is to freely choose to be Christ's pierced and wounded Heart. It is only from His Heart that the blood and water of the sacramental life of the Church is poured forth. It is this wounded Heart that shines forth the rays of God's purification and sanctification on the Church and world.

You are called, in a unique way, to be a source of this outpouring by being pierced yourself. Here are five suggestions on how God wants to use your priesthood as an instrument of His Divine Mercy. These five actions bring about the purification and sanctification of the Church and world. They enable you to more fully share in the priestly ministry flowing from the wounded Heart of Christ.

1. *Choose* to embrace suffering freely
2. *Rejoice* in the suffering you embrace
3. *Offer* your suffering in union with Jesus to the Father
4. *Purify* the world through your offering
5. *Sanctify* the Church through your ministry

Choose to Embrace Suffering Freely

Freely choose to share in the suffering of the Heart of Christ. You uniquely do this as a priest by allowing yourself to receive, and then embrace, suffering. First, choose to accept, freely, every form of injustice that comes your way. Accept every ridicule issued forth by the world and by your own people. When criticized or condemned by another, don't fight back or defend yourself. Don't try to justify your actions or give into anger. Do not do this. Instead, accept every humiliation and suffering as from the Lord, for they are fully deserved as a result of your sins. This is the first step.

Secondly, allow yourself to feel a pain that is much deeper than mere criticism or persecution. The unique priestly pain that more perfectly shares in Christ's suffering is to *feel the pain in the Heart of Christ that results from the rejection of the Gospel.* Let your love for God's people be so strong and all-consuming that you also experience what Jesus experienced. Let yourself experience the rejection of the Gospel. Sure, there are many who will run to you and will be open to the love in your heart, receiving the Gospel with joy. This will be a great consolation to you. But there are many who will not. There are many who will not open themselves to the Mercy of God shining forth from your own heart and priestly ministry. You will find, if you share in the love of the Heart of Christ, that you long for these souls with such a holy longing. This longing will produce the sweetest and deepest pain. Choose that unique priestly suffering and embrace it wholeheartedly.

Rejoice in the Suffering You Embrace

Once you choose to freely embrace the sufferings in the Heart of Christ, as experienced in your priestly ministry, you must then go one step further. Make sure that the *free embrace* is also done with great *joy*. Do not only accept these sufferings, rejoice in them. Rejoice in every piercing of the Heart of Christ in your priestly ministry, be they great or small. Rejoice and be grateful to our Lord that you feel the pain that His Heart felt. Your joyful embrace of these sufferings will be a powerful witness that will also produce strength for you, personally, to move forward with the sacrifice of your life as a priest.

Offer Your Suffering in Union With Jesus to the Father

Freely *choosing* the sufferings in the Heart of Christ and *rejoicing* in those sufferings are not enough. The next step is to *offer* this freely chosen sacrifice to the Father in union with the Sacrifice of Christ on the Cross. Jesus is most perfectly a Priest when He offers His sufferings to the Father. The offering of His humiliations and the sufferings that came as a result of His rejected love are what enable Him to fulfill His mission as the perfect Priest. Join Him in that offering, especially as you offer the Holy Mass. Make this constant and intentional offering and you will find that you are living your priesthood on a whole new level.

Purify the World Through Your Offering

The Church, the world and our own soul are in desperate need of purification. Purification leads to sanctification and your *free, joyful, priestly offering* will purify. In this threefold act, you will be made holy, the Church will be made holy, and the world will be invited to receive the purification it needs.

Priest of God, do not underestimate the role you play in the purification and sanctification of the world. This role, of being an instrument of The Divine Mercy, is more than the charism to preach and to celebrate the Sacraments, you must *become* the sacrifice with Christ, offering your life for the salvation of the world. Embrace your sacrificial role as a way of perpetuating the outpouring of The Divine Mercy of God, shining forth from the wounded Heart of our Lord.

Sanctify the Church Through Your Ministry

Once you have built a habit of daily *embracing*, *rejoicing* and *offering* all suffering to the Father, in union with the Sacrifice of Christ made present on the altar, you must seek to sanctify God's people through every other aspect of your ministry. Your ministry is powerful and deeply needed in our world. Countless souls look to you to find our Lord. Do not be negligent in your ministry. Be zealous and conscientious in every way. Pray daily and allow the fruit of your prayer to direct the ministry of Christ made present through your priesthood. Teach, sanctify and shepherd the people of God, and do not grow weary of this privilege. The Lord chose you, He wants to use you in unimaginable ways.

Below is a priestly prayer you are invited to pray so as to more fully share in the Divine Mercy of the Heart of Christ:

Dear suffering and persecuted Lord, my flesh is constantly tempted to reject the suffering I am offered. Dear Lord, instead of running from this pain, I desire to choose it freely. You Yourself said, "No one takes my life from me, I lay it down freely." Lord, in imitation of You I choose, this day, every pain and every suffering I am given. I resolve that these swords which pierce my heart, over and over, shall not be imposed upon me. Rather, I thank You for the spear and for the soldier who thrusts that spear into my heart. I thank You for the pain that this produces. And I thank You for the honor and privilege it is to receive these constant piercings, especially those caused by the rejection of Your

Gospel. Lord, I not only accept them, I choose them and I choose them freely.

Dear Lord of Mercy, *the pain I feel and now freely choose must produce joy. Therefore, Lord, I also choose to rejoice in this suffering. I rejoice in each and every thrust of the spear. I rejoice in each and every sharp and piercing pain. I am eternally grateful to You, dear Lord, for the honor of feeling such pain. I thank You for allowing me to share in Your humiliation and suffering. I thank You that I may be mocked and looked down upon, that I may be scorned and laughed at. And, dear Lord, on an even deeper level, I thank You that I can share in the suffering You felt as a result of Your burning love for Your people. It is this pain which is far greater than mere humiliation. The pain that comes from loving Your people and not being able to sanctify them as a priest, as a result of their rejection of Your Mercy, is the deepest pain of all. Thank You, Lord, that this rejection hurts so deeply as a result of my love for Your people.*

Dear Lord, our High Priest, *You are the Priest and You are the Sacrifice. As Priest, You offer the Sacrifice of Your physical life, but You offer something even greater. You also offer the Sacrifice of all Your interior sufferings and longings. Lord, I offer this priestly sacrifice to Your Father with You. I offer it in union with Your own Sacrificial offering on the Cross. You experienced this pain, rejoiced in it as the fruit of Your love, and You then offered it to the Father. May I make this priestly offering with You.*

Dear Lord of Holiness, *the fruit of Your Sacrifice is the purification and sanctification of Your Church. Purification comes first, then sanctification. It is for the fruit of purification that I pray the most. Please purify Your Church and the entire world through the offering of my priestly sacrifice. Purify, first, my own wretched soul. But, from there, I beg You to pour forth the rays of Your Mercy, flowing from Your wounded Heart, to touch and sanctify the world. Let the wound of Your Heart be opened wide so that the blood and water may, indeed, gush forth. May my heart be a continual incarnation of Your wounded Heart, dear Lord. May my heart, which is pierced and offered, become a font of*

Mercy for the Church and world in our day and age. Please purify priests, bishops, laity and the entire secular world through the new spring of blood and water which must gush forth. I thank You, dear Lord, for the honor and privilege of being an instrument of Your Divine Mercy in this world. Jesus, I trust in You.

1

Introductory Reflections

We begin, today, reflecting upon an introduction to *Diary of Divine Mercy of Saint Faustina.* This treasure reveals Jesus' own Heart. It reveals His infinite love and Mercy. Ponder each short daily reflection throughout the day so that, by the end of the Year, you will have pondered everything Jesus revealed to this great saint.

In the pages to follow, you will discover many of the beautiful truths of God's Mercy. Some may strike you to the heart, while other may not. Pay attention, especially, to those reflections that jump out at you. Some may be deeply convicting and be the cause for you to reexamine your life. Do not be afraid to let the Lord speak to you in a powerful way and do not resist His message of Mercy. If a particular message does strike you, and if this is the result of God speaking to you and challenging you, then listen. Pray over that reflection and let the Lord speak. Do not be offended and do not turn away.

This first chapter presents a basic introduction and overview of Saint Faustina's *Diary* and the message of Divine Mercy in general. These first ten reflections are offered as a way of introducing you, by way of an overview, to the Heart of our Lord as revealed through the six notebooks Saint Faustina filled with her inspirations and private revelations. As you read through this initial chapter, allow yourself to be open to the newness of the concept of Divine Mercy and the devotion that flows from it. God deeply desires to pour out His Mercy in our day and age and the revelations given to Saint Faustina are a gift by which God is speaking to us in a special way.

Reflection 1: "The" Divine Mercy

When speaking of Divine Mercy we refer to this gift from God as "The Divine Mercy." By pondering "The" Divine Mercy we are more aware of two things: *First*, The Divine Mercy of God is real, definite and concrete. It is not some abstract concept but it is a reality that we must understand and enter into. *Second*, there is only One Divine Mercy. It is "The" one and only gift of God. All that God has given us is a gift and for this gift we are to be eternally grateful.

Strive, today, to make this a glorious year of reflection on The Divine Mercy of God. Make a conscious decision to enter into all God desires for you this year.

Lord, Help me to be attentive to The Divine Mercy You pour forth day and night. Help me, during this year of reflection upon Your Mercy, to allow it to transform my life in a real and profound way. Jesus, I trust in You.

Reflection 2: Creation as an Act of Mercy

In preparation for a deeper understanding of The Divine Mercy, we begin with the first gift of God: The Creation of the World. God, in His goodness, created the world out of nothing. This act of creating everything out of nothing reveals, in part, that creation is a pure gift from the goodness of God. This first act of love is His first act of Mercy.

Ponder the gift of creation throughout this day. Try and let your heart be filled with gratitude for all God created out of nothing. All creation reflects the splendor and beauty of our God.

Lord, I thank You for the wonderful gift of creation. I thank You for creating all things out of love and for being the one and only source of all that is. All of creation reveals Your merciful love. Jesus, I trust in You.

Reflection 3: Creation of the Angels as an Act of Mercy

In addition to the creation of the material world, God created the spiritual world out of nothing. The angels, as well as every human soul, are gifts of pure love from God. In creating the spiritual world, God created beings who are capable of knowledge and love. The creation of angels is a particular act of Mercy toward humanity in that angels are created not only to know and love God, but also to know and love humanity and to draw humanity into the heights of Heaven.

Spend time today reflecting upon the gift of all celestial beings. Our guardian angels, as well as all celestial beings, are precious gifts beyond our imagination. Try to let this reality sink in this day and be grateful for their working in your spiritual soul.

Lord, I thank You for the gift of the celestial hosts of Heaven. I thank You for the abundance of Mercy You bestow upon humanity through these celestial beings. May I always be open to Your grace which comes to me through them. Jesus, I trust in You.

Reflection 4: The Incarnation and Birth

When the eternal Son of God took on flesh in the womb of the Blessed Virgin Mary, human nature was changed forever. By uniting Himself with humanity, God raised our dignity to a whole new level. The Incarnation established a new unity between God and man and this is an act of the utmost Mercy on God's part.

Ponder, today, the great miracle of new life. Think of the birth of a small child. And then try to imagine this little and helpless child being the Creator of the Universe and the Savior of the World. What a gift of God's Mercy!

Lord, I thank You with profound gratitude for uniting Your divine soul with fallen humanity. I thank You for uniting Yourself with me, a sinner. May I always be in awe of the Mercy bestowed upon me through Your Incarnation. Jesus, I trust in You.

Reflection 5: Redemption of the World

The Incarnation was the greatest act of Mercy ever known. The only subsequent act that surpassed it was the act of Jesus dying on the Cross destroying sin and death by His blood. The redemption of the world, through the blood of the Cross, is an act of love and Mercy that we will never fully comprehend. We could never be grateful enough for this act since we will never fully fathom the depth of this love.

Spend time throughout this day pondering the crucifix. Hold it in your hand, look at it, imagine it and meditate on it. And then try and close your eyes from time to time pondering the full reality of the Crucifixion. This was not an easy sacrifice. It was especially difficult to receive such brutality and to say, "Father, forgive them, they know not what they do." This is Divine Mercy.

Lord, help me to gaze deeply upon Your Cross and to discover, within that Cross, an ocean of pure Mercy. Wash me in this sacrificial love and help me to obtain eternal redemption. Jesus, I trust in You.

Reflection 6: Image of Divine Mercy

The *Diary* of Saint Faustina calls us to a new form of devotion in various ways. The first way is through meditation on the sacred image of The Divine Mercy. Saint Faustina was asked by Jesus to have an image of His merciful love painted for all to see. It's an image of Jesus with two rays shining forth from His Heart. The first ray is blue indicating the font of Mercy coming forth through Baptism and the second ray is red indicating the font of Mercy poured forth through the Blood of the Holy Eucharist. During this year discover this image, place it in your home and ponder its meaning.

Ponder, today, the image of The Divine Mercy. Ponder, especially, the fact that no image will even come close to expressing the full depth of love pouring forth from the Heart of our Saviour. Grow in a desire for that Mercy as you ponder this sacred image.

Lord, You have poured out upon the world Your infinite Mercy coming forth from Your divine Heart. May I bask in that Mercy now and always. Jesus, I trust in You.

Reflection 7: Instituting the Solemnity of Divine Mercy

The *Diary* of Saint Faustina calls us to a new form of devotion in various ways. The second way is through the celebration of Divine Mercy Sunday. Jesus told Saint Faustina that He desired an annual solemn Feast of Mercy. This Solemnity of Divine Mercy was established as a universal celebration on the Eighth day of the Octave of Easter. On that day the floodgates of Mercy are opened and many souls are made holy. Plan on making this solemn feast a day of great celebration this coming year.

Begin, today, looking forward to this culminating Feast of Mercy! Reflect upon the fact that the mere institution of such a solemn feast is a powerful sign of the desire in the Heart of God to pour down His Mercy upon us.

Lord, may I always honor and celebrate the wonderful Feast of Mercy. May my heart, and the hearts of all Your faithful children, be open to all that You wish to bestow upon us through this feast. Jesus, I trust in You.

Reflection 8: Pondering the Chaplet of Divine Mercy

The *Diary* of Saint Faustina calls us to a new form of devotion in various ways. The third way is through the Chaplet of Divine Mercy. The chaplet is a treasured gift. It's a gift that we should seek to pray each and every day.

Discover this wonderful chaplet of grace and Mercy and pray it often. Repeat its prayer over and over and allow yourself to receive all the grace God wishes to bestow upon you through this gift.

Eternal Father, I offer Thee the Body and Blood, Soul and Divinity of Your dearly beloved Son, our Lord Jesus Christ, in atonement for our sins and those of the whole world. For the sake of His sorrowful Passion, have Mercy on us and on the whole world. Jesus, I trust in You.

Reflection 9: Meditation at the 3 O'clock Hour

The *Diary* of Saint Faustina calls us to a new form of devotion in various ways. The fourth way is by honoring the hour of Jesus' death every day.

"Father, into Your hands I commend my spirit!" And Jesus breathed His last...

It was at 3 o'clock that Jesus took His last breath and died upon the Cross. It was Friday. For this reason, Friday should always be seen as a special day to honor His Passion and ultimate Sacrifice. But since it took place at 3 o'clock, it is also important to honor that hour each and every day. This is the ideal time to pray the Chaplet of Divine Mercy. If the chaplet is not possible, it's at least important to pause and give thanks to our Lord every day at that time.

Lord, thank You for the gift of Your ultimate Sacrifice on the Cross. Thank You for surrendering Your life into the Father's hands in this total gift of Yourself. May I always honor that moment of the day and daily strive to imitate this perfect Sacrifice of love. Jesus, I trust in You.

Reflection 10: Apostolic Movement of The Divine Mercy

The *Diary* of Saint Faustina calls us to a new form of devotion in various ways. In addition to our personal devotion, we are called to be apostles of Mercy. Are you an apostle of Mercy? The Apostolic Movement of The Divine Mercy is a call from our Lord to actively engage in the work of spreading His Divine Mercy. This is done by spreading the message and by living Mercy toward others. This is no small task. To live Mercy and to spread it requires a total union with the Heart of Christ. It requires a deep purification of our souls from all that is contrary to the love and Mercy of Christ.

Ponder, today, how well you are as such an apostle of our Lord. You will most certainly be made aware of areas where you need to grow in Mercy so that you can better bring that Mercy to those around you. Stretch yourself and commit to being a better sign of the Heart of Christ in our world.

Lord, I know I am called to be an apostle of Your most holy Mercy. I often fail in being a witness to this Mercy in both my words and deeds. Renew within my soul a longing to spread this precious gift to all. Jesus, I trust in You.

2

Reflections on Notebook One

This First Notebook of Saint Faustina begins her private revelations given from the Heart of Jesus to her. She writes in a beautiful and simple way. Though, as mentioned in the introduction to this book, her actual words are not quoted in these reflections that follow, the messages that she received and articulated are presented.

In truth, her messages are those contained in Sacred Scripture and in the Tradition of our Church. And if you were to read through the lives and teachings of the saints, you would find the same revelations. God has always spoke to us throughout the ages. He speaks the one Message of Truth, and He reveals that Message in love. The revelations to Saint Faustina are one new way that God continues to speak and reveal Himself to us, His sons and daughters.

The reflections in this first chapter, based on the First Notebook, are intentionally short and focused. They are a way for you, the reader, to slowly and carefully listen to the Heart of God spoken to this great saint. Read these reflections slowly and prayerfully. Ponder them throughout the day and allow the Lord to speak to You the message He wants to give

Reflection 11: Adoration of the Most Holy Trinity

To comprehend, experience and offer The Divine Mercy of God we must first adore the Most Holy Trinity. If we could but fathom just a glimpse of true adoration of the Most Holy Trinity, we'd be left speechless, silent, overwhelmed with peace, contentment and joy (See *Diary* #5).

Strive, today, to ponder the mystery of the Holy Trinity and the privilege and duty we all have to adore in a profound way.

From a prayer to the Most Holy Trinity by St. Catherine of Siena:

> *O Eternal God! O Eternal Trinity! Through the union of Thy divine nature Thou hast made so precious the Blood of Thine only-begotten Son! O eternal Trinity, Thou art as deep a mystery as the sea, in whom the more I seek, the more I find; and the more I find, the more I seek. For even immersed in the depths of Thee, my soul is never satisfied, always famished and hungering for Thee, eternal Trinity, wishing and desiring to see Thee, the True Light.*
>
> *O eternal Trinity, with the light of understanding I have tasted and seen the depths of Thy mystery and the beauty of Thy creation. In seeing myself in Thee, I have seen that I will become like Thee.*
> *(Act of Thanksgiving to the Trinity, from St. Catherine's Dialogue on Divine Providence).*

Jesus, I trust in You.

Reflection 12: Adoring the Trinity in Your Soul

Adoration and love of the Most Holy Trinity take place, first, within our souls. Deep within each one of us God offers an invitation to adore Him. It is there, within the soul, that The Divine Mercy of God is encountered. It is there that we begin to learn what Mercy is all about (See *Diary* #6).

Spend time, today, pondering the indwelling of the Most Holy Trinity. God is there, living within your own soul. Seek Him, love Him and adore His divine presence.

Most Holy Trinity, I love You and adore You as you live within my soul. May I seek You more deeply and come to love You with all my heart. Jesus, I trust in You.

Reflection 13: An Invitation Within the Silence

Within our souls we must seek to hear God speak. He speaks in the silence and in the depths. He speaks, first, an invitation. He speaks an invitation to know Him and to encounter The Divine Mercy flowing from His Heart. The invitation is only that: an invitation. Jesus' Mercy is not imposed or forced. For that reason, the invitation requires a response and our response will determine the depth of Mercy we open ourselves up to receive. The response must be that of loving and holy obedience to Him Whom we hear speaking (See *Diary* #7).

Ponder two things: 1) Do I hear the invitation from Jesus to receive His Mercy? Hearing is the first step. Without hearing we cannot respond. 2) How do I respond to that invitation when I hear it? Am I willing to accept it on the deep and all-consuming level that it was offered? If so, it will change your life.

Lord, I know You constantly speak to me in the silent depths of my soul. Help me to be attentive to Your voice amidst the noise of this world. And as I hear You speak, help me to be generous in my response accepting Your gift of unlimited Mercy and grace. Jesus, I trust in You.

Reflection 14: True Satisfaction Only Through Mercy

So often in life we seek satisfaction from the passing things of the world. Be it riches, fleshly pleasure, prestige, or anything else, we must come to discover that one thing and one thing alone satisfies. The Divine Mercy of God is what we seek. Everything else is an illusion of satisfaction. If we try to satisfy our souls with other things, we will be left in interior sadness, anguish and disillusion. The Mercy of God keeps calling out and inflicts a sweet pain until we respond (See *Diary* #8).

Reflect upon the "sweet pain" inflicted upon your soul every time you try to find satisfaction in something other than God's Mercy. It's "sweet" because it's a rebuke of love from God calling us to trust only in His Mercy. It's "painful" in that we should allow ourselves to see clearly that attachment to anything not of God does not sit well in our soul. Every attachment to things outside of God's Mercy will ultimately be experienced as a burden.

Lord, may I allow myself to feel and experience Your Mercy calling me to turn from all that is not of You. Help me to run to Your Mercy in all things and to turn from those things that ultimately weigh me down and are painful and burdensome. Jesus, I trust in You.

Reflection 15: God is Relentless in His Love

Do you put God off? Do you ignore His constant calling? Do you drown out His voice with countless distractions? Know that God never ceases to call you. Listen to Him. Sometimes we put God off because we have judged, wrongly, that we will find satisfaction in life by some other means. It could be anything or everything that this passing world seems to offer us. There are so many enticements that bombard us every day that we can easily set God aside and fail to see that radically following Him is the key to happiness. When we radically follow Him in all things we open ourselves to His Divine Mercy and our life is changed. Don't be deceived by the allurement of anything that is not part of the Mercy of God. Do not put Him off (See *Diary* #9).

Today, honestly look at what draws you here or there. What is it that you daily seek or are seduced by. Recommit to radically seeking our Lord and let Him alone suffice in your life.

Lord, I am constantly drawn here and there and daily find myself seeking things that have nothing to do with You and Your Divine Mercy. Help me to see clearly and to have the wisdom and courage I need to turn only to You and to the abundance of Your unlimited Gift of Mercy. Jesus, I trust in You.

Reflection 16: Total Abandonment to God

Fall down before God. Prostrate yourself before Him. If you can, do it literally. If it would be a distraction to others then do it interiorly. Fall down prostrate before God and beg Him to show you His Divine Mercy and His most holy Will. There are many times in life when a simple prayer or two are not enough. What we need is to totally abandon ourselves before God. Of course this is what we must do every day all day. But in order to carry this interior disposition of total abandonment to God, we need concrete moments when we make this our absolute and complete act of surrender (See *Diary* #9).

Reflect, today, upon how deeply you pray. Do you only offer a few prayers here or there? Or do you take time each week to make an act of complete abandonment and surrender to God. Do you intentionally lay your life before our Great God in total love and trust? If you are not sure, then make sure you do so today.

Lord, I abandon myself into Your hands and trust in Your perfect goodness and Mercy. I prostrate myself before Your Divine Majesty and surrender to Your loving care. Jesus, I am totally Yours. Jesus, I trust in You.

Reflection 17: Turn to Our Blessed Mother in Prayer

Turn to our Blessed Mother in confident prayer. She holds you close to her Immaculate Heart and will direct you to her Son, Jesus. She is the perfect Mother, the Mother of All Grace. Trust in Her maternal care and intercession. She knows how to unlock the graces of the Mercy of her Son. And she longs to do so for you, her precious child (See *Diary* #11).

Sincerely reflect, today, upon your relationship with Mother Mary, the Mother of Mercy. Do you trust in her maternal care and intercession? If you are not wholeheartedly in love with our Blessed Mother and if you do not completely trust in her motherly care, spend time today opening your heart more fully to all that God wants to bless you with through her care. Don't be afraid to turn to her. She will point you to her Son.

Dearest Mother, my Queen. The Lord has entrusted to you the storehouse of His Mercy. The King of Kings has set you on a throne and given you charge of His Mercy. May I come to you, this day and always, seeking that which you wish to bestow upon me. Thank you for bringing me the Divine Mercy of your Son. Dearest Mother, pray for me. Jesus, I trust in You.

Reflection 18: Mercy Given Through Priests

Mercy is given in numerous ways. Among the many channels of Mercy, seek it through God's holy priests. Let His priest listen to you, speak to you and direct you. Priests are weak and are sinners. But in their weakness they are given a special grace to direct souls. The priesthood is one of the most visible channels of Mercy in our world. Pray for priests and let God speak to you through them (See *Diary* #12).

Call to mind the priests God has placed in your life. Pray for them, support them and encourage them, but also be open to the ways God pours forth His Mercy on you through them. God comes to you through them in countless ways if you but have eyes to see and ears to hear.

Lord, I pray, today, for all priests. May your sons become holy and radiant in all that they do. Forgive their sins and fill them with virtue. Help them speak Your Word and administer Your Mercy with fidelity and zeal. Thank You, Lord, for the gift of the sacred priesthood. Jesus, I trust in You."

Reflection 19: The Lord Accepts You in His Mercy

If you have truly sought out our Divine Lord, then ask Him if He will accept you into His Heart and into His holy Will. Ask Him and listen to Him. If you have surrendered all and offered yourself to Him, He will respond to you telling you that He accepts you. Once you are given to Jesus and accepted by Him, your life will change. Perhaps not in the way you expect it to change, but it will change for the good in a way beyond what you could have hoped for or expected (See *Diary* #14).

Reflect upon three things today: 1) Do you seek Jesus wholeheartedly? 2) Have you asked Jesus to accept your life without reserve by your total surrender? 3) Have you allowed yourself to hear Jesus say to you that He loves and accepts you? Follow these simple steps and let the Lord of Mercy take control of your life.

Lord, I do seek You with my whole heart. Help me to find You and to discover Your most holy Will. As I find You Lord, help me also to let You draw me to Your merciful Heart so that I may be totally Yours. Jesus, I trust in You.

Reflection 20: Give Your Life to Jesus Every Day

Once Jesus has accepted you and taken possession of your soul, do not worry about what is next. Do not expect life to change dramatically right away, but do not be surprised if it does. All that matters is that you daily renew the gift of yourself to His merciful Heart and that you allow Him to daily renew His acceptance of you in His Heart (See *Diary* #15).

Look, today, at how often you renew the total giving of yourself to Jesus. Do you do this daily? Have you done so today already? Make this a daily habit and let the Lord work miracles in your life.

Lord, I do renew my total self-giving to You this day and every day. May I turn to You always and abandon myself to You in every circumstance of life. Jesus, I trust in You.

Reflection 21: You Are Loved. Believe it.

Being accepted by Christ and living within His merciful Heart will lead you to discover how much He loves you. He does love you more than you can imagine. Let yourself begin to discover that love. Savor it, believe it, understand it and seek it all the more (See *Diary* #16).

Spend time today pondering one simple fact. You are loved. You are loved by our Divine Lord Jesus with a greater intensity than you could ever imagine. Sometimes we fail to recognize this fact and, as a result, fail to let His love enter in. Ponder His love for you today and let it begin to sink in more deeply.

Lord, I know that You love me but I also know that I do not understand the full extent of Your perfect love. Lord, help me to see Your love more clearly and to allow that love to sink into the depth of my soul. Jesus, I love You. Jesus, I trust in You.

Reflection 22: Abundant Mercy Stretching Your Soul

Encountering Jesus in your soul will have the effect of leading you to long for more. Do you long for more of Jesus? Do you long for His Mercy? The desire for Him, the desire for more, stretches us and enables us to receive more of His Mercy every day. Let the desire for our Lord grow in abundance within you (See *Diary* #18).

Spend time, this day, looking at your heart. Is it daily being stretched by the abundant Mercy of God? Do you see your soul being filled each day to the point that it feels like bursting with gratitude and overflowing with love? If not, know that God wants to pour this abundance of Mercy into your life.

Lord, I am open to You and Your Mercy. But I know there is so much more that You wish to pour out upon me. I know You desire to fill my soul with Your grace to such an abundance that it overflows with love of You and with love for others. Help me to be open to this abundance of Your love and Mercy. Jesus, I trust in You.

Reflection 23: When God Seems Silent

At times, when we seek to know our merciful Lord all the more, He will appear to be silent. Perhaps sin has gotten in the way or perhaps you have allowed your own idea of God to cloud His true voice and His true presence. At other times, Jesus hides His presence and remains hidden for a reason. He does so as a way of drawing us deeper. Do not worry if God seems silent for this reason. It's always part of the journey (See *Diary* #18).

Reflect, today, upon how present God seems to be. Perhaps He's abundantly present, perhaps He seems distant. Now set that aside and realize the fact that God is always intimately present to you whether it feels like it or not. Trust Him and know that He is always with you regardless of how you feel. If He seems distant, first examine your conscience, admit any sin that may be in the way, and then make an act of love and trust in the midst of whatever you may be going through.

Lord, I trust in You because I believe in You and in Your infinite love for me. I trust that You are always there and that You care for me in all moments of my life. When I fail to sense Your divine presence in my life, help me to seek You and to trust You all the more. Jesus, I trust in You.

Reflection 24: The Purification of Your Soul

The greatest suffering we can endure is a spiritual longing for God. Those in Purgatory suffer greatly because they long for God and do not yet fully possess Him. We must enter into the same purification here and now. We must let ourselves long for God. We must see Him and realize we do not yet fully possess Him and that He does not yet fully possess us because of our sin. This will be painful but is necessary if we are to be purified of all that keeps us from His perfect Mercy (See *Diary* #20-21).

Reflect upon the fact that the spiritual purification of your soul is necessary. Ideally, we will all embrace this purification here and now. Why wait? Do you seek to grow in this purification? Are you willing to let your soul long for God and have Him as your one desire? If so, all else in life will fall into place as you seek Him and as you discover the Divine Mercy that awaits.

Lord, please do purify my soul in every way. Allow me to enter into my purgatory here and now. Let my soul become consumed with a longing for You and let that desire overshadow every other desire in my life. Jesus, I trust in You.

Reflection 25: Interior Suffering - A Path to Mercy

As you grow deeper in your relationship with God you will have many moments of struggle as well as many moments of consolation. Do not be afraid of moments of dryness and interior suffering. They are necessary and part of God's method of holiness for you. In those moments, raise your eyes to Jesus. See Him in His glory and beg for His Mercy (See *Diary* #22-23).

Honestly look at your soul this day. Ponder all that you experience interiorly. Ponder, especially, all that only you are aware of. Do you find pain and suffering within? If it is a result of your own sin then rejoice that you see this. If it is the result of God purifying you, then rejoice that He loves you enough to let you go through this spiritual dryness. Look to Heaven and give thanks for all that you experience interiorly, for that which is in your soul is the presence of God leading you to Himself.

Lord, at times I feel dry and dead inside. At times I wonder where You are and if You are with me. Help me to have hope and trust in those moments and to see them as a pathway to a deeper faith in You. Help me to turn to You in these moments so that Your gates of Mercy may be opened ever more widely. Jesus, I trust in You.

Reflection 26: Uniting Your Interior Cross With Christ

As you grow closer to God you will, at times, feel many things. Some will encounter feelings of rejection by God. God never rejects us but the interior feelings of rejection can be real. This leads some to despair. If you find yourself, now or in the future, struggling with despair, do not be afraid and do not give in. Let God come to you in that experience and be present to you as you suffer through it (See *Diary* #23).

Continue to look deep within your heart this day. What do you see? If it is painful to look inside, then know that this pain is a pathway toward God. It may not make sense and it may be hard, but God the Father chose the path of the Cross for the Son. By embracing His Cross both exteriorly and interiorly, Jesus united all human nature to His Godhead. Let your suffering become a means of your holiness this day and a source of your unity with God.

Lord, as I continue to look deep within at my heart, help me to see myself as You see me. Help me to sort out any pain and suffering I carry. And help me to freely unite that interior pain to Your Cross just as You did. In this act, help me to discover The Divine Mercy You won for the world. Jesus, I trust in You."

Reflection 27: Trials Transformed Into Virtue

At times God imposes trials upon us. This is done out of love to strengthen us and to deepen our love of Him. Look at what it is that you experience as a trial. Ask God if this is from Him and what good He wants to bring from that trial. Trials always have the potential of making us stronger. If you are experiencing a certain interior trial in life, know that it is in this moment, more than any other, that God wants you to renew your trust in Him. Do it even if you do not feel like doing so. Trials are the greatest opportunity for our faith, hope and love to grow (See *Diary* #24).

What is your greatest trial right now? Identify whatever that may be and know that Jesus understands. Reflect upon Him coming to You in this moment, embracing this trial with you and in you. His strength is perfect and He will lead you through all things. In the process, He will fill you with a greater faith, hope and love.

Lord, I know that my trials in life are a grace. They may not seem to be at the moment I endure them but they are. Help me especially with (state your current intention). I surrender this situation to You and thank You for Your perfect love and strength. Jesus, I trust in You.

Reflection 28: Temptations to Complain

At times we are tempted to complain. When tempted to question God and His perfect love and perfect plan, know that this temptation is nothing more than that…a temptation. In the midst of that temptation to doubt and question God's love, renew your trust and abandon your self-pity. In this act you will find strength (See *Diary* #25).

What is it you have complained about the most this week? What most tempts you to be angry or annoyed? Has this temptation led to feelings of self-pity? Has it weakened your trust in God's perfect love? Reflect upon this temptation and see it as a means of growing in love and virtue. Often times our greatest struggle is a disguise for our greatest means of holiness.

Lord, I am sorry for the times I complain, get angry and doubt Your perfect love. I am sorry for any feelings of self-pity I have allowed myself to fall into. Help me, today, to let go of these feelings and to turn these temptations into moments of deeper trust and surrender. Jesus, I trust in You.

Reflection 29: Moments of Consolation

Just at the right time, if we are wholeheartedly seeking God every day, we will find that we receive a moment of consolation. It may be an unexpected peace or joy, we may feel enlightened and encouraged, or we may just sense the presence of God in our lives. Whatever the case may be, remember the moments of consolation you receive. They will not accompany us every day, but they are given at certain moments to remind us God is with us. Remember those moments, especially when you struggle (See *Diary* #27).

Reflect, today, upon the last moment you experienced some grace or consolation from God. What was He telling you through that experience? Ponder it, sit with it, be grateful for it and remember it. Let God speak to you through those experiences and never forget what He says.

Lord, I thank You for loving me with a perfect love. I thank You for coming to me in the moments I need You the most. Help me to always savor those moments and to remember them when life is difficult. Jesus, I trust in You.

Reflection 30: Obedience to God

One key to holiness is obedience. Adam and Eve fell from grace by disobedience and we are restored to grace by obedience. Obedience can be hard and requires a deep interior decision. Look for opportunities to be obedient to Jesus, especially when you do not feel like doing so. Those are moments of great grace and conversion (See *Diary* #28).

Work at being humble today. Only through humility will we see the pride that leads to disobedience. Pride leads to an obstinate persistence in our sin and a refusal to be open to God's abundant Mercy. Reflect upon your humble admission of sin and your willingness to repent of that sin so that you can imitate our Lord and His Blessed Mother in their act of perfect obedience to the Will of the Father in all things.

Lord, help me to humble myself before Your Divine Mercy. In that humility, help me to see not only my sin, but also the grace and Mercy You bestow so as to enter into the glorious life of grace You call me to live.

May I obey Your perfect commands of love and so be filled with Your Mercy. Jesus, I trust in You.

Reflection 31: The Unfathomable Nature of God

We cannot come to know God in His essence. He is beyond us and is unfathomable. But we can get to know God by seeing His actions in our lives and in the world. Look at His attributes. Look at His works. Look at what He has done in your life and in the lives of others. He is Omnipotent, All-Knowing, All-Loving and bestows all that is good in superabundance (See *Diary* #30).

Reflect, today, upon the unfathomable nature and essence of God. Knowing that we can never fully comprehend the perfection of God is the first step in coming to know Him more intimately. Humble yourself, this day, before the great mystery of our God and let His untouchable nature touch you in your heart.

Lord, You and Your ways are beyond me. Yet in the mystery of Your divine presence I come to know You. Help me Lord, as I ponder Your divine essence, to be drawn into a deeper love of You. Jesus, I trust in You.

Reflection 32: The Mercy of Forgiveness

Throughout life you will be hurt by the sins of others. This is inevitable. The real question to ponder is what you do with this hurt. Will you hold onto it and brew over it? Or will you forgive? But forgiveness is not enough. You must let the Divine Mercy so enter your soul that you not only forgive, but also allow this Mercy to fill your heart with compassion. You must let God's Mercy inspire you to love deeply. You must come to pray for those who have hurt you and, in doing so, dispense the grace of God to them. You are a dispenser of God's Mercy when you allow forgiveness to flow from your heart to the hearts of those who have hurt you (See *Diary* #31).

Humbly ponder your calling to be a dispenser of the compassion of the Heart of Jesus to those who have sinned against you. This is a high calling and requires deep surrender and love. But it is the only way to freedom and is the only way God's Mercy will fill your own soul.

Lord, I choose, this day, to forgive all who have wronged me. Help that act of Mercy to flood my mind, heart, passions, feelings and every part of my soul. May I be a dispenser of Your perfect and unlimited love for all. Jesus, I trust in You.

Reflection 33: The Mercy of Purification

Imagine if you could see your soul as God sees it. What would you see? How might God see your soul? Certainly He sees His precious child and looks at you with the greatest of love. But He also sees your sin, even the slightest sin. These sins, even the smallest imperfection, must be purged from within by His burning love. The Mercy of God becomes deeply "painful" in a spiritual way as it purifies. But this purification is necessary and is freeing. Purification must take place either now or through Purgatory. Choose the purification of God's merciful love now and you will not regret it (See *Diary* #36).

Reflect, today, upon God's love coming to you to purify your soul of every sin, even the smallest imperfection you may have. See this as an act of abundant Mercy. Be ready to feel the sweet pain of being purified and do not run from this. Your purification fills the Heart of our Lord with immense joy!

Lord, help me to see my soul as You see it. Help me to let Your merciful gaze cleanse me of every sin. In Your compassion, dear Lord, replace the sin in my life with Your Mercy. And help me to never run from You. Jesus, I trust in You.

Reflection 34: Satisfaction Only in God

So often in life we can fall into the trap of believing that we are satisfied by worldly and passing things. We can even be fooled into thinking that our sins satisfy us. And, in a strange way, they do offer a temporary satisfaction of sorts. But this "satisfaction" is shallow and deceptive. When we come to the profound realization that nothing but God satisfies our souls, we will be blessed and we will be disposed to seek true satisfaction only in Him. This comes about only through a deep recognition of His Mercy (See *Diary* #42).

Do you long to be satisfied by the Mercy of God? Do you seek out His Mercy every day? Reflect upon the desires within your heart. What do you long for? Let God's grace free you from unhealthy and foolish attachments and desires this day so that your desire can be set on God and God alone.

Come to me, Lord, in Your abundant Mercy and free me from the desires of this passing world. Help me to desire You above all things and, in that desire, to be overwhelmed by Your divine love. Jesus, I trust in You.

Reflection 35: Perceiving the Passion of the Lord

Do you understand the Passion of our Lord? Do you perceive His sufferings in your soul? This may, at first, seem undesirable. But perceiving the sufferings and Passion of our Lord is a great grace. As we perceive His suffering we must then encounter it and embrace it as our own. We must live His sufferings. In doing so, we begin to discover that His suffering is nothing other than divine love and Mercy. And we find that the love in His soul which endured all sufferings enables us to endure all things in love. Love endures everything and conquers everything. Let this holy and purified love consume you so that you can endure, in love, whatever you encounter in life (See *Diary* #46).

Gaze upon the crucifix this day. Gaze upon the perfect Sacrifice of Love. Gaze upon our God who willingly endured all things out of love for you. Ponder this great mystery of love in suffering and love in sacrifice. Understand it, accept it, love it and live it.

Lord, Your Cross is the perfect example of sacrificial love. It's the purest and highest form of love ever known. Help me to understand this love and to accept it into my heart. And as I accept Your perfect Sacrifice of Love, help me to live that love in all that I do and in all that I am. Jesus, I trust in You.

Reflection 36: The Mercy of Spiritual Friendship

At times we experience life as difficult. Our spiritual life may appear to be dry or overwhelming. Our sins may seem to be too much to overcome. And our relationship with God may appear to be too difficult to foster. But these experiences are all graces that invite us to seek God and His Mercy all the more. One grace we receive, as we need it, is the friendship and guidance God gives us through other people. Look for Jesus in others. Let His Heart reach out to your own in the people He places in your life. God is there, not only in the saint, but also in the sinner. Seek to discover the presence of God in each and every soul (See *Diary* #53).

Reflect, today, upon the people God has placed in your life. Begin with family but think also about each and every person whom you encounter. Some may be encountered only once, others every day. Know that God dwells in each and every one of them. Do you seek to meet God in each person? Try to look beyond the surface and discover the indwelling of God in them. When you see Him, you will find much more joy in each and every person you meet.

Lord, You promise to come to each one of us and to live within us. Help me to constantly seek Your divine presence in each and every person I meet. Help me to find You in my family and friends, in those at work or within the community. Help me to see You in the stranger I meet in passing and in every soul around me. As I discover You, help me to love You in them. Jesus, I trust in You.

Reflection 37: Humility, Simplicity and Sincerity

There are three words to ponder today: humility, simplicity and sincerity. Humble souls see and know God because they do not turn to themselves in their need. They recognize that God is everything and, without Him, they are nothing. Simple souls do not get caught up in the complications of life. They are able to cut through the countless distractions and live a childlike trust in God. Sincere souls are honest souls who are pure in heart and pure in their intentions. Be honest and truthful in your Christian walk and God will overwhelm all that is not of Him in your life (See *Diary* #55).

Ponder these three gifts today: humility, simplicity and sincerity. How well do you live them in your life? If one stands out as the most challenging, then sit with that for a while. Let God speak to you as you open your heart to His Mercy.

Lord, I open myself to the gifts of humility, simplicity and sincerity. Help me to see each of them as a precious gift that You wish to bestow upon me. May my mind comprehend them and my will embrace them. Jesus, I trust in You.

Reflection 38: Our Daily Duty

Some may feel as though their lives are dull and monotonous. It's the same thing day in and day out. Sometimes we seek some new excitement and experience. But if we allow grace to accompany us, every day, throughout the simple, repetitive and monotonous aspects of life, we will discover that life is always new. Every experience is a new moment and a new grace. We will never tire of our daily duty because we will discover God alive and fresh in every moment, making all things fruitful and beautiful. When we live in the grace and Mercy of God, we will discover joy and excitement in the smallest and most repetitive of daily activities. This is a Mercy that enables us to love life every moment of every day (See *Diary* #62).

Reflect upon your daily duty. Are there things that you dread each day? Are there chores that seem thankless and tiresome? Try to envision our Lord walking with you through every moment of every day. See Him with you in every activity, be it great or small. Know that every action you do can become an act of love for God. When this happens, you will begin to discover greater joy in life.

Lord, I invite You to accompany me on my daily journey. I invite You into every big and small duty I have. Help me to make everything I do, be it big or small, living gifts of love to You. In that love, help me to joyfully discover and live in your Mercy. Jesus, I trust in You.

Reflection 39: Loss of Spiritual Consolation

It's easy to fall into the trap of thinking that, because we follow Jesus, we should be continually consoled and comforted in all we do. Is that true? Yes and no. In one sense, our consolation will be continual if we always fulfill the Will of God and know we are fulfilling it. However, there are times when God removes all spiritual consolation from our soul out of love. We may feel like God is distant and experience confusion or even sadness and despair. But these moments are moments of the greatest Mercy imaginable. When God seems far away, we should always examine our conscience to make sure it is not a result of sin. Once our conscience is clear, we should rejoice in the sensory loss of God's presence and the loss of spiritual consolations. Why? Because this is an act of God's Mercy in that He is inviting us to obedience and charity despite how we feel. We are given the opportunity to love and serve even though we sense no immediate consolation. This makes our love grow stronger and unites us more firmly to the pure Mercy of God (See *Diary* #68).

Reflect upon the temptation to turn from God the moment you feel down or distressed. See these moments as gifts and opportunities to love when you do not feel like loving. These are opportunities to be transformed by Mercy into the purest form of Mercy.

Lord, I choose to love You and all whom You put in my life regardless of the way I feel. If love of others brings me great consolation, I thank You. If love of others is difficult, dry and painful, I thank You. Lord, purify my love into a more authentic form of Your Divine Mercy. Jesus, I trust in You.

Reflection 40: Entering the Heart of Our Lord

A speck of dust or a grain of sand are somewhat insignificant in most circumstances. No one notices one speck or one grain in the yard or even on the floor of a home. But if either were to enter the eye, this grain or speck becomes immediately noticeable. Why? Because of the sensitivity of the eye. So it is with the Heart of our Lord. He notices the smallest of our sins. Often times we fail to see even our most grievous sins, but our Lord sees all things. If we wish to enter into His

Heart of Divine Mercy, we must allow the rays of His Mercy to shine on the smallest speck of sin in our souls. He will do so gently and lovingly, but He will help us to see and experience the effects of our sin, even the smallest ones, if we let His Mercy in (See *Diary* #71).

Look into your soul today and ask yourself how aware you are of the smallest sin. Do you let His Mercy shine within, illuminating all that is there? It will be a joyful discovery when You let Jesus reveal to you what He sees so clearly.

Lord, I pray that Your Divine Mercy so fills my soul that I see all that is within me as You see it. Thank You for Your gentle and compassionate Heart and for being attentive to the smallest detail of my life. Thank You for being attentive to even the smallest of sins that I need to overcome. Jesus, I trust in You.

Reflection 41: Feelings Versus Faith

At times, the truth can seem to be of little consolation to us. That may seem strange to say. But if we are honest, there are times when we suffer interiorly despite the fact that we know what we are feeling is not true. For example, we may KNOW that God is with us and loves us, but we may not feel that or experience that at one time or another. We may KNOW that God is in control of our lives, but we may feel like in our life He is nowhere to be found. This apparent contradiction between what we know and what we feel or experience can be hard to reconcile interiorly. But it is a grace to experience this apparent contradiction. It's a grace because when we do not feel the presence of God or, even worse, if we feel like we have been rejected by God, we are given, in that moment, an incredible opportunity for holiness. Why? Because faith is not about feeling, it's about knowing. It's about knowing the truth in all things, believing that truth and living in accord with that truth despite what we may feel or experience interiorly.

Though this can be hard to understand, it's a truth we must believe and embrace if we are to grow in perfection and holiness (See *Diary* #77).

Reflect upon the truths of our faith that appear to be in contradiction to what you feel. Which will you rely upon? That which comes through faith? Or that which directs your feelings? The best way to transform your misleading feelings is to make a profound act of faith in all that God has spoken and revealed. Make that act of faith and let God, in His time, redirect all that you interiorly feel and experience. Trust Him!

Lord, I offer You, this day, that which I feel and experience in my life. Specifically, I offer you (state an intention). Help me to rely upon You and all that You have spoken as my guide. Help me to allow Your truth to enter into my life and redeem me. Jesus, I trust in You.

Reflection 42: Unjust Treatment Offered as Atonement

There are many times in life when we are treated unjustly. As a result, our first instinct is to fight back, defend ourselves and see to it that justice is done. But is that what Jesus did? No, He remained silent and accepted all injustice as a sacrifice for the atonement for our sins. He was the Just One who took upon Himself all injustice. In doing so, He did two things. First, He appeased the justice of the Father as He offered this injustice for the atonement of sin. This is the central and deepest mystery of our faith. Second, He invites us to follow His example. In doing so, we are invited to accept unjust treatment and meet it with Mercy and forgiveness. This requires great inner strength and love. But if we are able to unite our own unjust suffering to that of Christ's, we will win more souls for God than if we fought back winning a temporary satisfaction of earthly justice (See *Diary* #81).

How have you been treated with cruelty and injustice? Reflect upon that which has been most painful to you and know that this suffering is an opportunity for you to atone for the sins of the world. You are enabled, by uniting your hurt to the suffering of Christ, to win many souls for God. This is the mystery of our redemption. It's a mystery we are invited to enter into, live and offer to God as a sacrifice of love. Take a step in this direction, today, and watch the hurt you have dissolve into Mercy.

Lord, I offer You, this day, my hurt, pain and all suffering. I especially offer You the injustices I have faced in life. May You remove all bitterness from my heart and replace it with Your Divine Mercy. Jesus, I trust in You.

Reflection 43: Patience in Hardship

What is of greater value to God? To be successful in all that you set out to do, or to endure every hardship of life in patience and peace? Many may struggle with this question and want to choose both. Certainly it is easy to see that if we set out to accomplish the Will of God and all that He wants of us, this will be of great value for the Kingdom of God. But what if that which God calls us to do is to embrace patience and peace in the midst of some apparent struggle of difficulty? Is this of great value? Yes, it is of the greatest value because in this process of growing in patient endurance we are made truly holy (See *Diary* #86).

What is it that is most difficult for you each and every day? What tries your patience more than anything? Do you look at this trial as an "obstacle" to happiness and fulfillment in life? If so, try to look at it from a different perspective. Try to see any difficulty as an opportunity for virtue and, in particular, an opportunity for personal growth in patience. Growing in that virtue delights the Heart of Christ and is of the greatest value for His Kingdom.

Lord, I surrender to You those things that are most difficult for me. I thank You for them and believe that they are what will help me grow in holiness more than anything. I especially offer to You (mention any personal difficulty). Receive it Lord as my offering to You and give me the grace to transform it into love and Mercy. Jesus, I trust in You.

Reflection 44: The Lord's Gaze Casts Out Fear

Do you know that our Lord gazes upon you, night and day, with perfect love and affection. Do you know that He knows every detail of your life and walks with you through everything? This may be hard to believe because we cannot hear Him audibly, see Him with our eyes, or touch Him with our hands. But His intimacy is much deeper than the physical world. His intimacy is one that looks into our soul and loves us. His gaze of love, if we let it, will cast out all fear in life (See *Diary* #90).

What is it that you fear the most? What is it that causes you the greatest anxiety? Today, try to identify the cause of your fear. And when you do, know that our Merciful Lord has already seen it all. He is aware of your situation and looks at you with love. The key is to look back at Jesus, to seek His face within your own soul, and to gaze back at Him with love. There, by looking intently upon our Lord, you will find the courage you need to let go of all that weighs you down and you will allow His grace to lift you on high.

Lord, help me to turn my eyes from all my fears. Help me, instead, to seek out Your loving gaze and to allow that gaze of love to cast out all that is not of You. Lord, if I could only see Your face, radiant and beautiful, living in my soul, I would be consoled and comforted in all things. Jesus, I trust in You.

Reflection 45: Holy Communion

Sometimes we do not feel like going to Mass or may be deeply distracted as we approach the Blessed Sacrament. Perhaps one of the best things to do in this case is to live in holy obedience. Jesus wants you to receive Holy Communion every Sunday and every holy day because He knows you need it. He knows that this Food from Heaven is necessary for you to obtain happiness. It is the Gift of Himself given freely and completely to you. And He commands you to attend the Holy Mass for your own good (See *Diary* #105).

Reflect, today, upon your attitude toward the Gift of the Holy Mass. Do you attend faithfully? That is, without fail? Are you perfectly obedient to our Lord's command? And when there, how do you enter into the Mass? Do you pray and seek Him inviting Him into your soul? After you receive Holy Communion do you kneel and truly pray? We could never be grateful enough for this sacred Gift. Make your next Holy Communion one that sets you down a path of holiness.

Lord, I thank You for this precious Gift of Holy Communion. I thank You for coming to me in such an intimate and perfect way. Help me to always be obedient to Your command to receive You faithfully. And each time I am privileged to receive You, help me to be fully attentive to Your divine presence. Jesus, I trust in You.

Reflection 46: Daily Duties are the Path to Heaven

It is true that our goal must be Heaven. We must constantly keep our eyes on this eternal reality. Why? Because in comparison to this passing world, Heaven is all that ultimately matters. So how do we keep our focus on Heaven without becoming complacent with our daily duties? Would it be proper to neglect our daily duties and responsibilities so as to spend all day at church? Certainly not. In fact, the way to Heaven centrally involves living our duties well. We must live them in fidelity, diligence and love. Living well while we are here on Earth is the best preparation for Heaven (See *Diary* #107).

Reflect, today, upon Heaven. See this glorious reality for what it is. It is eternal happiness! It is unending joy! Look, also, at all that God calls you to do each and every day. Be it small menial tasks or great and visible works, do everything for the love of God, seeing each responsibility you have been given as a central way by which you obtain eternal joy.

Lord, I invite You to enter into my life daily. I pray that everything I do may be done as an act of love for You and for others. May I fulfill all my responsibilities well and, through them, obtain the glorious life that awaits. Jesus, I trust in You.

Reflection 47: Recognizing the Needs of Others

Often times we can be so preoccupied with ourselves and our own problems that we fail to see the struggles and needs of those around us, especially those of our own family. At times, because we are so self-consumed, we run the risk of adding unnecessary burdens to those we are called to love and care for. We need to foster within our hearts true Christ-like empathy and compassion for each person we encounter (See *Diary* #117).

Do you see the needs of those in your life? Are you aware of their wounds and burdens. Do you sense when they are sad and overwhelmed? Do you add to their sorrow or do you seek to lift them up? Reflect, today, upon the great gift of an empathetic and compassionate heart. True Christian empathy is a human response of love for those all around us. It's an act of Mercy we must foster so as to lighten the burden of those entrusted to our care.

Lord, help me to have a heart full of true empathy. Help me to sense the struggles and needs of others around me and to turn my eyes from myself to the needs that they carry. Lord, You are full of compassion. Help me also to be filled with compassion for all. Jesus, I trust in You.

Reflection 48: Silence

Our tongue can build others up, or cut them down. Our tongue also has a direct effect upon our own soul. When the tongue speaks words inspired by God, we grow in holiness. When the tongue speaks words not from God, we do great damage to our souls and others. The goal is not so much exterior silence; rather, it's interior silence. Interior silence means that we think and pray before we speak. It means we are interiorly recollected and in tune with the voice of God speaking silently and gently within our conscience. This interior recollection of God is necessary if we are to dispose ourselves to speak the words of Mercy to others at the right time and in the right way (See *Diary* #118).

Seek, today, to become a person who is continually in tune with the voice of God within your own conscience. God's language is real and transforming. His language is one of silent but clear communication with us. God is always speaking, are you hearing? Try to silence your own thoughts and ideas today so that you can hear only what He has to say to you.

Lord, I offer You my words this day. May I speak only what You inspire me to speak. May I hear only what You wish for me to hear. Help me, Lord, to enter into a deep and continual recollection of You, and in the silence of my heart may I meet Your divine presence so that I may share You and Your Mercy with others. Jesus, I trust in You.

Reflection 49: Being Misunderstood

We are called to be saints. And if we walk down that road, we will be called to live heroic virtue. Heroic virtue will not always be understood by others. In fact, in the opinion of worldly wisdom, heroic and holy virtue is foolishness. But we must not allow the opinions of worldly "wisdom" to confuse us, tempt us or distract us from the road of true virtue (See *Diary* #126).

Are you misunderstood, at times, because you are striving to live a holy life? Do others give you this or that bit of advice which seems to be in contradiction to the voice of God in your own conscience? Reflect upon the road of virtue God is calling you down. The world does not understand the road of virtue, Mercy and forgiveness that we are called to embrace. The world does not understand that we must accept injustice at times in silence and trust. The world does not understand the joy we have when we suffer for the sake of Christ. Keep your eyes on the voice of God as He speaks to you in your conscience and do not let the opinions of others or the world lead you astray.

Lord, help me to walk the road of heroic virtue. At times, this road will leave me misunderstood. And, at times, others will tempt me to turn away from Your divine voice. Help me, at all times, dear Lord, to hear only You and to be obedient only to Your most holy Will. Give me wisdom, strength and courage to always follow Your divine ways of Mercy. Jesus, I trust in You.

Reflection 50: Hearing the Voice of God

It's true that, throughout your day, God is speaking to you. He is constantly communicating His truth and His direction for your life, and He is constantly bestowing His Mercy. The problem is that His voice is ever so gentle and silent. Why? Because He wants all of your attention. He will not attempt to compete with the many distractions of your day. He will not impose Himself upon you. Rather, He waits for you to turn to Him, to set aside all distractions, and to be attentive to His quiet but clear voice (See *Diary* #130).

Do you hear God speak? Are you attentive to His gentle interior promptings? Do you let the many distractions of your day drown out God's voice or do you habitually set those aside, diligently seeking Him all the more? Seek His interior promptings this day. Know that these promptings are signs of His unfathomable love for you. And know, that through them, God is seeking your full attention.

Lord, I love You and desire to seek You in all things. Help me to be aware of the ways in which You speak to me day and night. Help me to be attentive to Your voice and to be led by Your gentle hand. I give myself to You completely my Lord. I love You and wish to know You more fully. Jesus, I trust in You.

Reflection 51: Pure Love

Do you love with a pure love? What does this form of love look like? Pure love is one that flows directly from the Heart of Christ to and through your life. This holy love has beautiful characteristics. First, it is plentiful. When we love with the Heart of Christ we love in abundance. There is no limit to how much love we can share. It's like the brightness of the sun at noon casting rays on all below. Second, it's ingenious, doing what is pleasing to God. It is not cautious or calculated.

It does not hesitate or evaluate. Rather, the wisdom of love is immediate and knows in each moment how to radiate God's love. And third, it is happy. Even when love calls one to heroic sacrifice there is great delight in this total self-giving (See *Diary* #140).

Reflect, today, upon how fully you love with a pure and generous heart. Do you give of yourself in abundance? Is it a delight to serve without counting the cost? Do you easily find ways to show Mercy to others and delight in doing so? Ponder these questions today and pray that the Lord shines through all you do.

Lord, please purify my heart and make it holy. Let my heart be joined to Yours so that I may radiate all that You are. Shine through me in abundance and guide me in a pure love. Jesus, I trust in You.

Reflection 52: Daily Prayer

What is it that makes your soul beautiful? Prayer. What is it that keeps you from sin? Prayer. What is it that fills you with hope? Prayer. What is it that leads you on the road to holiness? Prayer. Prayer is the key to all things. Without prayer, each and every day, you are directionless in life and are left to your own wisdom and ability, which is a frightening state to find yourself in (See *Diary* #146).

Do you pray? Not just every so often, at Sunday Mass or before meals. But do you truly pray every day? Do you spend moments alone speaking to God from the depths of your heart and let Him speak back to you? Do you allow Him to initiate a conversation of love with you every day and throughout the day? Reflect, today, upon your habit of prayer. Reflect upon whether you can honestly say that your daily conversation with God is the most important conversation you have each day. Make this a priority, the number one priority, and all else will fall into place.

Lord, I know my prayer life is weak. I know I need to give more attention to my daily conversation with You. Help me to form a strong habit of prayer, each and every day, so that this life of prayer will become the guiding light of my life. Jesus, I trust in You.

Reflection 53: Difficulties in Prayer

There are both interior and exterior difficulties we encounter as we attempt to form a daily habit of prayer. Interior difficulties: discouragement, dryness, heaviness of spirit and temptations. These difficulties are overcome through patience and perseverance. Exterior difficulties: fear of what others may think or say, and setting time aside. These difficulties are overcome through humility and diligence (See *Diary* #147).

Try to set a daily time for prayer and do not be afraid if others become aware of this commitment. Make it a time where you set aside every distraction and diligently focus in on the voice of God. Try kneeling or, even better, try laying prostrate before our Lord. Kneel or lay prostrate before the crucifix in your room or before the Blessed Sacrament at church. If you do, you will most likely encounter immediate temptations and difficulties. Do not be surprised by this. You will find yourself thinking about other things that you should do and you may even worry that others will discover you are praying. Persevere, stay focused and pray. Pray deep and pray hard and you will see the good fruits of this commitment in your life.

Lord, give me the strength I need to persevere through any and every difficulty that tries to keep me from my prayer with You. Make me strong so that I can set aside any struggle or temptation that comes my way. And as I press on in this new life of prayer, please take my life and form me into a new creation in Your love and Mercy. Jesus, I trust in You.

Reflection 54: Praying for Others

It's easy to presume that everyone we know will go to Heaven. This, of course, should be our hope. But if one is to attain Heaven, there must be a true interior conversion. Each person who enters Heaven is there because of a personal decision to give one's life to Christ and to turn from sin. How do we assist those around us on this journey? The most important thing we can do is pray for them. At times, praying for another can seem futile and unproductive. We may not see any immediate results and conclude that praying for them is a waste of time. But do not let yourself fall into that trap. Praying for those whom God has put into your life is the greatest act of Mercy you can show them. And your prayer may actually be the key to their eternal salvation (See *Diary* #150).

Think about those whom God has placed in your life. Be it family, friends, co-workers or simple acquaintances, you have a duty to pray for them. Your daily prayer for those around you is an act of Mercy that can easily be exercised. Call to mind those in your life who may be in most need of prayer today and pause to offer them to God. As you do, God will pour grace upon them and He will also reward your own soul for this act of generosity.

Lord, in this moment I offer to You all those who are in most need of Your Divine Mercy. I pray for my family, friends and for all those whom You have put in my life. I pray for those who have hurt me and for those who have no one to pray for them. Lord, I especially pray for (mention one or more people who come to mind). Fill this child of Yours with an abundance of Mercy and help him/her on the way to holiness. Jesus, I trust in You.

Reflection 55: Creation Reflects the Mercy of God

Think of the most beautiful sunset possible, gleaming over the wide ocean in the evening with the sky radiant in color. Or think of the majestic mountain peaks piercing through a bright blue sky, or a mighty waterfall, pouring forth from the heights. All of these gifts of creation are glorious, beautiful and breathtaking. But none of them compares to the glory and majestic splendor of God's Mercy (See *Diary* #158).

God's Mercy, when properly perceived, will take our breath away and more. We will be left in awe of His perfect unfailing love for us. But sometimes we cannot see His Mercy for what it is. Reflect, today, upon your own experience of God's Mercy. Do you perceive all that He is? Have you had moments when you have encountered His Mercy in an overwhelming way within your own soul? If not, spend time seeking to comprehend Him. Humble yourself before Him and ask Him to peel back the veil of His infinite love for you.

Lord, I know You are merciful beyond what I could ever imagine. But there are many times when I do not understand You and Your ways. I feel distant and lost. Help me to know Your love. Help me to see the splendor and beauty of who You are. And help me, as I come to discover You, to be drawn into a burning love for You. Jesus, I trust in You.

Reflection 56: The Good News of the Day

The secular world is filled with bad news. The newspapers, talk shows, and other forms of media thrive on sensational and exaggerated tragic events to keep our attention. And we, for our part, are often eager to share the latest gossip or criticism. But what about the good news? What about the news of God's abundant Mercy? How often are you fascinated by this message and how often do you seek to tell the world about the Mercy of God? (See *Diary* #164)

Reflect upon that which you are most eager to share with others each and every day. Think about the joy you receive when you speak of the goodness and Mercy of God. Look for opportunities, this day, to share some joy about how great God is. Look for ways that God's beauty and goodness have been evident this week and speak of His workings to those God puts in your path.

Lord, help me to turn from the sensationalism and negativity of the secular world. Help me, instead, to turn my eyes to You and Your glory. Give me courage, wisdom and love so that I may speak of You freely and joyfully. Lord, You are the Good News that must be shared everywhere. Help me to be a willing instrument. Jesus, I trust in You.

Reflection 57: A Fire Within Your Soul

Is it possible to know that someone has a deep interior life of prayer? Even though this is "interior" and is a spiritual reality, is it possible to sense this externally? Most certainly it is. In fact, the deeper one's life of prayer the more that this interior life will shine forth for others to see (See *Diary* #172).

How about you? What does your soul radiate? When people see you, what do they sense? Certainly our perceptions of people can be wrong at times, but when God is alive in an abundant way, those who have eyes to see will see. Those who are hungry for God will perceive His presence in your life and be fed by Him through you. Reflect upon how radiant your interior life is. And reflect upon whether or not that burning flame within is shining forth for others to see. And if it is not burning brightly and intensely, today is a good day to kindle that fire within.

Lord, I invite You to come live in my soul. I invite You to fan into flame the spark of faith that I have. May Your love and Mercy become a blazing fire in me so that I may be consumed by You and so that others may sense Your love through me. Jesus, I trust in You.

Reflection 58: Purification of Sin

Sin is a topic that many avoid. We don't like to think about our sins. We don't like to admit to them, and we often rationalize them as if we do not have any. We can easily come up with excuses for this "sin" or that. But here is another perspective on sin. We should see our sin, no matter how grave or how small, as a little twig. And then we should see a huge and blazing fire. If you were to throw that twig into the fire it would immediately be consumed. The twig is our sin and God's Mercy is so powerful that it can easily and quickly consume it. We only need to be willing to admit our sins and throw them into that burning fire of Divine Mercy (See *Diary* #178).

Can you admit your sin? Do you see your sin? No excuses, just honesty. And are you willing to confess your sins, all of them, in the sacramental fire of Reconciliation? If you are aware of the power of God's Divine Mercy and His willingness to eliminate your sin, you will have no fear in honestly admitting it and letting Him consume it. Try to examine your conscience today and face that which you need to let God burn away.

Lord, Your Divine Mercy is infinite and most powerful. It is a flame of burning love. Help me to trust in You enough to face my sin honestly and to throw it into the fire of the Sacrament of Reconciliation. May I trust in this glorious Sacrament and, in so doing, may I trust in You. Jesus, I do trust in You.

Reflection 59: "Oh, Blood and Water…"

After Jesus' death, one of the soldiers came to Him and was ordered to make certain He was dead. So that soldier pierced His precious body with a lance and immediately blood and water gushed forth from His wounded Heart. This has been prayerfully reflected upon throughout the ages and has been seen as a sign of the Sacraments of Baptism and Holy Communion and the fact that the Blood of the Holy Eucharist and the Water of Baptism spring forth directly from the ultimate sacrificial gift of Jesus' perfect sacrifice of the Cross (See *Diary* #187).

Renew, today, your gratitude for these Sacraments of God's abundant Mercy. Ponder the fact that they were made possible only because Jesus was willing to sacrifice His life out of love for us. Let His sacrifice, this day, fill your own heart with gratitude and awe as you think about the price He willingly and freely paid so as to redeem us.

Lord, Your love is seen clearly in the Sacrifice of Your Cross. You held nothing back from us as You poured out Your Mercy to the last drop on the Cross. Help me to see and understand this great mystery of sacrificial love. Fill me with gratitude for all that You have done and help me to imitate this total self-giving toward others. Oh blood and water, which gushed forth from the Heart of Jesus, as a font of Mercy for us, I trust in You.

Reflection 60: Dealing With a Spiritual Drought

Does your soul feel like it is in a spiritual drought at times? Do you wish you could have greater spiritual consolation in your daily life. This is a common struggle and one that we should not worry about. The primary goal of our spiritual life is to do the Will of God. Often times, a certain spiritual dryness actually helps us live the Will of God more than powerful and emotional spiritual consolations. God knows what we need and will give it to us when we need it (See *Diary* #195).

Consider, today, how you feel inside. What does your spiritual life feel like today? Now set that thought aside and realize that there is only one thing that ultimately matters: doing the Will of God, not feeling the will of God. "Doing" must be our food and our strength. Contrast your *feelings* with your *doing* today and ask our Lord for grace to live out His Will.

Lord, I recommit myself to Your most holy Will this day. I commit myself to doing that which You command. May I see all Your commands as commands of love. May my embrace of these commands bring strength and peace to my soul, especially during times of spiritual dryness. Jesus, I trust in You.

Reflection 61: Where Happiness Comes From

Could you be happy if you were in prison? Or what if you were called at a young age to enter a cloistered monastery and live in seclusion throughout your life? Could you find happiness if you were living in the utmost poverty having barely enough to feed your family each and every day? The answer is "Yes." You most certainly can find happiness within any situation of life. How? Happiness is not dependent upon the external circumstances of life that are out of our control. It is not dependent upon wealth, physical freedom, or even vocational callings. Happiness is found exclusively in the fact that we are intimately united with our divine Lord, no matter what our vocation or life circumstances. The question is whether or not you are in love with God (See *Diary* #201).

Reflect upon your interior relationship with our Divine Lord. Do you know and love Him in a real and personal way? Do you daily communicate with Him and spend your day in His presence? Is your life of prayer alive and flourishing? Does your heart burst forth with a burning love? God loves you perfectly. Love Him back and you will find your source of your joy in life.

My dear Lord, help me to love you with a burning love. Help me to know You in the most intimate and personal of ways. I know that my happiness depends solely upon my love for You. May that love in my heart increase daily so that I may be one with You in all things. Jesus, I trust in You.

Reflection 62: The Small Sacrifices of Life

Do small sacrifices matter? Sometimes we can think that we should try to do great things. Some may have ideas of grandeur and dream of accomplishing some great feats. But what about the small, monotonous, daily sacrifices we make? Sacrifices such as cleaning, working, helping another, forgiving, etc.? Do the small things matter? Most certainly. They are a treasure we give to God like none other. Small daily sacrifices are like a field in the open valley, filled as far as the eye can see with beautiful wild flowers. One flower is lovely, but when we commit ourselves to these small acts of love all day, every day, we present to God a flowing field of endless beauty and magnificence (See *Diary* #208).

Reflect upon the small things today. What is it that you do each day that tires you and seems boring or unimportant. Know that these acts, perhaps more than any other, present you with a glorious opportunity to honor and glorify God in a magnificent way.

Lord, I offer You my day. I offer You all that I do and all that I am. I especially offer You the small things I do every day. May each action become a gift to You, offering You honor and glory throughout my day. Jesus, I trust in You.

Reflection 63: How do You Speak to Others?

When speaking to others, the love and Mercy of God must flow from our lips. But how? What should our speech look like? One way to examine our speech to others is to look at it in the light of how we should speak to God. When speaking to God we should speak with honesty, simplicity, humility and confidence. Think of a sincere child praying to God. This pure soul exudes these qualities well. So should we. And if we speak to God with these qualities, they will also be a good guide in our speech to others (See *Diary* #215).

Reflect upon the people and conversations that you have. Do you speak from pride or sarcasm? Do you struggle with gossip or carelessness? Think about what your speech would look like if it were honest, simple, humble and confident in God's grace. Joy will be present in each conversation guided by these virtues.

Lord, help me to speak with a merciful and kind heart. Help me to guard my tongue against malice and harshness. Forgive me for my past indiscretions and help me to be a mouthpiece of Your generous and merciful Heart to others. Jesus, I trust in You.

Reflection 64: Hearing the Voice of God

When you are at church, do you listen? Specifically, do you listen to the voice of God? Often times we sit and listen to the homily and our mind wanders and we miss all or most of what was said. Where does your mind wander? The truth is that sometimes a wandering mind is from the Lord. Sometimes there may be one thing said at Mass that our Lord then places on your heart to ponder. Do not be afraid to let Jesus take you on a spiritual journey while at Mass or while alone in prayer. He may often wish to speak a homily directly to your soul (See *Diary* #221).

Reflect, today, upon how well you reflect. True prayerful reflection is not simply daydreaming. It's not distraction that leads us to obsess or worry about this thing or that. Prayerful reflection is a way of letting God take hold of our imagination so as to lead us into His Truth. He often desires to lead us into a particular word of Truth that we need to know at that time. How well do you do this? Ponder your prayerful pondering and next time you pray do not be afraid to let God take control.

Lord, I know You speak to me day and night. Help me to hear Your sweet voice and to listen. Help me to allow You to take control of my prayer and to direct me into all You have to say. Jesus, I trust in You.

Reflection 65: Jesus My Master

Are you comfortable calling Jesus your Master? Some may prefer to call Him "friend" or "shepherd." And these titles are true. But what about Master? Ideally, we will all come to give ourselves to our Lord as the Master of our lives. We must not only become servants, we must become slaves. Slaves of Christ. If that doesn't sit well then ponder simply what sort of Master our Lord would be. He would be a Master who directs us with perfect commands of love. Since He is a God of perfect love, we should have no fear abandoning ourselves into His hands in this holy and submissive way (See *Diary* #228).

Reflect, today, upon the joy of being totally given over to Christ and being completely under His direction. Ponder every word you say and every action you do being lived in obedience to His perfect plan. We should not only be completely free from any fear of such a Master, we should run to Him and seek to live in perfect obedience.

Lord, You are the Master of my life. I submit my life to You in a holy slavery of love. In this holy slavery, I thank You for setting me free to live and love as You desire. I thank You for commanding me in accord with Your most perfect Will. Jesus, I trust in You.

Reflection 66: Justice Through Mercy

Some people, day in and day out, experience the harshness and cruelty of another. This is quite painful. As a result, there can be a strong desire for justice so that the person causing pain be held accountable. But the real question is this: What is the Lord calling me to do? How shall I react? Shall I be an instrument of God's wrath and justice? Or shall I be an instrument of Mercy? The answer is both. The key is understanding that God's justice, in this life, is implemented through His Mercy and through the Mercy we show to those who offend us. For now, accepting the darts of another in virtue is the way to God's justice. We grow in patience and strength of character as we live in this virtuous way. In the end, at the end of time, God will right every wrong and all will come to light. But, for now, our mission is to bring the justice of God by offering His unlimited and continual Mercy (See *Diary* #236).

Reflect upon any hurt you may have received from another. Reflect upon any words or actions that have stung you to the heart. Try to accept them in silence and surrender. Try to unite them to the sufferings of Christ and know that this act of humility and patience on your part will bring forth God's justice in His time and in His way.

Lord, help me to forgive. Help me to offer Mercy in the face of every wrong I encounter. May the Mercy You place in my heart be the source of

Your own divine justice. I entrust to You all that I cannot comprehend in this life and know that, in the end, You will make all things new in Your light. Jesus, I trust in You.

Reflection 67: Hidden Roses of Love

Some acts of love are meant to be shared only between lovers. Acts of the utmost intimacy and self-giving are precious gifts of love shared in the secrecy of a relationship of love. This is also the case with our love of God. We should regularly look for ways to express our most profound love of God in ways that are known only to Him. In return, God will lavish merciful graces upon us, interiorly, known to us alone. These mutual exchanges of love are powerfully transforming to a soul and the source of the greatest delight (See *Diary* #239).

Reflect, today, upon the intimacy of your relationship with our merciful God. Do you take great delight in showering Him with Your love? Do you do so, regularly, in the secrecy of your heart. And do you open yourself to the countless ways that God bestows these graces of love upon you?

Lord, may my interior acts of love for You be as a rose I place before Your Divine Heart. May I delight in offering You my love and may I rejoice, always, in the secret and profound ways that You lavish Your love upon me. Jesus, I trust in You.

Reflection 68: Rejoicing in the Goodness of Others

When others do well, how do you react? Most likely when a child does well it brings delight to your soul. But what about others? A sure sign of a merciful heart is the ability to sincerely find joy in the good that others do. Too often jealousy and envy get in the way of this form of Mercy. But when we delight in the goodness of another and rejoice when

Daily Reflections on Divine Mercy

God is at work in someone's life, this is a sign that we have a merciful heart (See *Diary* #241).

Think about the person that you may find it difficult to offer praise and honor. Who is it that is difficult to compliment and encourage? Why is it this way? We often point out their sin as the reason but the true reason is our own sin. It may be anger, envy, jealousy or pride. But the bottom line is that we must foster a spirit of joy in the good works of others. Reflect upon at least one person you find it difficult to love in this way and pray for that person today. Ask our Lord to give you a merciful heart so that you can rejoice as He works through others.

Lord, help me to see Your presence in others. Help me to let go of all pride, jealousy and envy and to love with Your merciful Heart. I thank You for working in many ways through the lives of others. Help me to see You at work even in the greatest of sinners. And as I discover Your presence, please fill me with a joy that expresses itself with authentic gratitude. Jesus, I trust in You.

Reflection 69: Struggles Tempt Us to Doubt

We all encounter struggles in life. The question is: "What do you do with them?" Too often, when struggles come our way we are tempted to doubt the presence of God and to doubt His merciful help. In fact, the opposite is true. God is the answer to every struggle. He alone is the source of all we need in life. He is the One who can bring peace and serenity to our soul in the midst of any and every challenge or crisis we may face (See *Diary* #247).

How do you deal with struggles, especially ones that turn into crises? How do you deal with daily stress and anxiety, problems and challenges, worries and failings? How do you deal with your own sins and even the sins of others? These, and many other aspects of our lives, can tempt us to turn from total trust in God and lead us to fall into doubt. Reflect upon how well you handle daily struggles and adversity. Do you remain confident each and every day that our Merciful Lord is there for you as the source of peace and serenity in the midst of a turbulent ocean? Make an act of trust in Him this day and watch as He brings calm to any storm.

Lord, You and You alone can bring peace to my soul. When I am tempted by the difficulties of this day, help me to turn to You in perfect trust placing all my cares on You. Help me to never turn from you in my despair but to know with certainty that You are always there and are the One to whom I must turn. I trust You, my Lord, I trust You. Jesus, I do trust in You.

Reflection 70: Identifying with the Suffering Christ

Which image of Christ are you more comfortable with? Which image do you more easily identify with? The image of Christ glorified as King of all? Or the image of the beaten and suffering Christ? In the end, we will fix our eyes on the Lord in glory and majesty and this will be our delight for eternity. However, while we are pilgrims in this earthly life, the suffering Christ should dominate our mind and our affection. Why? Because it reveals the closeness of Jesus to us in our own weakness and pain. Seeing His wounds disposes us to reveal our own wounds with confidence. And seeing our own brokenness in truth and clarity helps us love our Lord more deeply. He entered into suffering through His Cross. He wants to personally enter your suffering as you gaze upon His wounds (See *Diary* #252).

Look at the wounds of Jesus this day. Try to call His suffering to mind throughout the day. His suffering becomes a bridge to us. A bridge that allows us to enter His divine Heart which loved to the last drop of blood.

Lord, I gaze upon You this day. I gaze upon every wound and ever scourge that You bore. Help me to draw close to You in Your pain and help me to allow You to transform my own sufferings into an instrument of divine union. Jesus, I trust in You.

Reflection 71: Our Littleness and Nothingness

It is a grace from God to see ourselves as we are. And what will we see if we see ourselves this way? We will see our misery and nothingness. At first, this may not be all that desirable. It may even seem contrary to the dignity we have in Christ. But that's the key. Our dignity is "in Christ." Without Him, we are nothing. We are misery and nothingness by ourselves (See *Diary* #256).

Today, do not be offended or afraid to acknowledge your "nothingness." If it does not sit well with you at first, beg God for grace to see yourself as you are without Him. You will quickly see that without our divine Savior, you are truly miserable in every way. This is the starting point to a deep gratitude in that it allows you to more fully realize all that God has done for you. And when you see this, you will rejoice in the fact that He has come to meet you in this nothingness and has lifted you high to the dignity of His precious child.

Lord, may I see my misery and wretchedness this day. May I come to understand that without You I am nothing. And in that realization, help me to become eternally grateful for the precious gift of becoming Your dear child in grace. Jesus, I trust in You.

Reflection 72: An Incomprehensible Mystery

When God enters your soul, He acts in such a way that you will never fully comprehend His workings. His grace and Mercy are such that they remain a mystery deeper than the oceans and more vast than the upper limits of the Universe. Understanding the incomprehensible nature of God's grace is, in fact, the first step to wisdom. It's the first step to realizing the omnipotence of God and His infinite Mercy (See *Diary* #266).

Will you ever comprehend the grace of God? Will you ever fully grasp all that He has done for you? Certainly not. But if you can become all the more aware of the fact that you cannot comprehend God and His love, then you are on the road to wisdom. Reflect upon the incomprehensible workings of grace today. Face the great mystery of God's infinite Mercy. Let yourself become aware of this mystery so that you will begin to know that you do not know. And in that realization, you will be one step closer to understanding the Mercy of God.

Lord, Your ways are so far above my ways and Your wisdom is so far above what my mind can ever fathom. Help me, this day, to see the mystery of Your incomprehensible nature. And in seeing this mystery, help me to begin to understand Your Mercy all the more. Jesus, I trust in You.

Reflection 73: Growing in Our Desire for Jesus

The more we come to know Jesus, the more we desire Him. And the more we desire Him, the more we come to know Him. This is a beautiful cyclical experience of knowing and desiring, desiring and knowing (See *Diary* #273).

Do you desire to know your precious Lord? Do you long for Him in a burning way? Reflect upon this desire in your soul and if it is lacking, know that it's because you need to come to know Him more. Reflect, also, upon the ways in which you do sense a real knowledge of Jesus. What does that knowledge of Him do to you? Allow it to move from your head to your heart, and from your heart to all your affections. Allow Him to work on you, to draw you and to envelop you in His Mercy.

Lord, help me to come to know You. Help me to comprehend You in Your perfection and Mercy. And as I do come to know You, flood my soul with a longing and desire for more of You. May this desire increase my love of You and help me to know You all the more. Jesus, I trust in You.

Reflection 74: A Compassionate Heart

Is there a difference between "sympathy" and "compassion?" If so, what is the difference? And which is more desirable? Sympathy simply means that we feel bad for another. It means, in a sense, that we pity them. But compassion goes much further. It means that we enter into their sufferings and carry their burden with them. It means we suffer with them just as our Lord suffered with and for us. We must only seek to offer true compassion for others and to invite them to offer compassion to us (See *Diary* #279).

How well do you do this? How well do you offer true compassion? Do you see the hurt of others and seek to be there for them, encouraging them in Christ? And when you suffer, do you allow the compassion of others to flood your soul? Do you allow the Mercy of God to reach out to you through them? Or do you seek only pity from others allowing yourself to fall into the trap of self-pity? Reflect upon the difference in these two qualities and ask our Lord to make your heart one of authentic compassion for all.

Lord, please do give me a heart full of Mercy and compassion. Help me to be attentive to the needs of others and to reach out to them with Your own Divine Heart. May I long to bring Your healing grace to all those in need. And may I never soak in my own self-pity or seek that pity from others. But may I be open to the compassion Your Heart desires to offer me through the love of others. Jesus, I trust in You.

Reflection 75: Encountering Christ in Others

The Blessed Sacrament is truly sacred. It is revered and treated with the greatest respect. We would never throw our Lord away or discard Him on the floor or in some irreverent place. And yet we often fail to treat others with the same respect we show Jesus present in the Sacred Host (See *Diary* #285).

Do you realize that each person is a tabernacle? Each person is an image of God and is precious and sacred beyond imagination. We must see all people this way and we must seek to treat them with the greatest reverence and respect. In doing so, we honor our Divine Lord more than we could ever know. Reflect upon how you treat others this day. Reflect upon whether or not you treat them with the same love and respect you would show our Lord in the Sacred Host. Ask Jesus to help you to see His divine presence in everyone you meet.

Lord, may I love You always in all people. May I see You in every soul and honor Your divine presence within them. You, oh Lord, are alive in the heart of every creature. I love You and desire to love You more as I encounter Your divine presence in everyone I meet. Jesus, I trust in You.

Reflection 76: Unjust Accusations

Perhaps everyone has experienced an unjust accusation by another. It may be because another is honestly mistaken about the facts or about our motivation for what we do. Or, it may be more malicious and cruel. Being falsely accused can be quite painful and will most likely tempt us to react in anger and defensiveness. But what is the proper response to such nonsense? Should we weary ourselves with silly words that mean nothing in the Mind of God? Our response should be one of Mercy. Mercy in the midst of persecution (See *Diary* #289).

Have you experienced such an injustice in your life? Have others spoken ill of you and twisted the truth? Reflect upon how you react when this may happen. Are you able to receive these accusations as our Lord did? Can you pray for those who persecute you? Can you forgive even if no forgiveness is asked for? Commit yourself to this path, for you will never regret taking the path of Divine Mercy.

"Father, forgive them for they know not what they do." These were Your perfect words of Mercy spoken from the Cross. You forgave in the midst of Your brutal persecution. Help me, dear Jesus, to imitate Your example and to never allow the accusations, malice or persecution of another to distract me from You. Make me an instrument of Your Divine Mercy at all times. Jesus, I trust in You.

Reflection 77: The Lord Knows All Things

It is most certain that our Divine Lord knows all things. He is aware of every thought we have and every need we carry far more than we will ever realize. At times, as we come to realize His perfect knowledge, we may expect Him to answer all our needs even if we do not acknowledge them. But our Lord often wants us to ask. He sees great value in us discerning our needs and offering them to Him in confidence and prayer. Even if we do not know what is best, we must still bring our questions and concerns to Him. This is an act of trust in His perfect Mercy (See *Diary* #295).

Are you aware of your own needs? Can you articulate the challenges you face in life? Do you know what you should pray for and what to offer our Lord as your daily sacrifice? Reflect upon that which Jesus wants you to entrust to Him this day. What is it that He wants you to be aware of and present to Him for His Mercy. Let Him show you your need so that you may present that need to Him.

Lord, I know that You know all things. I know that You are perfect wisdom and love. You see every detail of my life and love me despite my weakness and sin. Help me to see my life as You see it and, in seeing my needs, help me to make a continual act of trust in Your Divine Mercy. Jesus, I trust in You.

Reflection 78: Desire for Happiness

The most basic desire we have is for happiness. Everything we do, in some way, is done so as to help us achieve this goal. Even sin is committed with an erroneous sense that it will lead us to happiness. But there is one source of human fulfillment and one source of authentic happiness. That one source is God. Seek our Divine Lord as the fulfillment of every human longing that you have (See *Diary* #305).

What is it that you seek in life? What is it that you long for? Is God the end of all your longings? Do you believe that God and God alone suffices and fulfills all you desire? Look at your goals, this day, and reflect upon whether or not God is the ultimate end of those goals. If He is not, then the goals you seek will leave you dry and empty. If He is, you are on the road to more than you could ever hope for.

Lord, please help me to make You and Your most holy Will my one and only desire in life. Help me to sift through the many longings I have and to see Your Will as the one and only goal that I must seek. May I find peace in Your Will and discover You at the end of every journey. Jesus, I trust in You."

Reflection 79: Our Blessed Mother of Sorrows

Mother Mary endured so much in life. She endured suspicion and ridicule at the miraculous conception of her Savior. She watched with a perfect motherly love as her Divine Son was rejected and misunderstood. And she stood by Him in His agony and death. And through it all, her motherly love was perfect and powerful. She stands by us, also, in all that we endure in life. And she gives us a perfect witness of love and compassion through her tender heart (See *Diary* #315).

Ponder the heart of the Mother of God this day. Ponder your Blessed Mother, the true mother of Jesus, as she loved her Son throughout His life. Imagine the sword of sorrow that pierced her heart countless times. And strive to understand the perfect and tender love with which she loved both her Son and those who treated Him so cruelly. Seek her prayers, this day, to imitate her love and ask her to shower that love upon you. She will not let you down.

Dearest Mother, my Queen, please pray for me and help me to know your motherly care. Help me to turn to you in all things so that I may receive the abundance of Mercy flowing from your pure heart. Give me the grace to imitate your kindness and tenderness and to stand by all those who are in need. Mother Mary, pray for us. Jesus, I trust in You.

Reflection 80: At the Hour of Our Death

If you have prayed the "Hail Mary" prayer, then you have prayed for your last hour in this world: "Pray for us now and at the hour of our death." Death is frightening to many people, and the hour of our death is not usually something we want to think about. But the "hour of our death" is a moment we should all look forward to with the utmost joy and anticipation. And we will look forward to it only if we are at peace with God, within our soul. If we have regularly confessed our sins and sought the presence of God throughout life, then our last hour will be one of great comfort and joy, even if it is mixed with suffering and pain (See *Diary* #321).

Think about that hour. If God were to give you the grace to prepare for that hour many months in advance, how would you prepare? What would you do differently so as to be ready for your final passing? Whatever comes to mind is most likely that which you should do today. Do not wait until the time is near to prepare your heart for your passing from death to new life. See that "hour" as an hour of the greatest grace. Pray for it, anticipate it and be watchful for the abundance of Mercy God wishes to bestow upon you, one day, at the glorious conclusion of your earthly life.

Lord, help me to be rid of all fear of death. Help me to continually remember that this world is but a preparation for the next. Help me to keep my eyes on that moment and to always anticipate the abundance of Mercy You will bestow. Mother Mary, pray for me. Jesus, I trust in You.

Reflection 81: Power and Mercy

Imagine a dictator of a country who has absolute power and is also a very angry, malicious and vengeful man. This is not someone you would want to upset. Now imagine the opposite. Imagine one who has absolute power and is also blessed with a heart of pure Mercy. This is our God. And in addition to our God having these qualities, He passes them on to His Mother. She is Queen and exercises her queenship with great authority. But it's an authority that is expressed in perfect Mercy. We should always trust in the power of God as it is made manifest through the mediation of our Mother of Mercy (See *Diary* #330).

Reflect upon that for which you are in need of Mercy. It could be sin, or it could be a heavy cross that seems too much to carry. It could be the need to forgive and to exercise charity toward a person who has wounded you. Whatever it is, turn to our Blessed Mother, the Mother of Mercy, and entrust your need to her glorious heart. With the authority entrusted to her by God, an abundance of grace will be given to you in your need.

Dearest Mother, Mother Most-Powerful, you have been entrusted with the grace of Heaven. As Queen, your Divine Son has given to you the glorious privilege of dispensing His Mercy. I beg of you, dear Mother, to bestow that grace in abundance so that we, your children, may know the Mercy and goodness of God. Mother Mary, pray for us. Jesus, I trust in You.

Reflection 82: Attachments

There are many things in life we can become attached to. Sometimes we can even become attached to things that are good. Most often, what we become attached to is our own stubborn will. We want what we want when we want it. One key to authentic holiness is to strive to be detached from everything but God and His holy Will. This requires much "letting go" in our lives and much surrender (See *Diary* #338).

What is it that you are attached to? What comes to mind first? What is it that you would not want to let go of? Even attachment to good things in life is a way of trusting more in creatures than in God. And, in fact, the only way to authentically love another, be it God, family, friends, or anyone else, is to detach from your selfish attachments so that the love of God can flood you and love others through you with His pure and perfect love.

Lord, help me to let go of all that is not of You. Help me, especially, to see my sin and to surrender it over to You. Help me to detach even from family in a holy way so that I am free to love them with Your Heart. May You, my Lord, be my one goal and love, and in this love may I discover how to love everyone with Your Heart. Jesus, I trust in You.

Reflection 83: Pray Always

Praying "always" may seem like an impossible task. Is it really possible to do so? Does God even expect this of us? It most certainly is and He most certainly does. No, we will not be called to spend all day, every day, at church in prayer. Not even those called to the cloistered monastic life do as such. But praying always is a must. It simply means that we have developed such a habit of closeness to God that our hearts are always with Him. We are always attentive to His presence and are always in communion with His grace. If we form this interior love for God, we will be praying always (See *Diary* #346).

Think about your day. What occupies your mind and heart most of the time? Do you spend excessive time daydreaming about things that have nothing to do with our Lord and the plan He has for you? Work at establishing a habit of prayer. Pray deeply and wholeheartedly at various moments of the day giving prayer your full attention. And then, throughout the day, try to let those moments of prayer sustain you and remain with you, carrying you on throughout all that you do.

Lord, help me to know how to pray. Instill within me a deep habit of prayer. Help me to regularly take moments, each day, when all I do is focus on You, seeking You out. And help me to bring those moments into everything I do so that my mind and heart may always be in communion with You. My Lord, I love You, help me to love You more. Jesus, I trust in You.

Reflection 84: The Blessed Host

It is impossible for us to love and adore Christ deeply enough as He is present in the Most Holy Eucharist. When we are before Him, present in the Most Holy Eucharist, we should see the Almighty God present in veiled form. He is: Mercy, Eternal Life, The Eternal God, The Savior of Sinners, The Living Water, The Fire of Pure Love, The Medicine for All Our Ills, All Sentiments of Love, The Hope of All, The Lifter of Burdens…and He is worthy of all our trust (See *Diary* #356).

What do you see when you gaze upon the Sacred Host? With your eyes you see bread, but with your soul you should see God. You should see God in all His glory and power and you should adore Him with all your might. Think about how you relate to our Lord as He is present in the Holy Eucharist. Pray that God will flood your mind with a true knowledge of Him and inspire your heart with a burning love.

Lord, help me to know and love You as You are present in the Most Holy Eucharist. Help me to understand the gift of Your Mercy made present through this Holy Gift. May I learn to adore You every time I am before Your presence in this Sacred Host. Jesus, I trust in You.

Reflection 85: Interior Mortification

One of the greatest gifts we can give to our Divine Lord is our willfulness. We often want what we want, when we want it. Our will can become stubborn and obstinate and this can easily dominate our whole being. As a result of this sinful tendency toward willfulness, one thing that delights our Lord greatly, and produces an abundance of grace in our lives, is an interior obedience to that which we do not want to do. This interior obedience, even to the smallest of things, mortifies our will so that we are made free to more completely obey the glorious will of God (See *Diary* #365).

What do you want with a passion? More specifically, what do you cling to in an obstinate way with your own will? There are many things we want that could easily be given up as a sacrifice for God. It may not be that the thing we desire is evil; rather, it's that letting go of our interior desires and preferences change us and dispose us to be more receptive to all that God wishes to bestow upon us.

Lord, help me to make my one desire that of perfect obedience to You in all things. May I cling to Your Will for my life in both great and small things. May I find in this submission of my will the great joy that comes from a heart fully submissive and obedient to You. Jesus, I trust in You.

Reflection 86: Melting the Hardest of Hearts

Imagine a large block of ice. Now imagine that there is a precious coin in the middle of that block. In order to obtain that coin, the block must melt away. So it can be with our hearts. Some hearts have become so hardened over time that there seems little chance of melting them away so as to bring forth the true value and dignity of that person. But Jesus is a radiant Sun whose rays shine forth with great intensity. Within His continual presence, even the hardest hearts will melt away (See *Diary* #370).

Do you know someone whom you have "written off" because of their continual hardness of heart? Do you know someone who appears to be unwilling to change, year after year? Do not lose hope. Know that if you continually act as a prism through which the grace and Mercy of God shines, even the hardest heart can be touched.

Lord, I pray, today, for those who are most hardened in their sins. You know the hearts of all and You know the minds of all. Please lead me to those in most need of Your Divine Mercy and use me as a channel of Your glorious and warming grace. Jesus, I trust in You.

Reflection 87: The Will of God in All Things

Wouldn't it be nice if you could do the Will of God always? If you could simply make the choice to perfectly say "Yes" to God in all things and in every situation? The truth is that you can. The only thing hindering you from this absolute choice is your own stubborn will (See *Diary* #374).

It's hard to admit that we are stubborn and full of self-will. It's hard to let go of our own will and to choose, instead, the Will of God in all things. Hard though it may be, we must make this our firm resolve. And when we fail, we must resolve again. Never tire of trying again and again. Your unfailing effort brings joy to the Heart of our Lord.

Lord, I do desire to embrace Your Divine Will in all things. Help me to be free of my own selfish will and to choose only You in all things. I abandon myself into Your hands. When I fall, help me to get back up rather than to give into discouragement. Jesus, I trust in You.

Reflection 88: Interior Suffering Transformed

Many people carry very heavy burdens within their souls. On the surface, they may radiate with joy and peace. But within their souls, they may also have great pain. These two experiences of our interior and exterior are not in contradiction when we follow Christ. Often times Jesus allows us to feel a certain interior suffering while, at the same time, He brings forth the good fruit of exterior peace and joy through that suffering (See *Diary* #378).

Is this your experience? Do you find that you can express yourself with great joy and peace in the presence of others even though your heart is filled with anguish and pain? If so, rest assured that joy and suffering are not mutually exclusive. Know that Jesus permits interior suffering at times so as to purify you and strengthen you. Continue to surrender that suffering and take joy in the opportunity you have to live a life of joy amidst such hardship.

Lord, I thank You for the interior crosses I carry. I know that You will give me the grace I need to continue down the path of acceptance and joy. May the joy of Your presence in my life always shine forth as I carry each and every cross I have been given. Jesus, I trust in You.

Reflection 89: The Power of a Generous Love

There are so many souls who are in need of our prayers and are in need of the Mercy of God. These are those souls who are stuck firm in their sin. We may pray for them but it seems to have little effect. What more can we do? Sometimes, the greatest intercession we can make is a heart filled with the most generous love. We must strive diligently to have the most pure and relentless love for these souls. God will see this love and will turn His gaze of love upon them as a result of the love He sees in our hearts (See *Diary* #383).

Who is that person in such need of the Mercy of God? Is there a family member, a coworker, a neighbor or friend who appears to remain obstinate toward God and His Mercy? Commit yourself to the most generous love you can offer that person and give it to God as your intercession. Allow God to gaze upon this person through your love.

Lord, so often I fail to love as You desire me to love. I am selfish and judgmental toward others. Soften my heart and then place in my heart the most generous love I have ever felt. Help me to turn that love to those in most need of Your Divine Mercy. Jesus, I trust in You.

Reflection 90: Unity With All

We are made for unity with one another. When there is a lack of unity, the effects are felt in families, communities and among nations. What is it that unites us more than anything? First and foremost, we are united with other souls through our Baptism (See *Diary* #391).

Think about the most basic fact that you share an unbreakable bond with each and every person who is baptized into Christ Jesus. Regardless of whether or not another is embracing their baptismal calling, the unity still remains. Think about that unity and cling to it. Allow yourself to see each and every baptized person as a true brother or sister in Christ. This will change the way you think about them and act toward them.

Lord, I thank You for the wonderful family You have created through the Sacrament of Baptism. I thank You that I am blessed to share in this family. Help me to love all Your children as a result of the simple fact that they are my brothers and sisters in You. Jesus, I trust in You.

Reflection 91: Prayer for Another Opens the Door

Only God knows what another truly needs. We cannot read another's soul unless this special grace were given to us by God. But each of us is called to pray fervently for others. At times, if we are open, God will place on our hearts the need to pray fervently for another. If we feel called to enter into special prayers for another, we may also be surprised to find that God will suddenly open the door for a holy and heartfelt conversation that this person desperately needs (See *Diary* #396).

Has God placed a certain person on your heart? Is there a particular person that often comes to mind? If so, pray for that person and tell God you are ready and willing to be there for that person if it be His Will. Then wait and pray some more. If God so desires, you will find that, at the right time and the right place, your openness to this person could make an eternal difference.

Lord, give me a fervent heart of prayer. Help me to be open to those whom You place in my path. And as I pray for those in need, I make myself available to You to be used as You will. Jesus, I trust in You.

Reflection 92: Creativity in Prayer

Often times, our days are filled with activity. Families are often occupied with one event or another. Chores and work can pile up and we may find, at the end of the day, that we have had little time to pray to God in solitude. But solitude and prayer can happen at times throughout our busy day. Though it's important to look for moments when we can be alone with God, giving Him our full attention, we should also look for opportunities to pray, interiorly, in the midst of our busy lives (See *Diary* #401).

Do you find that your life is full of activity? Do you find that you are often too busy to get away and pray? Though this is not the ideal, it can be remedied by looking for opportunities within your busyness. At a school event, while driving, while cooking or cleaning, we always have the opportunity to raise our minds and hearts to God in prayer. Remind yourself, this day, that you can pray during most moments of the day. Praying continually, this way, may provide the solitude you so desperately need.

Lord, I long to be in Your presence throughout my day. I long to see You and to love You always. Help me to pray to You, in the midst of my activity, so that I may always be in Your company. Jesus, I trust in You.

Reflection 93: The Meeting of Love and Sin

Where do love and sin meet? They meet in the persecution, ridicule and malice inflicted upon our Lord. He was the Incarnation of perfect love. The Mercy in His Heart was infinite. His care and concern for all people was beyond imagination. And yet the soldiers mocked Him, laughed at Him and tortured Him for entertainment and fun. He, in turn, loved them with a perfect love. This is a true meeting of love and sin (See *Diary* #408).

Have you encountered the sins of others? Have you been treated with spite, harshness and malice? If so, there is an important question to ponder. What was your response? Did you return insult for insult and injury for injury? Or did you allow yourself to be like our Divine Lord and face sin with love? Returning love for malice is one of the most profound ways we imitate the Savior of the World.

Lord, when I am persecuted and treated with sin, I find myself hurt and angry. Free me from these tendencies so that I may imitate Your perfect love. Help me to face all sin I encounter with the love overflowing from Your Divine Heart. Help me to forgive and so be Your presence to those who are guilty of much sin. Jesus, I trust in You.

Reflection 94: Facing the Evil One

If you wish to avoid the fierce hatred of the evil one, then refrain from striving for holiness. Satan will still hate you, but he will not hate you as much as the saint. But, of course, this is foolishness! Why would anyone avoid holiness so as to avoid the hatred of the evil one? It is true that the closer we come to God, the more the evil one will seek to destroy us. Though it's good to be aware of this, it's nothing to fear. In fact, attacks from the evil one should be seen as signs to us of our closeness to God (see *Diary* #412).

Reflect, today, upon any ways that you have felt overwhelmed by fear. Very often, this fear is the fruit of you letting the trickery and malice of the evil one affect you. Instead of letting fear affect you, allow the evil that confronts you to be the cause of your increase in faith and trust in God. Evil will either tear us down or become an opportunity for us to grow in God's grace and strength.

Lord, fear is useless, what is needed is faith. Increase my faith, I pray, so that I will be daily under the control of Your gentle inspirations and not under the control of the fear caused by the attacks of the evil one. Jesus, I trust in You.

Reflection 95: Trusting in the Mercy of God

If you dropped an object into the middle of the vast ocean you would know, with deep certainty, that this object would get wet. The immensity of the ocean would consume it. So it is with the Mercy of God. It is immense and infinite. Therefore, if you trust in His Mercy, you can have a deep certainty that you will obtain it (See *Diary* #420).

Do you trust that God will bestow His infinite Mercy upon you? The goal is to be certain of this. We do not arrive at this certainty because of our own goodness; rather, we arrive at it as a result of the unfathomable and infinite Mercy of the Most Holy Trinity.

Lord, I love You and I desire to trust in Your perfect Mercy to the point that there is no doubt in my mind and heart that You will bestow this precious gift. Help me to trust in Your Mercy because of Your infinite goodness. Purify me of all doubt, dear Lord, and help me to trust You more. Jesus, I trust in You.

Reflection 96: The Great Plan God Has For You

We can all, at times, have dreams of grandeur. What if I were rich and famous? What if I had great power in this world? What if I were the Pope or the President? But what we can be certain of is that God does have great things in mind for us. He calls us to a greatness we could never imagine. One problem that often arises is that, when we begin to sense what God wants of us, we run away and hide. God's Divine Will often calls us out of our comfort zone and requires great trust of Him and abandonment to His Holy Will (See *Diary* #429).

Are you open to what God wants of you? Are you willing to do whatever He asks? Often times we wait for Him to ask, then think about His request, and then become filled with fear over that request. But the key to fulfilling the Will of God is to say "Yes" to Him even before He asks anything of us. Surrendering to God, in a perpetual state of obedience, will free us from the fear we can be tempted with when overanalyzing the details of His glorious Will.

Dear Lord, I say "Yes" to You this day. Whatever You ask of me, I will do. Wherever You lead me, I will go. Give me the grace of complete abandonment to You no matter what You ask. I offer myself to You so that the glorious purpose of my life may be fulfilled. Jesus, I trust in You.

Reflection 97: The "Excuse" of Our Weakness

If you were asked to build a rocket ship from scratch, you may object stating that you are not competent in this area and, therefore, cannot do what you are being asked to do. We often have the same response to God regarding His Will. We can easily feel as though we are being asked too much by our Lord, but this is foolish thinking since our Lord would never ask us to do that which He will not also provide the grace to accomplish (See *Diary* #435).

What is it that you feel unqualified to do? Perhaps it's a matter within your family, or an activity you are called to assist with at church. Or perhaps our Lord has placed something on your heart that you avoid considering out of feelings of inadequacy. But if we trust Jesus, we must trust that we will be able to fulfill His perfect Will in our lives. We must trust that He would never call us to something beyond what we can accomplish through His grace.

Lord, I say "Yes" to you again this day. I, once again, renew my commitment to fulfill Your holy Will. May I never let worry or a lack of confidence keep me from fulfilling the holy mission You have given to me. Jesus, I trust in You.

Reflection 98: Being an Instrument

When God calls us to fulfill some mission, who is at work? God or us? The truth is that we are both at work, God is the source and we are the instrument. We make a free will effort, but it is God who shines through. Just as a window can act as a source of light in the house, it is not the window that shines, it is the Sun. Similarly, we must surrender ourselves to God so that He will shine through us, but we must always remember that we are only a window through which God will shine in our world (See *Diary* #438).

Do you want God to shine through you brightly? Do you want His rays of love to radiate and enlighten others? If you do, then humble yourself so that you can become His instrument of grace. Recognize that you are nothing more than an instrument, not the source. Be open to the Source of all Grace and He will shine through with great power and splendor.

Lord, I offer myself to You as a window for Your merciful Heart. Shine through me, dear Lord. May I be a true instrument of Your grace and may I always remember that You and You alone are the source of all grace and Mercy. Jesus, I trust in You.

Reflection 99: The Scourge of Sin

Why was it that Jesus suffered as He did? Why did He receive such a severe scourging? Why was His death so painful? Because sin has consequences and is the source of great pain. But Jesus' voluntary and sinless embrace of suffering transformed human suffering so that it now has the power to purge us and free us from sin and all attachment to sin (See *Diary* #445).

Do you realize that the extreme pain and suffering Jesus went through was on account of your own sin? It's important to acknowledge that humbling fact. It's important to see a direct connection between His suffering and your sin. But this should not be a cause of guilt or shame, it should be a cause of gratitude. Deep humility and gratitude.

Lord, I thank You for all that You endured in Your holy Passion. I thank You for Your suffering and Cross. I thank You for redeeming suffering and transforming it into a source of salvation. Help me to allow the sufferings I endure to change my life and purge me of my sin. I unite my sufferings to Yours, dear Lord, and pray that You will use it for Your glory. Jesus, I trust in You.

Reflection 100: The Desire for Good

God smiles upon us and lavishes rewards upon us for the love we offer to Him and to others. Our works of love, when inspired by His grace, are transformed into treasures in Heaven. But that's not all that is transformed into treasures. Even our desire to do good and to serve God is transformed. God sees all things, even our smallest sincere desires, and transforms all into grace (See *Diary* #450).

What do you desire in life? What do you long for? Do you find that your desires are attached to sinful acts? Or do you find that your desires and longings are for the good things of Heaven and the works of God. Seek to transform even your desires and you will be richly blessed!

Lord, I offer you my heart and every desire within it. Help me to long for You and for Your holy Will to be fulfilled in this world. May I desire what You desire and long for an abundance of Mercy in our world. Jesus, I trust in You.

Reflection 101: God Speaking Through Others

Very often, God wants to speak to You a particular message that you need to hear. It may happen that, as you listen to a homily, read a book, hear something on the radio or talk with a friend, something particular will jump out at you that does not seem to affect others. Pay attention to this inspiration, it is a gift to you of God's Mercy and a revelation of His love for you (See *Diary* #456).

Reflect upon anything, lately, that has gotten your attention. Have you heard something that seemed to be spoken just for you? Is there something that has been on your mind? If so, spend time with that thought and try to discern if it is from the

Lord and what He may be saying to you through it. This may be God's voice speaking to you and an act of His great Mercy.

Lord, I desire to hear Your voice. Help me to be attentive to Your word as it is spoken to me. When You speak, help me to listen and to respond to You with generosity and love. Jesus, I trust in You.

Reflection 102: God Uses the Weak

If you were God, and you had some glorious task you wanted accomplished, who would you choose? Someone with manifest gifts? Or someone who is weak, humble and appears to have very few natural gifts? Surprisingly, God most often chooses the weak for the greatest tasks. This is one way through which He is able to manifest His almighty power (See *Diary* #464).

Reflect, today, upon whether you have a high and lofty view of yourself and your abilities. If so, be careful. God has a hard time using someone who thinks this way. Seek to see your lowliness and humble yourself before the glory of God. He wants to use you for great things, but only if you allow Him to be the one who acts in and through you. That way, the glory belongs with Him and the work is accomplished according to His perfect wisdom and is a fruit of His abundant Mercy.

Lord, I offer myself for Your service. Help me to always come to You in humility, acknowledging my weakness and sin. In this humble state, please shine through so that Your glory and power will do great things. Jesus, I trust in You.

Reflection 103: Knowledge of God is Beyond Words

Communion with the Trinity must be the central purpose of our lives. And though we may converse and speak words to

Them, the deepest form of communication is beyond words. It's a union, a giving of ourselves and a basking in Their Mercy. Knowing and conversing with the Trinity must take place in the depths of our souls through a language that is understood in a way that words cannot contain (See *Diary* #472).

Do you know God? Do you know the Father, Son and Holy Spirit? Are you in daily communion with Them, speaking to Them, hearing Them? Reflect upon your knowledge of the Divine Persons of the Trinity. Each "speaks" in His own way. Each one calls to you, communing with you, loving you. Let your soul come to know the Persons of the Holy Trinity. A relationship with Them will fulfill the deepest longings of your soul.

Most Holy Trinity, Father, Son and Holy Spirit, please come and dwell within my soul. Help me to know You and love You in the depths of my being. I desire to be in communion with You and to hear You speak Your mysterious language of love. Most Holy Trinity, I trust in You.

Reflection 104: The Chaplet of Mercy

Prayer is essential to our Christian walk. When you pray, it is good to speak from the heart, pouring out your soul to God. But prayer must also follow your faith and all you know of God. It must reflect your true knowledge of God and call upon His Mercy. The Chaplet of Divine Mercy is one such prayer that perfectly reflects your faith in the Mercy of God. (See *Diary* #475-476).

Do you pray? Do you pray every day? Is your prayer centered in faith and truth, enabling you to continually call on the Mercy of God? If you do not pray the Chaplet of Divine Mercy, try it every day for a week. Be faithful and trust in the faith revealed in the words spoken. You will see the doors of God's Mercy open if you commit yourself to this prayer.

Eternal Father, I offer You the Body and Blood, Soul and Divinity of Your dearly beloved Son, Our Lord Jesus Christ, in atonement for our sins and those of the whole world. For the sake of His sorrowful Passion, have Mercy on us and on the whole world. Jesus, I trust in You.

Reflection 105: The Effects of God's Indwelling

What would you experience if God were to fully dwell in the depths of your soul? Peace, joy and amazement! And from these gifts, and from the indwelling of the Trinity, you would have courage in the face of hardship, strength to cast out fear and an impenetrable defense against the evil one, against his lies and his snares. You will not be free from temptation and suffering, but you will overcome them since God alone dwells within you, and He will be your protection and joy (See *Diary* #480).

Has the Most Holy Trinity taken possession of your soul? If so, there will be no room for sin or fear. You will see the fruits of this indwelling in your daily life and you will be at peace. If you do not see God at work in your life in this way, invite Him to enter. This is not a onetime invitation; rather, it must become your daily habit and sincere desire. Do not tire of inviting God to dwell within you.

Lord, Your presence in my life is the greatest Mercy I could ever receive. There is nothing greater than You living in me. I thank You that You desire to be one with me and to take possession of my life. I give myself to You freely and without reserve, for You are my God and my all. Jesus, I trust in You.

Reflection 106: Sleeping in Christ

Each night, as you go to sleep, you are invited to sleep in the grace and Mercy of our Lord. You are invited to rest in His arms so as to be rejuvenated and refreshed. Sleep is an image of prayer and, in fact, can become a form of prayer. To rest is to rest in God. Every beat of your heart must become a prayer to God and every beat of His Heart must become the rhythm of your rest (See *Diary* #486).

Do you sleep in the presence of God? Think about it. When you retire to bed, do you pray? Do you ask our Lord to surround you with His grace and to embrace you with His gentle arms? God has spoken to the saints of old through their dreams. He has put holy men and women into a deep rest so as to restore them and strengthen them. Try to invite our Lord into your mind and heart as you lay your head down to sleep, this night. And as you wake, let Him be the first one whom you greet. Allow each night's rest to be a resting in His Divine Mercy.

Lord, I thank You for the rhythm of each day. I thank You for the ways You walk with me throughout my day and I thank You for being with me while I rest. I offer to You, this night, my rest and my dreams. I invite You to hold me close to You, that Your Heart of Mercy may be the gentle sound which soothes my weary soul. Jesus, I trust in You.

Reflection 107: Revealing Your Soul in Confession

God sends to us His representatives in the person of His priests. Though priests are not perfect, they are God's representatives nonetheless. This is especially true in the Sacrament of Reconciliation. It's essential that we approach that Sacrament with confidence and honesty. We must allow the confessor to see the sin in our souls so that he can enter, cleanse and heal by the sacred power of absolution (See *Diary* #494-496).

Do you go to confession? If so, how often? Do you clean your house more often than you clean your soul? The Lord has given you an immeasurable gift in the Sacrament of Reconciliation. He invites you to receive this gift with an open heart. Do not fear this invitation; rather, run to it with eager anticipation of the many graces our Lord wishes to bestow. And do so as regularly as you can.

Lord, why do I fear Your Mercy as it is bestowed through the Sacrament of Reconciliation? Why do I fear Your sacred Mercy poured forth through the act of absolution? Give me courage and humility so that I may confess my sins clearly and completely and so be cleansed and restored to Your Heart. Jesus, I trust in You.

Reflection 108: The Voice of the Church

God has spoken to the saints in numerous ways including through many interior graces and inspirations. But even the greatest mystic, living on the heights of holiness, must ultimately submit to the Voice of God spoken through His Church. The Church, especially in the person of our Holy Father, is the clearest channel of the Voice of God in our world. Through the Church we will be led to Heaven. We must always strive to be in perfect union with Christ as He is alive and made manifest to us through His Church. We must let ourselves be led by God through our bishops, pastors and all to whom He has entrusted our pastoral care. Giving authority to the Church was God's idea and plan; it must also become ours (See *Diary* #497).

Do you see the wisdom of the plan of God as He has chosen to reveal Himself to us through the Church? Do you believe in the Church as the Mother and Teacher of your faith? Do you especially trust in the words of our Holy Father, the Pope? Make an act of faith, this day, putting your wholehearted trust in the Voice of God spoken through His Church and you will begin to more fully understand the countless mysteries of life that God has revealed.

Dear Lord, I desire to be obedient to You in all things. I desire to hear Your Voice and follow Your commands. Help me to have the wisdom to discern You speaking and acting through Your Church. May I see beyond the person of the priest, bishop and the Holy Father so as to discover Your guiding hand. Jesus, I trust in You.

Reflection 109: The Arms of God

When a child is frightened or gets hurt, the natural place of comfort is the arms of a parent. This is the first thing a crying child looks for. So it must be with us. The arms of our Father in Heaven, and Jesus our Savior, are what we must run to in our need. We should not hesitate to turn to God in all things, especially when tempted to despair, or when we recognize our weakness and sin (See *Diary* #505).

When burdens weigh you down, or when you get angry or are tempted to despair, where do you turn? Some turn to sinful fleshly comforts, others to harsh words, and others run to God. Run to God in every moment! Ideally, we run to Him when life is good and when we are filled with great joy and consolation. But God also wants us to run to Him, immediately, when life is hard. Make the arms of God the first thing you think about when you find yourself in need.

Lord, I do run to You. I pray that I will daily build a habit of running to You in all things. I pray that I will turn to You with my every need. I cling to You, Divine Lord, and seek to rely upon You always. Jesus, I trust in You.

Reflection 110: The Rays of Mercy

The Mercy of the Heart of Jesus shines forth with great radiance. This was the image of Divine Mercy seen by Saint Faustina. The open Heart of our Lord burst forth with an outpouring of light and grace on the world. Jesus wants to continue to shine forth on the world, and He wants to rest in your heart so that He may shine on others through you (See *Diary* #514).

What is in your heart? Is it bitterness and pain? Is it sin and darkness? Or is it the Heart of our Lord? Does Jesus live in your heart? These questions are so very important to answer honestly. If you cannot honestly say that the Heart of Jesus rests in your heart, then this is an important revelation to ponder. Seek to let His Heart melt away any sin and dispel any darkness. In their place, let His light shine forth. When the Heart of Jesus rests in yours, your heart will radiate Mercy and bathe others in its rays.

Lord, as I look at my heart, I see sin and darkness at times. Come live in my heart, dispel all darkness and wipe away all sin. As You take possession of my heart, shine forth Your Divine rays of Mercy upon me, and upon a world in need. I give my heart to You, dear Lord. Jesus, I trust in You.

Reflection 111: The Lies of the Evil One

The devil will tempt us in many ways. One common way the devil likes to attack us is to remind us of our sins, including those we have confessed. He loves to try to convince us that we are on the wrong path, that we are not pleasing to God, that we are liars and sinners. And while it's true that we are sinners, the evil one always fails to see our sin through the lens of God's Mercy. To overcome his deceptive temptations, while he reminds us of our sins, we need only to remind ourselves of the Mercy of the Heart of Jesus. As we gaze upon His Heart, we will have no fear about admitting our sin. This act of honesty will not produce anxiety, despair and doubt as the evil one desires. Instead, facing our sin in the light of the Mercy of God, will refresh us and lift our spirits, filling them with an abundance of hope (See *Diary* #520).

Think about the ways that the evil one may tempt you to despair over your sins. To mourn for your sins is a good and healthy act, but never in despair. Christian mourning leads to the Mercy of God, and the contrition you feel in this holy act lifts your burden and fills you with joy.

Precious Lord, free me from the deceit and attacks of the evil one. Keep me safe, oh God, and help me to never forget the abundance of Your Mercy. As I see that Mercy, help me to daily repent of my sin so as to rob from the evil one all weapons of his malice. Jesus, I trust in You.

3

Reflections on Notebook Two

We now enter into Notebook Two of the six notebooks that make up the *Diary* of Saint Faustina. The reason for having more than one notebook is simply that when one notebook was filled by Saint Faustina she began with a new one. Therefore, there is nothing particularly different from one notebook to the other. However, for the purpose of this current book of daily reflections, each reflection will begin to be lengthened, starting here with Notebook Two, so as to help you, the reader, enter more deeply into the beautiful mysteries of faith and our shared spiritual life that have been revealed in these writings of Saint Faustina.

You are invited once again to take one reflection each day and to ponder it throughout the day. Try to pray the prayer for each reflection each morning, noon and evening. Allow each mystery reflected upon to become a source of wisdom and understanding for you.

Reflection 112: Love of God Increases Our Desire for God

When you love God and rejoice in that love, your desire for God will increase. The more you know Him, the more you will want to know Him, and the more you want to know Him, the more you will know Him. Similarly, the more you love Him, the more you will want to love Him, and the more you want to love Him, the more you will love Him. Finally, the more you serve Him, the more you will want to serve Him, and the more you want to serve Him, the more you will serve Him. Knowledge, love and service increase the desire for these, and the increase in desire for these three increases each one (See *Diary* #525).

Do you want to know, love and serve God with all your heart, mind, soul and strength? Hopefully you do. How is this achieved? It's achieved by growing in these virtues and allowing them to increase your desire for them all the more. Look, today, at your desires. Inquire, within, about the desires of your heart. If you do not see a wholehearted desire to know, love and serve God, then commit yourself to these ends by choosing them. From there, the Lord will take over and direct you in accord with His own merciful Heart.

Lord, increase my desire for You and for Your Divine Will. Help me to know, love and serve You with my whole being. Increase, also, my desire for You in these ways. Jesus, I trust in You.

Reflection 113: An Offering to the Everlasting Father

The greatest prayer we can make is the "prayer of offering." A prayer of offering is a sacrifice offered to the Father in union with the One Sacrificial Offering of Christ on the Cross. We do not offer ourselves, by ourselves. We offer ourselves in union with Christ Jesus. Specifically, we must offer our prayers, fasting, mortification and daily work to God. Pray prayers every day. Mortify your fleshly desires regularly through fasting and other forms of self-denial. And do all your daily work as a gift to God and as a result of His daily will. Offer all of these to the Father with the Son, and God will accept your offering as a pure and holy sacrifice (See *Diary* #531).

When you pray, do you make your prayer an offering? Too often we pray for this need or that and stop there. It is good to present our needs before God. He knows our needs even before we present them, but He still wants us to ask Him to meet our specific needs. But don't stop there in your prayer. The Lord wants you to go further. He wants sacrifice from you. Reflect upon whether your prayer becomes a daily sacrifice to God. If this sacrificial language is not part of your daily thinking, begin to make it so. Think and act sacrificially in your daily life and prayer and the Lord will receive your sacrifice, using it in powerful ways for your own holiness and for the holiness of the entire Church.

Lord, You not only offered the perfect sacrifice of Your life to the Father, You also set for me a perfect example of true prayer. Help me to daily offer to You the sacrifice of my life so that, through this sacrifice, You may make me holy and bring greater holiness to Your Church. Jesus, I trust in You.

Reflection 114: Detachment From the World

The "world" is referred to in Scripture many times, especially by Jesus Himself. He said that the world will hate you and will not understand you. The world will, in fact, persecute you. This could become the cause of fear and distress for some. It causes these effects within us when we are overly concerned about looking good in the eyes of the world and acting so as to win its esteem. Do not fall into this trap. The world will love you only if you become worldly, taking on its secular and sinful values. Instead, keep your eyes fixed on Heaven. Live as though you are in the world, but not of it. Allow the Lord to shield you from worldly enticements so that you will live only in Him and for Him at all times (See *Diary* #537).

Seriously ask yourself, today, how much influence the opinions of the world have on you. Do you find yourself dreaming of being well regarded and respected in the public eye? If so, be very careful with this desire. Sure, if you have given yourself completely to Christ and, as a result, many people speak well of you, this is good. But it's not all that common. More often, when we commit ourselves to Christ and to His holy mission, we will find that we are misjudged, scorned and even persecuted. It may be only in small ways, but don't be surprised if it becomes more pronounced as you draw closer to the Will of God. Do not worry about this. Keep your eyes on Christ and be concerned only about His judgment of you. His "opinion" is all that matters because His opinion is Truth.

Lord Jesus, You were not controlled by the opinions of others. You did not allow the false values and pressures of the world to direct You. Help me to keep my eyes on You and Your Will in all things. Give me courage to be concerned only with pleasing You. Jesus, I trust in You.

Reflection 115: The Will of God Will Keep You Safe

The Will of God is much more than a future plan God has laid out for you. It's more than His hopes and dreams for you. His Will is your path to holiness and it is a source of the greatest consolation and joy. His Will is both active and passive (permissive). It's active in that He has definite plans for you and calls you to discern those plans and embrace them. It's passive in that He will permit certain evils to befall you as a result of your own sins and those of the whole world. Do not fear when God permits some evil or some suffering to come your way. Jesus Himself is the perfect example of one who experienced the effects of the permissive Will of the Father. Do not be surprised or scandalized by what God permits. His passive and permissive Will invites you to trust in Him in all things and allows you to grow in faith and trust of Him no matter what your future holds. Do not be afraid of that which God permits. (See *Diary* #541).

Reflect upon any way that you are confused or even scandalized by what God has allowed to happen in your life. Know that He knows what He desires and He knows what He permits. Do not be afraid of His permissive Will. Do not be afraid to accept all that befalls you with faith and confidence. What God permits is done so as to manifest His providential care for you and as a way of increasing your own faith and trust in Him.

Lord, when I suffer, I sometimes doubt Your love and care for me. I question whether You are there, sustaining me and leading me. Give me the grace I need to endure all the effects of sin in our world. Help me to face the effects of my own sin and those of the world with courage and confidence in Your protective hand. Jesus, I trust in You.

Reflection 116: God's Dependence Upon Us

God is wholly independent in that He perfectly sustains Himself. The Father, Son and Holy Spirit form a perfect unity through which they are interconnected and interdependent. And this interdependence is all They need. However, the Trinity freely chose to become dependent upon each one of us in a unique way. By choosing to enter into our lives, uniting with us, and forming a bond of love with us, God, in a certain way, makes Himself dependent upon our trust. His dependence upon our trust relates to the depth of love and the bond He forms with us. Without our trust, God has limited Himself in how deeply He can unite Himself with us. Therefore, God offers Himself to us freely and without reserve, but requires our full participation for this perfect gift of love to become complete (See *Diary* #548).

Do you understand your role in the life of the Holy Trinity? The Father, Son and Holy Spirit offer you perfect love, but will not impose that love upon you. They invite you to freely reciprocate this love. Only in this free choice, on your part, to accept Them in trust, can God fulfill His choice of being one with you. Allow God to fulfill His longing of union with you. Do not reject this love nor be hesitant to reciprocate it.

My God, Father, Son and Holy Spirit, I thank You for the gift of Your life and Your love. I freely accept this perfect Gift of Yourself. Help me to daily grow in trust of You so that I may receive You and offer myself back to You with the same generosity that You have shown me. Jesus, I trust in You.

Reflection 117: The Enclosure of Your Heart

Some religious sisters and monks live a cloistered life within the confines of an enclosure. No one may enter that enclosure without good reason, unless they are a member of that community of faith. Others may enter only with the permission of the superior. It may be that a sister is gravely ill and in need of the Sacrament of Anointing, or it may be that a workman must enter for a needed repair. The image of an enclosure is analogous to our soul. We must give the key to Jesus and allow Him to safeguard it. He will only allow those who belong to enter in (See *Diary* #554).

What is it that you allow into your soul? Do you allow the Lord to guard you and govern your inner thoughts and your heart? Too often, we allow many worldly things to enter. We open wide the door to the enticements of sin and filth. Give the key to your soul to our Lord. He will guard you and keep you safe. He will welcome all those with whom He desires you dwell, and open the door to those who come to heal and restore. But He will diligently protect this sacred space of your soul from that which does not belong, if you let Him.

Lord, I do give You the one and only key to my soul. I choose You as my guardian this day. Allow me to commune, freely, with those whom You have invited into my life and set before me. Help me to love them and to serve them with all my heart. As I give You this key, I thank You that You will protect me. May I trust You and never seek to welcome that which displeases You, and that which You do not welcome. Jesus, I trust in You.

Reflection 118: An Obstinate Heart

One of the primary ways we stop the Mercy of God from entering into our lives is through *obstinacy*. Specifically, when we obstinately hold onto our own opinion, as a result of our pride, and therefore fail to be open to the truth, we shut the door to grace. This is a particularly dangerous sin because obstinacy, by its very definition, implies there is an unwillingness to repent and change. The obstinate person remains, day after day, year after year, closed to the grace of God. The only cure for an obstinate heart is humility before the Truth of God. Coming to God, with a sincerely open heart, ready and willing to change our convictions the moment He speaks, is the first step to being rid of this sin. Humble yourself by listening, setting aside your own firm opinion, being open and willing to change. This may be difficult at first, but you will be truly grateful you did (See *Diary* #560).

What are you obstinate about? Is there a long-standing thought you hold against another? Is there something that you are *convinced* you are right on? Make sure that God feels the same way. Seek, today, to be open to change. The first step is to ask the Lord to open your eyes to see. The second step is to let yourself see this tendency within your heart.

Lord, I know I am obstinate. I see it within my soul. I hold on to my will and refuse to listen to others out of pride. Give me the grace of an open mind that I may shed my stubbornness. Help me to humble myself before You and others and help me to be ready and willing to listen to Your Truth. Jesus, I trust in You.

Reflection 119: Interior and Exterior Mortifications

Mortification is a practice of denying your will so as to grow in greater detachment from the passing things of this world. We must seek to detach from everything but God and His holy

Will. It's not that everything we like or desire is bad, but if we want true holiness, our desire for God must transform every other desire and direct them all. Interior mortification consists of ways in which we deny our own thoughts or will. For example, saying a kind word when we do not feel like it, or holding our tongue when it is hard to hold. Exterior mortification consists of practices such as fasting from foods we like or giving things up for Lent and throughout the year. These practices are essential to the spiritual life if you are serious about your relationship with God (See *Diary* #565).

What are you most attached to? What seems to control you and direct your desires the most? It could be a sinful tendency, or it could be a passion for some natural hobby. Start with your sinful tendencies and look for ways to mortify your desires so as to become strong enough to overcome these sins. Look also at your natural passions and likes. Choosing to freely sacrifice these, to a certain extent, from time to time, is a positive and holy way to grow in holiness. Look for ways to do this and God's Mercy will flow more abundantly.

Lord, I desire to desire You alone and above all other desires. Purify me and free me from my many attachments in this life. Help me to have the courage to make daily sacrifices to You so that my mind and will are more prepared to receive Your Mercy. Jesus, I trust in You.

Reflection 120: Pure Love of God

The ultimate purpose of your life is love. And, more specifically, it is first to love God with a pure love. For love to be pure, it must be freed from all selfishness. Pure love looks only at the one being loved. When we love God with a pure love, we will find that we are drawn to God for His sake, because He is glorious and worthy of our love, and because loving Him is right and just. When we can love in this way, selflessly and focused only on God's greatness and beauty, then we will discover something else quite glorious. We will discover that, as a result of our pure love of God, we are also filled with a joy so abundant and powerful that we need no other reward. The joy that fills us as a result of loving God with a pure love becomes so strong that it overflows into a profound and sincere love for others. This is the greatest satisfaction in life. We truly need nothing else to be happy beyond measure (See *Diary* #576).

Are you happy? If not, what do you blame for your lack of happiness? It's easy to point and assign blame. However, we must realize that happiness comes only as a result of our choice to love God with a pure heart of love. Reflect upon whether this is something you are experiencing in your life. Ponder the love and affection you have for God. Think about how strong or how weak this love is. And remind yourself that, if you love God purely and above all else, this love will order your life so perfectly that the joy you experience will satisfy you above any other earthly consolation. If you want to be happy, seek to love God with a complete and pure heart.

Lord, I know my love for You is far from perfect. Help me, this day, to turn my eyes and heart more fully to You so that my love of You may be purified, allowing me to love You above all things for Your own sake, because You do deserve my total love. In my love of You, I thank You for the joy that this produces. May that joy overflow so abundantly that I find perfect satisfaction and happiness in this love. Jesus, I trust in You.

Reflection 121: The Secret Inner Garden of Your Heart

Imagine that your home had an inner, hidden courtyard in which you had a garden. No one knew about this secret garden. It was a place where you planted, tilled, labored, weeded and harvested. The produce from this garden was then secretly distributed to many to nourish and delight them. This is an image of the depths of your soul. The home symbolizes your whole self. The inner and hidden garden symbolizes the inner and secret depths of your soul. The gardener is our Lord and He is the one who secretly enters, tilling, planting, weeding, growing and harvesting the many good fruits that come forth from your life. He desires to enter in secrecy, doing much labor in your life that no one knows about. The result, if you let Him in, will be experienced by the abundance of virtue that overflows, affecting the lives of many (See Diary #581).

Do you allow our Lord to enter into the inner and secret garden of your own soul? Do you allow Him to labor within you, bringing forth an abundant harvest? This work He desires to do in you is a work seen only by you. It's a holy secret of grace working in your life. The Lord offers it out of His perfect love for you. Tell Him, this day, that you will let Him in and then allow yourself to watch as He does amazing things in this inner courtyard, transforming it into a garden bursting forth in abundance.

Lord, I see this courtyard and I am aware of it being overgrown with weeds of all types. There is much work to do. But, this day, I say "Yes" to You. I accept the labor of perfect love that You offer me and I return to You my gratitude for the miraculous work You desire to do. Help me to be patient with You and to adore You as you prepare the soil, plant Your virtues and bring forth a harvest. I thank You, my dear Lord. Jesus, I trust in You.

Reflection 122: If You Could Choose

If you could choose between all the wealth in the world or an intimate and loving relationship with Jesus, which would you choose? Do not answer that too quickly. We may know that choosing Jesus is the right answer, but would you choose Him? Imagine the power and worldly "freedom" you would enjoy if you had unlimited earthly wealth. And yet, the truth is that all the wealth in the world cannot produce one bit of happiness. It may make life easier in some ways, but far more complicated and burdensome in others. Many holy men and women have chosen a life of complete poverty because they discovered the riches produced by an authentic and transforming relationship with Jesus and they wanted nothing to get in the way. He offers this wealth to all of us. But most do not accept. Will you? (See *Diary* #587)

Do you understand the riches bestowed upon you if you choose to allow the abundant love of Jesus to flood your soul? Do you believe that this relationship is worth abandoning all else so as to attain it? Is your one desire in life the burning love of Jesus? If it is, this love will utterly transform you and the love from that relationship will flow forth from you, affecting every action you do and every other relationship you have. Choose our Lord as your most intimate lover and make Him the true center of your life.

Lord, I am aware of the fact that I can never fully grasp the depths of Your perfect love for me. Nonetheless, I choose Your love this day and I desire to make You the center of my life. Come fill my heart with such a burning love that I come to realize that You are all I need in life. For in coming to know You, my Lord, I come to love You and all your creatures. Jesus, I trust in You.

Reflection 123: The Blessing of Humiliations

Who, in their right mind, would want to be humiliated? What would you do if you were humiliated? Most people would be tempted to seek ways to avoid humiliation. Some would become deeply hurt as a result. Others would become angry and defensive. And though the source of one's humiliation may not be fair, it's important to understand that humiliations can become an invitation to the deepest depths of God's grace and Mercy. Humiliation has the potential to produce humility when embraced properly. Though anger and hurt may also result, humility must be the goal. What matters most is that we shed any pride, anger or hurt that we experience and allow ourselves to enter into the depths of humility. This necessary quality will enable us to rely solely upon God, seek consolation and peace only from Him, and allow Him and His holy Will to be the one and only source of our joy in life. Nothing could be better for the soul than the humility that comes from humiliations (See *Diary* #593).

What is it that humbles you the most? What wounds your pride and causes you to be angry or defensive? What do you stew over and think about obsessively? If something comes to mind, then this may be something very specific that the Lord wishes to turn into a source of grace and Mercy. Everything, be it sin, injustice, hurt, etc., has the potential to be turned into grace by our Lord. He truly is that All-Powerful. Identify that which wounds your pride the most and try to look at it from a new perspective, letting the Lord turn it into a source of grace.

Lord, my pride is wounded so many times. There are so many experiences I have that do not sit well with me. Help me to allow all those things that are out of my control to become transformed by You and Your grace so that they may no longer weigh me down, causing hurt and anger. Take these humiliations, dear Lord, and transform my heart through them so that, in my humility, I may come to know You more intimately and surrender to You more fully. Jesus, I trust in You.

Reflection 124: The Mercy of Intercessory Prayer

Do you want to see The Divine Mercy of God pour forth upon the world in an abundant way? Hopefully and presumably the answer to that question is an easy, "Yes." It's important to know that, in some ways, you are responsible for whether or not that happens. Specifically, Jesus has chosen to make His abundance of Mercy flow forth as a direct result of your intercession for others. It's true. Your personal choice to pray for others has a direct result on Jesus offering them special graces. This is a grace offered others in addition to the many other graces He offers in other ways. Do your part and others will be blessed in abundance. Ignore your part, and they will not receive the specific grace you could have won for them through your prayers (See *Diary* #599).

Reflect, today, upon the person or people God has entrusted to your intercession. This is no small responsibility. God has chosen you for this task. And through your prayers, others will be blessed. Who is it that God wants to bless through your prayers? Make a concrete decision to pray for them and trust that the Lord's Mercy will be bestowed as a direct result.

Lord, I pray that You will show me who You wish me to pray for. Place on my heart this desire. Help me to be faithful in my intercession and to trust in the power of that prayer. Here and now I offer (think of a person) to You. And I especially offer this person to the Immaculate Heart of Your Mother for her perfect prayers. Mother Mary, pray for us. Jesus, I trust in You.

Reflection 125: The Victim Soul

Do you know that our Lord chooses certain people for a specific mission of suffering? He picks certain people, who are few in number, to more fully resemble His innocent suffering here on Earth. These holy souls suffer in many and varied ways. They are the continuation of the innocent suffering of Jesus Himself. They have a very specific mission on Earth and it is a mission requiring the greatest sacrifice imaginable. The good news, for these chosen few, is that the crown of glory that awaits them in Heaven makes every act of suffering here on Earth worth it. Through their suffering, completely embraced in joy, and offered to the Father through the Son, they make up that which is "lacking in the sufferings of Christ" as St. Paul explains to us (Colossians 1:24). Though this unique vocation is only given to a few in a profound way, we are all called to share in Christ's sufferings so as to also share in His glorification (See *Diary* #604).

What do you do with your daily sufferings? Do you "offer it up?" This invitation from Jesus, to unite our sufferings with His, is a true calling that has more potential for grace than anything else. It's what makes us most like Him. It is the greatest sacrifice we can offer and the most powerful prayer we can pray. Think about the sufferings you encounter in your life. No matter what they are, do not run from them. Try to embrace them and offer them up, joyfully, to our Lord.

Heavenly Father, I give to You, this day, all my joys, works and sufferings. I especially offer You the sufferings I endure. I offer You all the small and great ways in which I experience suffering, hardship and pain in my life. May these become a sacrifice of love, offered in union with the one and perfect sacrifice of Jesus, Your Son. Transform this offering and make it a source of grace in this world. Jesus, I trust in You.

Reflection 126: Filial Fear – The Good Fear

Do you have fear in your life? It's important to know that some fear is quite unhealthy, stemming from a form of pride, while another form of fear is quite healthy, resulting from your profound love of God. The "holy fear" is *filial fear*, which is the fear of a child of God. This particular form of fear is present when your love of God is so deep that you *fear* doing anything that would harm your relationship with Him. It's not that you are afraid *of* God, rather, you have a holy desire to avoid all sin. This form of holy fear must also enter into every relationship of love you have for others. You should deeply desire to avoid all that harms each and every relationship you have been blessed to receive. This is a gift of God's abundant Mercy (See *Diary* #610).

Consider your love of God. Is it strong enough to produce the healthy desire in your heart to avoid all that might hurt that relationship? This holy fear must become a driving force to develop a profoundly personal relationship with our Lord. Consider, also, your relationship with others. Do you have a healthy desire to eliminate anything that is an obstacle to your wholehearted love of them? Seek this gift of God's Mercy and the Lord will draw you closer to Himself and to others.

Lord, I do love You and I desire to surrender to You everything in my life that keeps me from loving You with my whole heart. Give me a holy fear so that I may draw closer to You and learn to love others as You love them. Jesus, I trust in You.

Reflection 127: The Love of God Through Obedience

You are called to love God with your whole heart, mind, soul and strength. But how do you do this? What does an active loving of God look like in our lives? Ultimately, we love God through holy obedience. We must obey His Divine Will above all else. Perhaps that seems like a strange concept, that love of God is best expressed in holy obedience. But it is. It's expressed in holy obedience because of one simple fact: The Will of God is perfect, perfect for us, exactly what we need, it's what we were made for, and we must enter into perfect submission to His Will. In the end, the only way we will understand this form and depth of love is by living it (See *Diary* #616).

How well do you do with the practice of holy obedience? When you think about this, does it inspire you, or turn you off? Holy obedience can be a difficult virtue to embrace and live wholeheartedly. It can be difficult to accept and to embrace as a good. Look at your inner reaction to the idea of striving to obey God in all things. If you can rid yourself of any resistance to this practice, you will find great joy in loving God in this perfect way.

Lord, I want to obey You in all things. I thank You that Your law is perfect and, when embraced, completely refreshes my soul. Help me to always love You in this holy way so as to make Your Will my own. In this act, I imitate Your perfect obedience to the Will of the Father. Jesus, I trust in You.

Reflection 128: The Sweetness of Encountering Jesus

Have you encountered the sweetness of Jesus? He, with the Father and the Holy Spirit, come to you in the secret depths of your soul. There, in this hidden place, they desire to communicate with you. Their communication is beyond words and concepts. It's a communication of profound love that leaves the soul at peace and with a delight of the greatest sweetness. Their encounter with you is not an emotion; it's a spiritual union (See *Diary* #622).

How deep is your relationship with Jesus, the Father and the Holy Spirit? Is it something more intellectual? Is it based only on the fact that you believe in them, for the most part? Or is it something that goes much deeper? The goal must be to come to know God in a real and tangible way. But that knowledge of Him must also be personal. It must become a relationship that is lived and that sustains you in all things. If the Blessed Trinity lives within you, and if you allow yourself to embrace that relationship wholeheartedly, then you will discover an inner sweetness that overwhelms any suffering or hardship you endure. The sweetness of that love will carry you, day in and day out, to the glories of Heaven.

Lord, I long to know You, to love You and to become one with You. I desire to have You live within my soul, refreshing me with the sweetness of Your presence. Take my life, sweet Jesus, and unite me with Your perfect Heart of love. Jesus, I trust in You.

Reflection 129: Do Not Be Afraid

"Do not be afraid; just have faith" (Mark 5:36). These four words, "Do not be afraid," are spoken countless times throughout the Scripture. We should pay attention to them. Fear can paralyze us and lead us into many forms of foolish thinking and acting. The person who acts out of fear truly acts like a fool. That may seem harsh at first, but it's not if you understand what it means. It simply means that a person acting out of fear cannot act rationally. Fear does great damage to a person's ability to stay calm, remain focused and think clearly. That's why the Scriptures speak so directly regarding this important spiritual point. Fear must give way to faith and trust in God (See *Diary* #626-627).

What is it that causes you the most anxiety, worry and fear? It's a struggle we all deal with. There is no shame in admitting it. So what is it? Identify that which overwhelms you the most and you will identify that which God wants you to surrender in trust the most. Go to the heart of the struggle. Sincerely place that worry and fear into the Hands of God and trust. Trust that God is All-Powerful and capable of handling every situation. He may not change things the way you think they should be changed, but He will lift your burden and enable you to move forward without the fear that can easily paralyze and confuse you. Do not let fear dominate your life. Trust in God and let that trust transform you.

Jesus, I do want to trust You and to entrust all my many burdens to You. I especially turn to You with (pause and state that which causes the most fear and anxiety). Please enter into this burden and lift it by Your gentle hand, replacing it with peace and great inner calm. Jesus, I trust in You.

Reflection 130: Correcting Others in Love

There is little doubt that each one of us will encounter, from time to time, the sin of another. It could be in their words, actions or the omission of what they ought to do. Sin hurts and requires correction. Very often, when we are sinned against, we tend to get angry. But the anger we have is not always "holy anger" and is not, therefore, always from God. We can easily allow our wounded pride to be the source of a harsh, or even subtle, correction of another. This, then, becomes *our* sin. But sin must be confronted and God will, at times, call us to correct others. Our correction may even be severe. But when it comes from the holiness of God, inspiring and guiding us, our correction of the other will not wound them, it will be an act of Mercy. They may need severity, and God may inspire us to be severe, but we must always be careful that what we offer ultimately flows from the Mercy of God (See *Diary* #633).

Reflect upon any moments of contention that you have encountered lately. Were words spoken, or actions done that were based more on unhealthy emotion than on love? Examine how you react when hurt by another. Do you look at them with Mercy and seek to offer the Mercy of God, even if it must come, in that moment, in the form of a holy rebuke? Do not be afraid to let God use you to offer this form of Mercy. It may be hard to distinguish from the sin of anger, but we must strive to offer this Mercy for the good of those we are called to love.

Lord, I offer myself to You so that You can use me as an instrument of Your Divine Mercy. When I am sinned against, help me to forgive immediately. But help me, also, to know how best to address the sins of others. Help me to know how to offer correction in love for their good. Give me courage and wisdom, dear Lord, and use me as You will. Jesus, I trust in You.

Reflection 131: The Great Work of Small Sacrifices

Is it better to do great works, or small sacrifices? It's easy to conclude that some great work for God is far better than any small sacrifice. But is it? That all depends upon the Will of God. Sometimes we take on some "great work" for God but, in the end, it's not part of His plan. A work is great only when it is done because God inspired it and remains the one leading it. Conversely, if God inspires a very small sacrifice on your part and you accept it and live it, then you can be assured that this small sacrifice will do more good for the salvation of souls than any other sacrifice you could ever dream up on your own. In fact, trying to force the Will of God to conform to your own will, inevitably, does more damage for the Kingdom of God than good, even if *your* idea seems holy (See *Diary* #639).

What is it that God is inspiring you to do? How are you called to serve His holy Will? Look for His inspiration in the smallest of things. It may be a kind word spoken to another, or a small hidden sacrifice that only you are aware of. And if He is calling you to do something "great" that others will notice, do not be afraid of this, but do not be overly proud of it either. Do all things, great or small, in accord with the Will of God and you will find that all things you do are truly great!

Lord, I believe that greatness is found only in Your holy Will. Help me to set aside my own ideas and agendas so that I may seek only that which is in Your perfect Heart. Help me to humbly embrace every small sacrifice You ask of me, and to have courage to do those things which seem to be beyond my ability. May I listen to You and respond generously to whatever You say. Jesus, I trust in You.

Reflection 132: The Incomprehensible God

One common tendency we all have is curiosity. We easily become curious about almost everything, desiring to know. Magazines, news articles, shows, daily gossip sessions, etc., all have as their aim the satisfaction of our curiosity. This curiosity must turn into a desire to know God and all He speaks to us. But, with that said, we must also <u>know</u> that we cannot know. The wisdom and Will of God are so far beyond our limited minds and hearts that we will never be able to understand their mystery. Life is a mystery. Struggle and hardship are mysteries. Love is a mystery. And yet, as we humbly face the countless mysteries of life, we also face the incomprehensible mystery of God. Interestingly, knowing that we do not know, and understanding that we cannot understand, present us with the great mystery of God. In the face of this incomprehensible Mystery, we are in the presence of God. This is a gift! This silencing of our understanding before the mystery of God enables us to face life in faith. Faith is a way of knowing without fully comprehending. It's a gift enabling us to walk through life in darkness, yet with clarity and certainty (See *Diary* #651).

Do you find that you do not understand God or His ways? Do you look at your life and wonder, "Why this?" or "Why that?" or "Where is God in all of this?" God and His ways are a mystery. But, as a mystery, you are invited to enter in with the darkness of faith. This will only make sense if you let the Holy Spirit penetrate your thoughts and teach you in a new way. Your "understanding" of the Mind and Will of God will not so much be like other forms of knowledge; rather, your knowledge will be new, certain, clear, deep, and yet mysterious at the same time. Allow yourself to be taught by faith and you will be able to face any and every mystery and hardship that you encounter in life.

Lord, oh Incomprehensible Mystery! I stand before You in awe and in darkness. Yet in the darkness of my understanding, I reaffirm my faith and trust in You. As I face the mystery of my life and, even more so, the mystery of Your life, I allow You to consume me with the gift of faith. Help me to believe without seeing and to know without understanding. Most importantly, I desire and choose to give my life to You, oh Incomprehensible Mystery, and I choose You above all else. Jesus, I trust in You.

Reflection 133: Actions on Our Own

We cannot do anything good on our own. This is a fact. All we can do on our own is sin. In fact, the only way to please God and to do good things for Him is to rely upon Him for everything. We must have a relationship of complete dependence upon God in all things. It's easy to think that we will please God if we simply try harder with an action we have undertaken on our own and believe is good. If we do this or that and do it well, we will please Him. But this is not true. God is not looking for us to do something of our own choosing for Him, and to try and try again until we accomplish it. No, He is only looking for one thing: obedience to His Will in all things. And the only way we can be obedient to that which He calls us to, is by becoming completely dependent upon Him in every way (See *Diary* #659).

Reflect upon the joyful discovery of the Will of God. When we discover what He asks of us, and then accept His Will, we will also, necessarily, enter into a relationship of trust and utter dependence upon Him. This act of depending upon Him to fulfill His Will produces an abundance of peace and joy. Reflect upon whether you see this total dependence upon God alive in your life. Where you see it lacking, surrender more deeply in trust, giving up that which you cling to by your own will, choosing instead the Will of God as He makes it known to You.

Lord, I choose this day to become completely dependent upon You and Your most holy Will. I choose, further, to give up my own will and all that I try to do on my own. May my surrender and dependence upon You become the source of my enduring peace and joy. Jesus, I trust in You.

Reflection 134: The Sweetness of Our Joint Labor

A honey bee works diligently, day after day, and a colony of bees all work toward the same natural end. They work to produce honey. This is no small task and requires constant work on the part of thousands of bees to produce a small amount of honey. But, in the end, their efforts pay off and honey is made and stored in the hive. So it is with our lives. We are all called to serve the Lord individually, but we also do so in communion with others. Religious congregations, dioceses, parish churches, families and friends are all called in various ways to serve the Lord as a community of faith. When each one does his or her part, the Lord accomplishes an abundance of good fruit so as to bring the sweetness of His love into a world in much need (See *Diary* #664).

Do you see yourself as a "lone Christian?" Or do you see yourself as a member of the family of God, seeking to do your humble part so that the Church, as a whole, can complete Her mission. The Church is called to bring the sweet love of our Lord into a world starving for love. Reflect upon whether you are doing your small part. Your part is all that you are responsible for. It is nothing other than embracing the Will of God each and every day and each and every moment of the day. Small acts of love, the daily choice to trust, the humble submission of your will. You can fulfill your mission in life and when you do, the Lord will add this to the works of all His sons and daughters and, through His whole Church, He will transform the world, bringing forth His glorious Kingdom.

Lord, as a single bee produces only a tiny bit of honey, so also do my actions and service to You produce only that which You have given me to accomplish. I offer my love and service to You so that You may unite it with the love and service of others, producing, together, an abundance of Mercy for a world in such need. Jesus, I trust in You.

Reflection 135: Conversing with Jesus

Do you converse with Jesus? This is a form of prayer that is most fruitful. "Conversation" with God is not the highest form of prayer, but it is a form of prayer that we often need to begin with. Conversation with God is especially fruitful when we carry some form of burden or confusion in life. When this is the case, it can be helpful to speak about this openly and honestly with our Lord. Speaking with Him, interiorly, will help bring clarity to whatever obstacle we are facing. And when the conversation is complete, and when we have heard His clear response, we are then invited to enter deeper into prayer by submitting ourselves to that which He says. Through this initial exchange, followed by a complete submission of mind and will, true adoration of God is brought about. So if something is on your mind, do not hesitate to speak openly and honestly with our Lord about it. You will find that it is an easy and fruitful conversation to have (See *Diary* # 670).

Think about that which bothers you the most. What is it that seems to weigh you down. Try getting on your knees and pouring your heart out to Jesus. Speak to Him, but then be silent and wait on Him. In the proper way and at the proper time He will answer you, when you're open. And when you do hear Him speak, listen and obey. This will allow you to walk down the road of true adoration and worship.

Dear Lord, I love You and adore You with all my heart. Help me to confidently bring my concerns to You, laying them down before You and listening to Your response. Dear Jesus, as You converse with me, help me to heed Your voice and to respond with true generosity. Jesus, I trust in You.

Reflection 136: The Power of a Grateful Heart

If you were to examine the content of your prayer life over the past month, what would you see? Hopefully there would be many moments to surrender, intercession, praise and adoration. And hopefully there were also many moments in which your prayer consisted of deep thanksgiving to God. Being grateful, truly grateful, and expressing that gratitude in prayer is powerful. We have so much to be grateful for and yet, so often, we become more focused in on our problems than on the countless blessings God has bestowed upon us. Even in the midst of life's darkest hour, there is much that a holy soul can find to be grateful for. Offering prayers of gratitude to God, with much sincerity, has the potential to lift our spirits to the heights of authentic spiritual joy (See *Diary* #675).

What are you grateful for? Better put, in what ways has God blessed you in abundance? If you are not immediately aware of your blessings from God, that is a good sign that you may need to spend more time "counting your blessings." It's good to keep our eyes on the innumerable blessings God has bestowed upon us, to see them, name them and be joyful in them. The more we see them, the more we grow in gratitude, and the more we grow in gratitude, the more we are blessed.

Lord, I thank You with profound gratitude for the countless blessings in my life. Help me to daily become more aware of those blessings and to be grateful for them. Help me to see that life itself is a gift and that You are active in my life day and night. Help me to especially see these blessings when life is hard, or when some burden weighs me down. May I be filled with a grateful heart and always rejoice in Your goodness. Jesus, I trust in You.

Reflection 137: Power in the Cross

When you pray, do you ever sit and gaze upon the crucifix? From an outside perspective, the crucifix is a puzzling reality. Why would we lift high and honor such a horrific event? The brutal murder of the Son of God may not be, at first, something we are attracted to. Yet, the crucifix has a power and a draw for those who gaze upon it in faith because it is not only a horrific and brutal murder, it is, first and foremost, the complete victory over sin and death. The Crucifixion of our Lord was the greatest act of love ever known, because in that act, He destroyed death and sin forever for those who turn to Him with complete abandon. The crucifix is also a sign to us of the self-giving we are called to live. We are each called to enter upon that cross and die with Christ, giving ourselves to others. For in dying with Him, our sins are atoned for and we are able to share in the victory of His Resurrection. Gazing upon the Crucifixion of our Lord transforms us as it opens the doors of the Mercy won by this selfless act of love (See *Diary* #681).

Try praying before the crucifix. Try sitting in silence and gazing upon it. To "gaze" is more than to simply "look." When we gaze we seek to look beyond the image we see and to peer into the love that brought Jesus to that moment. We see a God of infinite love who was willing to go all the way to save us from our sins and love us with a perfect love.

Lord, I do desire to gaze upon Your perfect act of love and to see Your Heart, bursting forth with Mercy upon me and upon the whole world. Help me to understand the unfathomable gift of Your Sacrifice and to enter into an eternal gratitude for this gift. Jesus, I trust in You.

Reflection 138: God's Mercy is Infinite

Perhaps it's no surprise to hear it said that the Mercy of God is infinite. But "infinity" is quite a concept to grasp. In fact, some would argue that it is *impossible* to grasp. Delving into something that is infinite and has no bounds is beyond what we could ever fathom. So it is with the Mercy of God. Being infinite, we should realize that we will spend eternity, an infinite existence, seeking and receiving this Mercy that will never end. Right now, on Earth, our experience of the infinite Mercy of God is quite limited. It's as if we can take in a thimble full while the endless oceans await (See *Diary* #687 & 692).

Do you ever spend time reflecting upon infinity? Think of outer space, which never ends. And how could it? What would be at the other end of the end of space? So it is with God's Mercy. How could it ever end? How could it ever be exhausted? His Mercy is as vast and wide as God is Himself. Reflect upon the essence of God, and as you marvel at His infinite nature, allow yourself to be drawn into His unending gift of Love. For when you can begin to grasp it, you will desire it. And when you desire it, you will have begun your journey into infinity.

Lord, Your love for me is beyond what I can ever imagine. Help me to at least understand that I will never understand, fully, the depth of Your love. Help me to see that Your Mercy is endless and help me to begin my journey into eternity with You. Jesus, I trust in You.

Reflection 139: Providence makes it Happen

Sometimes we tend to push the Will of God faster than God has chosen to move. As a result, we end up doing our own will and not that of God's. The key is patience. We must patiently wait upon the Lord for him to act *in* us so that He is the one doing all things *through* us. In fact, the act of patience is something that God desires greatly in our lives. Through patience, we are able to let go of our own will and our own ideas and watch the Lord accomplish so much more than we could ever do on our own. We must be diligent, and respond to the Lord when He opens a door or points the way, but we must wait for Him to do the opening and pointing (See *Diary* #693).

What are you impatient with in life? What is it that you want God to move faster at? Reflect upon this inner struggle and know that the virtue of patience opens the door to the guidance and grace that God wants to give. Let Him do things in His time and His way and you will discover that His ways are far above yours.

Lord, I know that Your ways are infinitely above mine and that Your thoughts must be chosen over my own (see Is. 55:8). Give me the grace of patience in all things. Help me to wait on You and to trust that Your Mercy will be bestowed in abundance in accord with Your perfect wisdom. Jesus, I trust in You.

Reflection 140: Being Misunderstood

In your relations with others, do you sometimes feel misunderstood? It could be by a close family member, a friend, a coworker, etc. The problem is that the content of your mind, heart, will, intention, and all of your past experiences are what go into directing your actions. And no one understands all of this except God. We do not even fully understand what we do and why we do it most of the time. As a result, it is easy for others to fail to understand us and what takes place within us. It can also be easy for others to misunderstand us and even judge us. This can be hard to take but we must not let it bother us. Instead, we must direct our concern only to that which our Lord thinks. His Mind and

His judgment are all that matters. And the misunderstanding we may experience at times from others must be seen as an act of the permissive Will of our Lord, primarily to test and strengthen our Mercy for others (See *Diary* #700).

Can you think of a time in which you recently experienced the misunderstanding of another? If so, rather than letting yourself become angry or hurt over this, allow it to test the depths of your own merciful heart. Accept this humiliation with grace and give thanks to God that He has permitted you to share in the same act of misunderstanding and judgment that He took upon Himself. In this, you are blessed to be invited to share in the distribution of His Divine Mercy.

Lord, give me a merciful heart. When I am misunderstood, help me to accept this as an opportunity for grace, forgiveness and Mercy. Thank You for loving me enough to allow me to endure such a test. I give myself to You, dear Lord, so that You can work in and through me to be a witness of all that You endured. Jesus, I trust in You.

Reflection 141: The Mercy of the Angels

Only in Heaven will we understand the gift of the angelic hosts. These magnificent spiritual beings were created by God out of love. Some were created for the sole purpose of eternal worship and adoration of the Most Holy Trinity. They never tire of this calling and worship God with an ever deepening love and communion. Other angelic beings were created to bring the love and Mercy of God to us. The Guardian Angels and Archangels are two such creations that are constantly interceding for us, protecting us and guiding us into the Will of God. Our knowledge of them is not necessary for their continued attentiveness to our love and care. But humbly acknowledging their mediation and calling upon them is an act of pure faith and trust in God. They are here with us and we must call on them, trust in them, hope in them and love them.

Doing so is the Will of God and an acknowledgment of one central way through which He pours forth His Divine Mercy (See *Diary* #706).

Do you call on the angels to come to your aid? Do you pray to your guardian angel and St. Michael the Archangel, in particular? We must trust in their powerful mediation and sacred ability to guard and protect us in accord with the Mind and Will of God. Speak to these angels today, and allow yourself to become more fully consecrated to their care.

Lord, I thank You for the gift of the holy angels. I thank You for Sts. Michael, Raphael, Gabriel, my guardian angel and for the whole host of Heaven. I pray that I will continually be open to the workings of these angelic beings in my life. Through their mediation, keep me safe from all evil and direct me in accord with Your holy Will. Jesus, I trust in You.

Reflection 142: The Lord's Peace Dispels Evil

It is important to recognize the existence of the evil one, satan. And it's important to realize his anger and hatred. His hatred is of greater intensity than we may be able to understand. It is beyond his control to cease hating us and seeking to destroy us with all his powers. Why is it important to know this? Because when we receive some attack from the evil one, either directly or through the "inspired" anger of another, we tend to react with fear, scandal, or anger ourselves. We tend to want to fight back. But if we understand the intense hatred of the devil, we will realize that he desires to draw us into his hatred and anger. Therefore, the best response to any experience of his hatred is to turn from him and his attacks and to remain at peace with God. The peace of our soul will dispel him and all he seeks to do to us. His anger is not worth even a moment of our attention or engagement (see *Diary* #713).

How do you react to the evil one and his attacks? Do you recognize his insidious but vile ways? Can you discern his attempts to steal your peace and turn your focus to fear rather than faith? Reflect, today, upon the crucifix and turn your eyes to this saving act of perfect love given by our Savior. By turning to the Lord in all things, His peace remains and He will dispel the dark attacks of him who hates us.

Lord, I turn my eyes to You and give my mind, heart, feelings and passions to You and You alone. Free me from foolish fear and from all attacks from the evil one. May I discern his evil ways and reject their effects by trusting in You and You alone. Jesus, I do trust in You.

Reflection 143: Trust, Trust and More Trust

Every reflection of this book ends with a prayer and each prayer ends with the prayer, "Jesus, I trust in You." But do you? Trust is not only a one time act. It's not something we do or do not do. It's something we must do on a continually deepening level. There is no limit to the depths of the trust to which we are called. The deeper your trust, the more the Heart of our Divine Lord will be drawn to pour forth His Mercy. One essential aspect of growing in trust is seeing our misery and sin. When we see our sin without trust in God's Mercy, we are left in despair. But when we see the horror of our sin and trust in His Mercy to the same extent, He enters in and transforms our souls into His holy and pure dwelling place of love (See *Diary* #718).

Do you trust in God and in His abundance of Mercy? If you do, you will also be aware of your sin to a great extent. Do you see your sin? Are you aware of your miserable condition? If so, do not despair; rather, see it as a graced opportunity to trust all the more in God and in His perfect love for you.

Lord, I do trust in You but I do not trust You enough. Help me, first, to be aware of my wretchedness and sin. But in seeing this miserable condition, help me to turn to You rather than to despair. May my trust never end and may it grow continually deeper so that Your Heart may be opened and so that You will pour down Your grace upon me. Jesus, I trust in You. Jesus, I trust in You. Jesus, I trust in You.

Reflection 144: Your Holiness is a Gift to Others

Jesus deeply desires to pour forth His Divine Mercy into your soul. He desires to transform your sin and make you His perfect dwelling place. This is a gift beyond what we can grasp, but one we are invited to accept. Accepting the countless graces from our Lord is not only for our good, it's also for the good of others. Jesus wants you to become holy in every way out of love for you, as His precious child. But He also wants you to become holy for the good of others. The holier you become, the more abundant is the Mercy of God in your life. And the more abundant the Mercy of God in your life, the more others will be blessed by God's Mercy through you (See *Diary* #723).

Do you seek holiness? If so, it's easy to think of this goal in a selfish way. It's easy to seek holiness and Mercy for our own good. But if the gift we experience is truly the Mercy of God in our souls, then we will be compelled to let Him distribute this overflowing Mercy to others through us. Mercy cannot be kept in a selfish way for selfish purposes. It must be received so that we become an instrument to others. Reflect upon yourself being this instrument today, and offer yourself to God for this holy purpose.

Dear Lord, I thank You for the abundance of Your Mercy in my life. I thank You for loving me as Your precious child. Help me to be transformed by Your love and, in turn, to become an instrument of Your overflowing grace to others. Jesus, I trust in You.

Reflection 145: Lost in the Admiration of Love

Falling in love can leave one "spellbound." This form of human love may leave you speechless to a certain extent, not finding it necessary, or even possible, to accurately express what you feel. But the love of God is beyond any experience of human love and, thus, when experienced on a profound level, you will find yourself sitting back in awe and admiration of the God whom you love. No words will be able to capture or express your admiration and amazement of the glory and splendor of the God with whom you have been drawn to love. Your silence and awe will say far more than you could articulate in any other way (See *Diary* #729).

Have you fallen in love? More specifically, have you fallen in love with your God? "Falling in love," as it relates to God, is not only a human passion or emotion, it's a spiritual yearning that consumes your soul and leaves you content in His presence. The experience of this spiritual union with God is all that you need in life to find fulfillment and it will be the source of all that you do in life, in that your actions will be solely directed toward the love of God, your beloved. Reflect upon the depth of your love of God and if you do not see this love alive in your life, tell the Lord that you desire it and seek Him with all your might.

Lord, I love You and desire to be loved by You. I know my love is far from perfect. Lord, help me to seek You more intimately and to encounter You in the most intimate of ways. May my spirit be filled with a longing for You, and as I meet You may I gaze upon Your glory and splendor. May I truly become "lost" in my deep admiration of You, my God. Jesus, I trust in You.

Reflection 146: Praying with the Passion of Christ

All of us are aware of the sacred Passion of our Lord. But few are able to gaze upon His Passion with true feeling and love. In our prayer, we must learn to meditate upon the Passion of our Lord with great devotion. This is not so much something we do by our own effort; rather, it's something that we allow our Lord to do in us. We must allow Him to reveal to us the great suffering He went through and, in that revelation, we must allow our whole being to become consumed with love of Him who died this horrid death out of love for us (See *Diary* #737).

Do you spend time meditating on the Passion of our Lord? Perhaps it's easier to look at the Resurrection and His triumphal victory over sin and death. But the way to the Resurrection and Glorification is through the Passion. Reflect, today, upon how willing you are to allow yourself to be drawn into every pain and every suffering that our Lord endured. Seeing His Passion for what it is allows you to love Him more deeply. The more you become aware of His suffering, the more you will desire to console His wounded Heart through your love and submission to His holy Will. Let every aspect of the Passion of Christ speak to you and change you. The result will be a deeper love of God and an abundance of Mercy for those suffering all around you.

Lord, help me to become aware of Your holy Passion. Help me to see the love that enabled You to endure such torment. May I see in Your Passion Your endless love for all and may I, in turn, love those who suffer with the same love I have for You. Jesus, I trust in You.

Reflection 147: Mercy through Deeds, Words and Prayers

Do you want to become an instrument of the unfathomable Mercy of God? If so, you do this by your deeds, your words and your prayers. First, you must constantly be on the "lookout" for opportunities to show Mercy by your deeds. Too often, when given the opportunity (such as to forgive another), we turn the other way. But we must be vigilant and committed to seeking these opportunities out and rejoicing when they are given. Second, your words can bring forth grace and Mercy, or they can wound and harm. We do harm by harshness or even by our failure to speak when we ought. We bring forth Mercy when we speak words of truth in love, even challenging words, so as to make present the Truth of God. And third, we often forget about the power of praying and offering sacrifices for others. Interceding for the world as a whole, and for individuals in particular, is a way of turning the key and opening the doors of God's grace. Do not neglect this essential act of Mercy (See *Diary* #742).

Reflect upon your deeds, words and prayers. Can you point to concrete ways by which our Lord has used you to bring His Mercy to others. Try to identify a few of them and if you struggle with this examen, it is a good sign that the Lord wants to increase His daily outpouring of Mercy through you.

Lord, I consecrate to You my words, my actions and my life of prayer. Use me as You desire and help me to be attentive to Your daily inspiration. Help me to sincerely seek out opportunities, each and every day, all day long, by which I can spread Your perfect love in this world. I give myself to You, dear Lord. Jesus, I trust in You.

Reflection 148: Mercy for Those in Purgatory

When a loved one dies, it is easy to instantly presume they are in Heaven and are no longer in need of our prayers. But one of the greatest gifts we can offer to those who have gone before us is our prayers. It's true that every person who dies in a state of grace (meaning they do not have unrepented mortal sin), will enter into the glories of Heaven, eventually.

However, what we may often forget is that in order to enter into the full glory of the presence of the Most Holy Trinity, every last sin, no matter how small, must be purged away. This is Purgatory, and Purgatory is a clear and definitive teaching of our faith. But Purgatory, itself, is so easily misunderstood. It's not a place we go to be punished as a result of God's anger. Rather, it's a state in which we enter our final purification on account of God's love. It is His burning love that has the effect of purifying us of every last attachment we have to sin. Every bad habit, every omission of charity, every foul thought, everything that cannot enter into Heaven with us. Purgatory is an act of God's Mercy and we are called to help pour forth that Mercy on others through our prayers, sacrifices, and indulgences offered on their behalf after they pass from this Earth (See *Diary* #748).

Think about your loved ones who have gone before you. Let your love for them compel you to pray for them, especially today. Trust that the prayers, sacrifices and indulgences you offer for them are the greatest gift of Mercy you can give.

Lord, I pray for (mention a loved one who has passed) and pray for Your Divine Mercy to flood his/her soul. Purify every sin away and grant entrance into the glories of Your Heavenly Kingdom. I pray also for all holy souls in most need of Your Mercy. Jesus, I trust in You.

Reflection 149: Interior Inspirations

There are countless opportunities all around us to share the Mercy of God with those in need. But it is all too easy to miss these opportunities to do so. One primary way that we allow ourselves to become instruments of Divine Mercy is by seeking to continually be attentive to the many interior inspirations sent to us by the Holy Spirit. It's not so much a matter of looking for these opportunities ourselves; rather, it's a matter of becoming so aware of the workings of God, that we allow the Holy Spirit to inspire us here and there, leading us to the many opportunities to act as an instrument of the Mercy of God (See *Diary* #756).

Are you attentive to the interior inspirations sent to you by the Holy Spirit? These inspirations are often subtle and quite gentle. But if you can learn to discern them, God will use you for an abundance of good works. Reflect, today, upon your habit of seeking out His voice. Allow yourself to become drawn to His gentle promptings and to respond with a generous heart.

Lord, I turn to You and seek Your gentle but clear voice. As I hear You speak, give me the strength to follow Your commands so as to embrace Your holy Will and to become an instrument of Your Divine Mercy in our world. Jesus, I trust in You.

Reflection 150: Avoiding the Trap of Human Opinion

Does it matter what others think of you? In other words, should you be concerned about the "opinions" of others? Yes and no. No, we should not be concerned in the sense that the only "opinion" that matters is that which is true. And the Truth is that which is in the Mind of God. And that Truth is not an opinion, it is the Truth. So, no, we ought not worry about opinions that do not reflect the Mind of God. However, we should be concerned about another's opinion insofar as our love for them should draw us to help them arrive at the truth. Some are obstinate and hold to their opinion over the truth no matter what. This is beyond our control. But others are open and if we see an open mind and heart, we should also be open to any way that God wants to use us to help them shed their erroneous views in exchange for that which is in the Mind of God (See *Diary* #763).

Reflect, especially, upon the tendency you have to become overly concerned about what people think or say about you. Do you allow this to influence you in an unhealthy way? Do you allow it to affect your own choices and focus in life? Remind yourself, this day, that all that matters is the truth. What is in the Mind of God? That's what you should be concerned about. Recommit yourself to that truth and you will experience an immense amount of freedom.

Lord, I turn to You who are the one and only source of all Truth. I seek to know and believe only that which resides in Your Mind. I choose this Truth over all the opinions of the world, and I choose to let go of my own opinions, preferring only to embrace what You reveal. Give me the grace to live always in the Truth. Jesus, I trust in You.

Reflection 151: Spiritual Kinship

In order to be truly close to someone else, and to understand them on a deep level, is it necessary to speak continually and to share every detail of your mind and heart? Not if both souls are intimately united with God. In that case, very little has to be said in order for each person to recognize a shared unity and to understand the other. When God is alive in each person, it is His presence that unites them and enables them to know the other. This produces the blessing of a spiritual kinship which could never be attained in any other way, not even after years of constant talking and sharing. The unity that comes from a shared knowledge of God is far superior and far more effective in establishing a beautiful friendship than any other means (See *Diary* #768).

Think about your friendships. What is the basis of those relationships? Hopefully your friendships are grounded in your life of faith and love of God. Reflect upon how easily you are able to speak about your faith with your friends. While it's good to offer friendship and love to all people, it's also healthy to seek out those with whom you can share a spiritual kinship. Allow the Holy Spirit to draw you to others with whom you can share this depth of love and spiritual friendship and the Lord will bless you with an abundance of His Mercy through them.

Lord, I thank You for the gift of those people in my life who have a strong faith in You. Help me to rely upon those friendships and, in them, to discover Your merciful Heart. Help me also to be an instrument of Mercy to all whom You have placed in my life. Lord, You are my closest friend and I thank You for this precious gift of Your friendship and Your love for me. Jesus, I trust in You.

Reflection 152: The Mystery of the Grace of Suffering

Human suffering is one of the greatest mysteries of life. The *Diary* of Saint Faustina, as well as the whole spiritual tradition of our faith, reveals much about this profound mystery of suffering. First, from a purely secular point of view, suffering is far from desirable. In fact, it is typically avoided at all costs and seen as the greatest of tragedies. However, from a Christian perspective, suffering itself has been transformed by Christ and made the greatest instrument of grace ever known. It was through His intense suffering on the Cross that the salvation of the world came about. And by freely embracing all suffering, He made it the means and source of all grace. By so doing, Jesus also invites us to see our sufferings as an opportunity for grace. By embracing it, uniting it to His Cross, and offering it to the Father, our suffering is also able to take on infinite value and become a channel of the Mercy of God. Suffering, freely embraced by a Christian, must become a sign of one's closeness to Christ and a path to holiness (See *Diary* #774).

Suffering can be very difficult and yet unavoidable most often in life. Rather than run from it, reflect, today, upon the fact that God is able to use your suffering for good. This is a mysterious calling and requires the greatest of faith and trust. But when entered into, you will discover that the power of God overshadows and transforms even that which is most painful in life.

Lord, help me to entrust to You all suffering. Help me to have hope in You and to fix my gaze upon Your Cross during the most troubled times of life. Use me Lord, and use my suffering as a source of my holiness and for the upbuilding of Your Church in holiness. Jesus, I trust in You.

Reflection 153: Seeing our "Littleness"

Little children can't wait to grow up. When they have a birthday, they are filled with joy that they are one year older. And yet, as little children, they are still dependent upon their parents in many ways. The same is true of us in a spiritual sense. We often want to "grow up" and to become great saints, attaining great things for God. And yet, we must often remind ourselves that we are still children. In our "littleness" before God, we are now and ever will be fully dependent upon Him for all our needs. Recognizing this fact is essential to becoming a great saint and growing in holiness. We become great by becoming small (See *Diary* #779).

Reflect upon your littleness before God. Compared to the glory and power of the Almighty, we are small and weak. But God sees our littleness and He desires that we run to Him in complete confidence. Entrust yourself to His Mercy and run to Him. Realize that it is only by humbly admitting your total dependence upon Him that you are made strong through His embrace.

Lord, I do run to You and cling to You in my need. You are All-Powerful and glorious beyond measure. May I rely upon You in all things and continually seek You with my whole being. Jesus, I trust in You.

Reflection 154: Silent and Humble Adoration

Imagine the scene of our Blessed Mother in the humble state of the Nativity. She had no home at that moment other than this place where animals gathered. Yet in the stillness of that holy night, she was at home as she gazed upon her Child with the deepest adoration and love. She gazed in silence as He lay sleeping on the hay. This must be an image of your soul. You are called to enter into the humility of the inner dwelling place of your heart. Deep within, you must see this Precious Child, resting in peace. Remain silent and attentive, keep your eyes fixed on Him in adoration, and allow yourself to become consumed with delight at His presence within your soul (See *Diary* #785).

Reflect upon your humble and silent prayer. As you sit quietly before Jesus, or even as you go about the duties of your day, are you attentive to the divine presence of your Savior living within you? Do you see Him sleeping there in the stillness? Our souls must become a place of prayer and silence so that we can humbly keep our eyes upon our Lord within this holy dwelling place. If you keep your eyes upon Him, as He dwells silently within you, you will then go about your day with the peace and joy that only this holy Child can bring.

Lord, bring humility and stillness to my heart. May I discover You resting there in peace and adore You with a profound love. May I always keep my eyes upon You and never become distracted by the many temptations of this world. May the adoration I offer You who dwell within me become a source of the love and service I offer to all. Jesus, I trust in You.

Reflection 155: Facing Judgment with Grace

One painful experience you may face is that of the rash judgment by another. At times, others will look at you with judgment and disdain for reasons out of your control. Perhaps they will identify some small fault and magnify it in such a way that they use it as the lens through which they see your whole life. This can be quite painful and can evoke much disordered emotion. But it doesn't have to. The only thing you can do in the face of rash judgment is to forgive and seek to offer Mercy. But how do you do this? It is only possible if you are first hidden within the Mercy of the Lord. If you allow your eyes and heart to gaze continually upon His Mercy, and if you allow Him to cover you with that Mercy, then one effect will be that the harshness of others will not enter into your soul. Instead, when pierced with this lance, your heart will pour forth the Mercy that our Lord has poured upon you in abundance (see *Diary* #791).

Reflect, today, upon two things: 1) Are your eyes fixed, intently, upon the Mercy of God? Does His Mercy cover you, shield you and hide you from the cruelty of the world? 2) If so, when you are an object of scorn or ridicule, do you allow the Lord to open your heart so as to pour forth His Divine Mercy? He wants to use your heart to be an instrument of His own sacred and pierced Heart. You allow Him to use you only when you first allow Him to consume you with His Mercy.

Lord, consume me with Your Mercy. May I find in You my dwelling place and may my heart become fully united with Yours. As my heart becomes one with Yours, dear Lord, use it as a source of Mercy for others. When pierced, allow it to pour forth Your grace in abundance. I give my heart to You for Your perfect purpose and Will. Jesus, I trust in You.

Reflection 156: The Lord is Our Refuge

There are times in life when fear enters into your life. You may have some daunting task before you, or may be walking down a path of the unknown. These, and many other experiences in life, can become a cause for fear and anxiety. Fear of the unknown can especially become all consuming. But it need not be if the Lord is with you and is your constant Refuge. Jesus desires that you turn to Him in childlike trust and simplicity, knowing that He will lead you through life every step of the way. We need not fear if our eyes and heart are fixed on Him. He will never leave us (See *Diary* #797).

What is it that you fear the most in life? What is it about your future that worries you? Does that which is unknown to you cause much anxiety? Know that the Lord desires to free you of these heavy burdens by inviting you to take refuge in His Sacred Heart. By turning to Him, as a child, you will be freed of the fears that are quite burdensome. Ponder your fears this day and then turn to the Lord in perfect abandon. As you do, He will lift them from you, replacing them with His perfect peace.

Lord, I turn to You in my anxiety and fear. I trust You in all things and pray that You increase my capacity for faith and hope in You. Please become my refuge and give me the confidence of a child, to turn to You in my time of need. Jesus, I trust in You.

Reflection 157: Moral Decision Making

Do you ever struggle with making the right moral decision? This happens as a result of our fallen human nature. We are easily confused in life and can easily fail to grasp the Mind and Will of God. So what should you do? Know that your conscience is a sanctuary to which the Lord must be invited. When invited, He will come and dwell there to teach you all things. When facing decisions in life, pray, seek counsel from others, and seek the many truths revealed through Scripture and our Church. These are all sources of the Mercy of God. Afterwards, if you have truly sought the Lord and His holy Will, act as your conscience commands. Listen to it, trust it, and act on it. If in the future you see that you have erred, do not hesitate to change. But do not hesitate to move forward in the way that you hear our Lord directing you. He is a God of abundant Mercy and the pure and holy intention you have gives much joy to His Heart (See *Diary* #800).

Do you struggle with making decisions in life? Do you worry that you are offending our Lord? If so, let go of these worries for they may be the result of a scrupulous conscience. Instead, do your due diligence by seeking the reasonable advice of others whom you trust, seek guidance from the Scriptures and from our Church, pray and abandon yourself to God and His holy Will, and then trust your conscience and act. Think about that decision that you may struggle with right now. Work through this process and leave the rest to our merciful Lord.

Lord, help me to seek Your holy Will in all things, to come to know your holy Will and to act on it with full confidence. Give me, also, the grace of humility to change when I see that I have erred. Bless me, dear Lord, with a clean conscience so that I may glorify You always in freedom and love. Jesus, I trust in You.

Reflection 158: The Content of Your Speech

The content of your daily speech is a clear reflection of the content of your soul. So what does your speech reflect? Very often you may find that your conversations throughout the day have been about superficial and worldly matters. Though some casual conversations of this sort are normal and healthy, you should also be able to point to regular conversations that speak of the glory of God and your life of faith. You should be able to see daily words of charity and holiness. And you should see words that build others up (See *Diary* #804).

Reflect upon your conversations of the past week. What have they been about? Have you fallen into the trap of being cunning or harsh? Have you criticized or put others down? If so, these conversations reveal your soul. At times, your conversations may not fall into the category of sin, but may be dominated by worldly and unimportant things such as a fascination with wealth, or entertainment, or jokes or the like. Though none of these may be evil in and of themselves, if they are the dominant content of your speech then there is little room for the Lord. Seek to make your words and daily conversations a reflection of your deep love of Christ. Let your speech become an outpouring of the Mercy of God alive in your life. This is one key way through which God reveals the sanctity of your soul and uses you to bring holiness to others.

Lord, I surrender to You my speech. I give to You every thought I have and every word that comes forth from my mouth. Please use my words to reveal Your glory and the Mercy that permeates Your Heart. May this Mercy also permeate my heart and flow forth from my lips as an invitation to holiness for all. Jesus, I trust in You.

Reflection 159: Mercy at the Hour of Your Death

Every time we pray the "Hail Mary" prayer, we pray for the sacred hour of our death. In so doing, we entrust that hour to our Blessed Mother so that she will intercede for us at the moment we need it the most. Another holy prayer to pray in preparation for that hour is the Chaplet of Divine Mercy. Too often we fear the moment of our death. And though this is understandable to a certain extent, we must allow our Lord to reveal to us the importance and sacredness of that holy moment. Everything in this life must be but a preparation for this last hour of our earthly life. If we have sought the abundant Mercy of God throughout life, then we will be assured of His Mercy at our passing to the next. If we have not, we must still trust that His Mercy is infinite and, as long as we have breath and life, He offers to flood us with His holy gift (See *Diary* #811).

Do you fear the hour of your death? Or do you fear the hour of the death of your loved ones? While this is normal and understandable, we must strive to see that hour as an hour of great Mercy. God loves, with a profound love, the soul who is in this last hour of life. He looks with holy anticipation upon the soul desiring the full and imminent union that awaits. Reflect upon your sacred hour. Know that our Lord desires to begin your preparation for this moment today by continually increasing His Mercy within you. Allow that Mercy to pour forth and allow it to prepare your heart for the moment that you are privileged to see our Lord face to face.

Blessed Mother, please pray for me now and at the hour of my death. Dear Jesus, I desire that my heart be always prepared for the moment when You call me to Yourself. May all I do in this life become a preparation for that moment of passing, and may I receive in this hour an abundance of Your Mercy. Lord, please also give me the grace to help prepare others for this sacred hour and to pray for them fervently when that time comes. Jesus, I trust in You.

Reflection 160: The Mercy of Confession

Have you discovered the great joy of going to Confession? Some do not consider the Sacrament of Confession to be a great joy. Instead, they see it as a painful and humiliating experience. But perhaps some need the humiliation of an honest confession to help break them out of their sin. Others, those who sincerely seek the abundant Mercy of God, will take great delight in going to Confession because they see the glorious effect it has upon their soul. Seek to love Confession. Pray that it becomes something that you long for as you anticipate the wonderful fruits of this holy purification (See *Diary* #817).

When is the last time you went to Confession? If it has been a while then this reflection is for you. The Lord is calling you to receive the Mercy He has infused into this glorious Sacrament. By going to Confession and receiving absolution you are encountering Jesus Himself. It is He, hidden within the priest, who absolves you and cleanses your soul. Do you believe this? Do you want this grace for your soul? Reflect upon that which deters you from Confession. It may be inconvenience, or a busy schedule, or fear, or distrust of a particular priest. Whatever it is, keeping you from this Sacrament, allow the Lord to remove it. The Lord loves you and is calling you to His Merciful Heart. Rejoice in that fact and foster within your soul a holy longing to receive all that He wishes to bestow through this sacred gift of Mercy.

Precious Jesus, I entrust myself to Your Mercy and pray that I will be open to this gift as You desire to bestow it. I pray that I may have a burning desire for the Mercy You wish to offer me through this Sacrament. Humble me Lord, and help me to confidently open the wounds of my soul to Your healing grace. Jesus, I trust in You.

Reflection 161: The Singular Love Given to You

When pondering the love and the Mercy of God, it is tempting to see His love in a more general way, as if it were something evenly distributed to all people in the same way. But God's love for you is something so much more than a general gift to all people. It is deeply personal and singular, being offered specifically for you, out of love for you. God does not see you as one of many; rather, He sees you as a singular focus of His love. Each and every person is loved by God in this singular and unique way. Thus, you are loved as His one precious child for whom He has offered His life. Know that God loves you as you. He knows every detail of your life and pours His grace upon you (See *Diary* #824).

How aware are you of the unique and singular love God has for you? His love is personal in that you are an object of His burning Heart of Mercy. God is fully capable of loving each and every person in this way, seeing each one as His precious child and loving each person in their uniqueness and even in their sins. Let yourself, today, experience this personal and abundant love of God in your life. It will sustain you in all things and help you to always know that you are loved above all.

Lord, I love You and adore You and thank You for loving me with a perfect love. Help me to receive Your unique gift of love offered to me as Your precious child. May I return this love for You by acknowledging You as my one and only Lord and God. Jesus, I trust in You.

Reflection 162: Light Dispels the Darkness

Light dispels the darkness. Scientifically speaking, we know that light and dark are not opposing forces; rather, dark is the absence of light. And when light enters in, the darkness is no more. So it is with the Mercy of God. Without Mercy, our souls are dark. We fall into doubt, confusion, fear and despair when Mercy is absent. In this case, we are left in utter darkness where the filth of sin can reign. But God desires to bring the light of His Mercy. When this happens, and when we open our souls to this gift, the darkness of doubt, confusion, fear and despair vanish. They cannot remain where the Light of Mercy resides (See *Diary* #831).

When you look at your soul, what do you see? Is there darkness? Do you see its foul effects? Do you see doubt, confusion, fear or despair? Do you see sin? If so, the Lord desires to dispel the darkness that breeds these burdens and bring forth His merciful Light. Reflect upon the part of your soul that appears to be in most need of His Mercy. Know that

He wants to enter that area of your life and waits on you for the permission to do so. He will wait for you to let Him in.

Lord, please come into the darkness of my soul. Bring forth the bright rays of Your Light and dispel all that is not of You. Come refresh me and renew me, Lord. Help me to see and to know Your great love. I desire to live in the Light of Your Mercy, dear Lord. Jesus, I trust in You.

Reflection 163: Glorifying God in Your "Wretchedness"

Do you see the wretchedness of your own soul? Some may be offended by such a question. But if we understood the Mercy of God, and realized that it is our "wretchedness" that enables Him to be glorified the most, we would not shy away from such a thought. Many want to be holy and to see themselves as holy. It's easy to think, "If I am good, God will be pleased." But what we fail to realize is that God is glorified most when we see our littleness, our nothingness, and our wretchedness before Him. It is then that He can manifest His glory to the greatest extent through us. True, we have infinite dignity and value as persons as a result of being made in God's image and as a result of God taking on our human nature. But in our actions, we are sinners incapable of doing anything good. When we realize this, we open the door for God to enter in and manifest His Mercy. We let Him act through our weakness and do glorious things. This is the way we give glory to God (See *Diary* #836).

When you consider your holiness, do you tend to think highly of yourself, as if you have done many good things for God? This is pride. Humility is the virtue that allows you to see your weakness and complete dependence upon the Mercy of God. It enables you to realize that without Him, you can do nothing. It enables you to cry out with St. Paul, "Wretched man that I am" (Romans 7:24). But in that cry, you also perceive the unlimited Mercy of God using you in your weakness and, thus, become an image of His glory.

Lord, help me to see clearly my weakness. Help me to humble myself before Your greatness and, in that act, to be open to Your transforming power in my life. I give my littleness to You, dear Lord. Manifest Your glory through me as You desire. Jesus, I trust in You.

Reflection 164: Longing for the Souls of Sinners

When you see someone with manifest sin, what is your reaction? Many people react with disdain and harsh judgment. When someone breaks the law, we harshly condemn them. When someone lives an immoral lifestyle, we belittle them. Very often, our attitude toward the sinner is merciless. This is a problem. True, we must see sin for what it is and work to oppose it, especially when it affects others. But we must always hold in our hearts a deep love for sinners. We must have a longing for their repentance and always see the innate dignity they have as persons (See *Diary* #842).

What is your reaction toward the sinner? Be honest and look first at how you react interiorly. We are all sinners. Some sins are more manifest than others and some live sinful lives in an open and obstinate way. But should we allow ourselves to condemn them? We must judge an objective action for what it is, but the person must never be judged. This is solely up to God. Reflect upon your attitude toward those with more manifest sins. Pray that instead of becoming harsh and critical you will long for their conversion and love them wholeheartedly despite their actions.

Lord, give me a heart of mercy for sinners. Help me to love them with a burning love and to suspend my temptations to judge. May I long for all people with Your Heart of Mercy desiring their holiness. May I also be aware of my own sinfulness and daily seek Your merciful Heart. Jesus, I trust in You.

Reflection 165: The Perfect Contrition

When we become aware of our sins we may have various reactions. We may remain indifferent, or repent out of fear of God's justice. But the ideal response is to turn to God with love and to have true sorrow as a result of that love. If we have a burning love for God, we will become attentive to even the smallest sin we carry. And every sin we see, we will desire to be rid of. This burning love brings us to an act of perfect contrition by which our love of God purifies the smallest speck of sin on our souls (See *Diary* #852).

Do you see your sin? If so, how do you react to it? The way you react to your sin is a good measure of your love of God and Your trust in His Divine Mercy. If you react with indifference, your love is lacking. If you react in guilt and fear of punishment, your love is lacking. But if you react with trust in God and a total abandonment to His Divine Mercy, then the love you have in your life will become the source of even more Mercy poured upon you. Think honestly about your reaction to your sin and pray that the Lord will bless you with such an abundance of love for Him that you will be overjoyed at seeing that of which you need to repent.

Lord, give me such a perfect love for You that I become aware of every sin in my soul that displeases You. As I see my sins, even the smallest of sins, give me the grace to run to You in trust so that Your Mercy will purify me and make me holy. I love You my dear Lord, help me to love You more. Jesus, I trust in You.

Reflection 166: The Power of Your Unity with Christ

Imagine being All-Powerful, or being an intimate friend of one who is All-Powerful. There is a story of Pope St. Leo I, who lived in the fifth century, which reveals the power of God. It is said that Attila the Hun and his violent army sought to sack Rome. Pope St. Leo met Attila and "persuaded" him to turn back. Later, when Attila's army asked why he turned back, Attila stated that he had been alarmed by a figure dressed as a priest who stood at the pope's side. This figure was holding a drawn sword and acted as if he would strike Attila dead if he advanced. In fear, Attila turned around and left.

This short story reveals the power of God to defend us against all wickedness. Though an angel may not appear in physical form next to you, you can be assured that if you are immersed in the Mercy of God, there is nothing you need to fear. All the powers of Heaven will be on your side. The Lord will defend you against every evil and will give you strength to accomplish all that gives Him glory (See *Diary* #858).

Reflect, today, upon two things: 1) Your unity with Christ; 2) The power that flows from that unity. Do you trust that the Lord will protect you from all evil? Do you realize that fear is useless when you have faith and are clothed with the Mercy of God? Reflect upon this fact and surrender yourself more fully to the Lord who must become your Sole Commander in life.

My Lord and my Sole Commander, I trust You with my life. I entrust to You my whole being, especially all things that tempt me to fear. Give me confidence in Your Divine Mercy and help me to rely upon You in all things without reserve. Jesus, I trust in You.

Reflection 167: Desiring the Lord to the Greatest Degree

When you pray, and when you pray long and hard, the Lord will enter in. He will commune with you and unite His Heart to yours. You will experience these effects in various ways. One common effect is that the closer you are drawn into union with Christ, the more you will desire this union. And the more you desire this union, the more you will be drawn into union. Your prayer has a cyclical effect upon your union and your desire. This is good to be aware of so as to allow our Lord to use your desires to be drawn into greater holiness of life (See *Diary* #867).

What do you desire the most in life? What is the treasure you seek? This is an important reflection to make in an honest and sincere way. "For where your treasure is, there also will your heart be" (Mt. 6:21). If the Lord is your greatest treasure in life, then your heart will be drawn to Him in a powerful way. You will desire intimacy with Him and that desire will draw you close. Reflect, honestly, upon what you desire and allow the insight you gain to reorder the priorities you have.

Lord, please help me to make You the central Treasure of my life and to seek You and to desire You with all my heart. As I am drawn to You, increase my desire, and as You increase my desire, draw me closer. Lord, I pray that every aspect of my life may ultimately become consumed with a longing to serve You and Your holy Will. Jesus, I trust in You.

Reflection 168: Evoking the Mercy of God for Others

There is one thing, and one thing only, that has the power to free sinners from the fires of hell. That one thing is Mercy. God offers His Mercy freely and in abundance, but He has also chosen to offer His Mercy in response to our prayers when they are prayed with the utmost faith and childlike confidence. Jesus cannot refuse a heart that is pure and is filled with love for sinners. Your heart must become this way. You must strive to love sinners with such a burning love that the Lord is "obliged" to answer your request for Mercy. He obliges Himself out of love in response to the love you have in your heart (See *Diary* #873).

Do you realize that you have a certain "power" over the Mercy of God? This is only so because the Lord wills it. He has willed to respond to the love you have in your own heart with an outpouring of His Mercy upon those whom you love. Your love, when pure and unwavering, becomes a door through which the Heart of Christ pours forth His grace. Reflect upon your love for sinners and place that love before the Lord as your powerful prayer. He will see your love and respond with abundant generosity.

Lord, I love You and I love sinners. Help me to love all people more deeply and to offer that love to You as my pure prayer. May the love in my heart be the cause of Your own outpouring of grace and an instrument of Your Divine Mercy. Jesus, I trust in You.

Reflection 169: Calm in the Presence of the King

Meeting someone of great power can be cause for excitement. For example, meeting with the president of a company you wish to work at, or meeting someone famous for the first time, or meeting with the bishop or the Holy Father may all cause a certain excitement. But it could also cause a certain fear and anxiety. Of course the most important and "influential" person you will ever meet is your God. God is Omnipotent and Omniscient, that is, All-Powerful and All-Knowing. He is also All-Loving and, in that perfect love, descends from His throne of grace and majesty to converse with you, to care for you, and to fulfill every need that you have. He comes to fill you with the abundance of joy. Each "meeting" with our Lord must be one of great excitement in that it must be taken seriously, with attention and love being offered back to this most important Person you will ever come to know (See *Diary* #885).

What is your interior experience when you go to Him in prayer? Is it an encounter in which you are overly casual and unprepared? Is it an encounter that gives you fear and anxiety, looking for ways to avoid Him? Or do you allow yourself to be comforted and consoled by the fact that the God of the Universe cares for you enough to step down from His throne of grace and converse with you in your weakness and sin? The Lord's perfect humility should delight and amaze you and give you courage to turn to Him with your whole heart.

Lord, I am amazed at Your love for me. You who are the God of the Universe come to me in my weakness and sin. You are attentive to me and offer the perfect care of a loving Father. Help me to always be in awe of the humility You manifest as You descend from Your throne of grace and enter my soul. Jesus, I trust in You.

Reflection 170: Fidelity on Good Days and Bad

It's easy to love God when we feel like it and when life is going well and is quite easy. But when life is challenging, we are immediately tempted to turn in on ourselves and, in so doing, turn from our love for God. But a true sign of holiness is that we love God no matter what we feel or experience throughout our day. Come rain or shine we must not waver in our love for our God and others (See *Diary* #893).

Do you allow your emotions to dictate your faith? Do you allow the difficult circumstances of life to take you away from your absolute fidelity to your God? This is a real temptation and one that many fall into. Reflect, today, upon how you deal with difficult days and difficult moments. Seek to renew your faithfulness and love in the most challenging moments and you will discover that this act transforms you in ways that "easy living" never will.

Lord, I give You this day and I give You my whole heart this day. No matter what I feel or experience today or tomorrow I commit to You to remain faithful in all things. I promise not to allow daily hardships or burdens to weigh me down and damage my faith. My Jesus, I love You and choose to remain faithful to You always. Jesus, I trust in You.

Reflection 171: Comparing Earth to Heaven

Try to imagine what you will think about this time on Earth when you get to Heaven. Will you miss this life? Will you want to return? Will you wish you made more money while here or had more worldly success? Most likely not. Compared to Heaven, this world is pitiful. That doesn't mean that our lives cannot be glorious here, it just means that Heaven will be infinitely more glorious. For that reason, we must constantly put our eyes upon building true treasure that will last forever. Our only concern must be Heaven and doing all that the Lord calls us to do here and now so as to attain that glory. Do not spend one moment wasting time on things that will mean nothing to you in Heaven. Instead, spend all your time "building your Heavenly mansion" through a life of pure faith and charity, growing in an immense love of God. You will never regret increasing your love of God, here and now, when you get to Heaven (See *Diary* #899).

What occupies your daily thinking and dreams? What is the object of your hope and greatest desire? Try to honestly assess this and do not be afraid to admit it if you discover that your primary goals are those things that are passing and, ultimately, unimportant. As you discover this, turn your eyes to Heaven and to the love of God. Consider practical ways that you can refocus your life so that it is fully given to the purpose you were made for, namely, to love God with your whole heart, mind, soul and strength and to love your neighbor as yourself. Unless this is your central goal in life, you have the wrong goal. Pray and surrender to God and redirect all things to Him.

Lord, I desire to make You and Your holy Will the central focus of my life. I choose nothing other than to love You and my neighbor. Help me to be diligent in building Your Kingdom on Earth so that I may enjoy Your Kingdom eternally in Heaven. Jesus, I trust in You.

Reflection 172: Patient Submission

Are you patient? Both patience and impatience are born from a struggle within your will. There are many times in life when your will is drawn by something other than God, wanting something that God is not leading you to. Patience is a virtue that enables you to step back, take a deep breath and redirect your will to that which God alone has chosen for you. Patience is the gift of strength within you to deny your own immediate tendencies in deference to that which the Lord gently speaks to your heart. When you have patience, you are not controlled by the confusion caused through your disordered emotions or untamed feelings and desires. Patience brings order, focus and purpose. And the gift of patience, when it enables you to submit your will to the Divine Will, gives God immeasurable glory (See *Diary* #904).

How patient of a person are you? What controls your actions and influences your decisions the most? Are you more controlled by your disordered desires, or by God? Reflect upon this question today and make an act of submission of your will to the Will of God. Making this choice will immediately strengthen you and bring forth the virtue of patience in your soul.

Lord, I am so very impatient at times. I allow many feelings, emotions and passions to control me and to dictate my actions. I surrender my will to You this day. May Your Divine Will be done in all things rather than my own. Jesus, I trust in You.

Reflection 173: Unity with One is Unity with Three

The Blessed Trinity is described as having one Divine nature, yet remaining three distinct Persons. As a result, the three distinct Persons share in a perfect unity. In fact, they could not be "united" if they were not distinct from each other. So it's necessary to speak of God as the Three in One. Each one of us is called to share in this same unity. We do not share in the very nature of God by taking on His Divine nature strictly speaking. However, since our humanity has been united with God in Christ, so also our personhood is invited into communion with Him. We are called, as individuals, to enter into a spousal relationship with God. We are called to share in the profound unity of the Holy Trinity. Christ is to live in us, with us and through us. And as we become one with Christ, as a result of His union with our human nature, so also we become one with the Father and the Holy Spirit. This unity with God is the greatest act of Mercy we will ever know (See *Diary* #911-912).

Ponder, today, the mystery of unity. It can be a hard concept to understand and an even harder reality to live. But this is your calling. By the Incarnation, God the Son united the Divine nature with human nature. And by His death and resurrection, He set humanity free from the effects of sin so that we can be drawn up into His divinity. Ponder this. Pray over it. Seek to understand it and ask the Lord for knowledge. The more you grasp this glorious reality, the more you will desire to share in it.

Most Holy Trinity, Father, Son and Holy Spirit, I desire to be one with You. I long to be drawn into Your very life sharing in the Communion you share in Your inner Life. Oh, Holy Trinity, I love You and trust in You.

Reflection 174: The Timing of God is Perfect

When we desire to accomplish the Will of God in this world and do wonderful things for Him, we can sometimes seek to do things our way according to our timing. But to truly accomplish the Will of God you must pray hard, surrender yourself to His holy Will, and then even surrender the fulfillment of His Will. It's not a matter of just doing what you think best, when you think best; rather, it's a matter of accomplishing His holy Will as He directs it, when He directs it. Nothing more and nothing less. This is an act of trust and it will be rewarded with God accomplishing great things in accord with the perfect plan He has set forth, in accord with His timing (See *Diary* #916).

Do you want to do great things for God? If so, tell Him so and make an act of total surrender to His Will. And then wait, and wait and wait. Keep trusting and keep surrendering and trust that He will inspire you to action when the time is right. Reflect upon your patience with the Will of God today. God will always wait for the perfect moment to inspire you to act. If you can patiently wait on Him, you will see an abundance of Mercy flow from Heaven.

Lord, in surrendering myself to You and entrusting myself to You as an instrument for Your glory, I pray that I may act only when and how You direct me to act. Help me to always know that You are perfect in Your wisdom and orchestrate all things in a harmoniously beautiful way. I trust in Your Will and choose it over my own will, today and always. Jesus, I trust in you.

Reflection 175: Love is Found in the Details of Life

How nice it is when you have a friend that you trust with every detail of your life. We long to know others and we long to be known by others. When you find someone in whom you can confide even the smallest struggle or express the smallest joy, you have found a true friend. The Lord desires to be your closest friend. You must work to foster a "detailed" relationship with Him. He knows all things and knows you better than you know yourself. But this should not prevent you from pouring your heart out to Him. You must express to Him even the slightest concerns you carry and rejoice with Him over the smallest of joys. Speaking to God about the details of life brings joy to His Heart (See *Diary* #921).

When you speak to God, are you honest? Do you trust Him? Do you open every part of your life and face it in His presence? The Lord knows all but He wants to hear it from you in prayer. Speak to Him today. Reflect upon how often you go to Him with the smallest concern or the slightest joy. Give joy to Him today as you speak to Him as your closest friend and confidant in life.

Lord, You know all things and You know me through and through. As I recognize this fact, help me to always be fully honest with You. Help my prayer to always reflect the truth of my heart. And as I speak to You about the details of my life, I allow You to enter in, to help, to heal and to rejoice in all that You reveal. Jesus, I trust in You.

Reflection 176: Combating the Sin of the World

When God looks at the world, what does He see? Most certainly He sees the beauty of His creation, the perfect order of His design and the presence of His sons and daughters. But He also sees the horror of the multitude of sins. Even the slightest sin or imperfection cannot escape His sight. Imagine trying to take in the sins of the world with one glance. But in His perfect Mercy He allows Himself to be consoled by those humble and holy souls who are specially chosen by Him. Yes, all people are chosen, but certain souls respond to the heights of holiness more than others, and in so doing, combat the evils of our world in a powerful way. This is one of the unique callings of those living in the cloistered religious life, hidden from the world with a single focus on interior conversion. We may not see the benefit to such holy souls, but God does and His wrath is turned into Mercy, especially on account of these and all holy souls (See *Diary* #926).

Reflect upon the fact that you are one of these chosen souls. You may not be called to the hidden life of a cloister, but you are called to achieve great sanctity. As God sees the holiness of your life, His justice is satisfied and His Mercy flows forth. Though the things you say, the thoughts you have and the prayers you pray may never be known by another, God who sees all things sees your heart and the holiness that you achieve in life. This holiness will do more than all the words and actions you could ever accomplish on your own. You are a chosen soul. Fulfill that mission and you will become a powerful instrument of the Mercy of God.

Lord, I thank You for choosing me for holiness. I accept this calling and seek to serve You with my whole heart. My life is Yours, dear Lord, do with me what You Will. Jesus, I trust in You.

Reflection 177: Holy Obedience

One of the greatest safeguards against doing our own will rather than God's is holy obedience. Those in religious life are blessed to live this in a literal and external way, allowing the external practice to be interiorized so as to become certain that they are living the Will of God. But obedience must be lived in every life, not only religious. Obedience is achieved in many ways. It's achieved in family life when we submit our will to the preferences of others, subjecting ourselves in a form of obedience so as to foster love and unity. It's achieved in a profound way when we submit our will to the voice and teaching of our Church. We will never go wrong by living holy obedience to that which the Lord speaks through His Church. When we live this obedience, the Will of God will not be imposed upon us from outside; rather, we will hear Him speak first in our heart and then it will be confirmed exteriorly (See *Diary* #932-933).

Do you hear God calling you, gently and subtly, to submit to the preference of another? You ought not submit to those things that are contrary to the Will of God, but there are numerous opportunities each day to die to yourself and "obediently" embrace the will of another. If you can do this always in regard to the Will of God spoken through His Church, you will see the gates of Mercy opened and your humble submission will bring you great holiness.

Lord, it is so very hard at times to let go of my own will and to embrace the will of another. Help me to see these small acts as acts of true love and holy submission to You. May I allow You to mold my will into Yours as I act in holy obedience, especially when this requires great sacrifice. I also choose Your Will as it is revealed through Your Church and always submit to that revelation over my own ideas. Jesus, I trust in You.

Reflection 178: Sanctity is Never Achieved on our Own

Do you aspire to holiness of life? If so, you cannot do this on your own. You need the help of another, and even many others. The Lord has given us numerous ways to be directed by the loving hand of others. Some are blessed to have a spiritual director of many years who directs them in accord with the Mind and Heart of Christ. But most are called to rely upon the general direction offered by Christ through His Church. We do so when we find a confessor to whom we regularly confess our sins. We do so when we study the lives of the saints and learn from their wisdom. We do so when we listen attentively at Mass seeking to soak in the words our Lord wishes to speak. And we do so when we allow people of true holiness to come to know our souls so as to offer their humble counsel (See *Diary* #938).

How do you allow the Lord to direct your soul? Do you listen to Him speak to you in Confession? Do you listen attentively at Mass, through the wisdom of the saints and through the teachings of the Church? Do you seek out those people whom God has placed in your life to help you on your way? Reflect, today, upon the ways that God wants to use others to help direct your life toward holiness and embrace this gift as His act of abundant Mercy.

Lord, You and You alone are my Director and Guide. But You choose to guide me through the mediation of others. May I always be willing to humble myself so as to receive the many helps You offer me through this journey of life. I pray I will never turn away from these instruments of Your Mercy and grace. Jesus, I trust in You.

Reflection 179: Dealing with Interior Desolation

"The Lord giveth and the Lord taketh away..." (Job 1:21). How true this is. There are times in life when we experience the abundant consolation of God. It may be at moments of great family joy, or when we experience the unconditional love of another. At times we sense the powerful presence of God in our life of prayer and are filled with joy. But there are many other moments in life when God seems distant and our souls feel desolate. Do not worry about this. If this is caused by sin, then face that sin, confess it and move on. But if it's not a result of any sin, then know it's an opportunity for you to deepen your faith and your love of God despite how you feel. This is a true grace and we should be grateful that God loves us enough to call us to faith even when we feel very little inside (See *Diary* #943).

What do you experience in your soul right now? Do you sense the closeness of God and does that closeness give you great consolation? Or do you feel dry and desolate as if God is hidden from you? We must rejoice in each experience and know that God offers the grace we need for each moment. Renew your faith this day no matter how you feel. Do it especially in moments of much desolation. Your act of faith in those moments will open the gates of God's Mercy to you and to the world more than you may realize.

Lord, I love You now and always and renew my love for You no matter how I feel. In good times and in difficult ones I choose to love You, to have faith in You and to trust in You. You are the God of consolation and the God of desolation. I choose You no matter what. Jesus, I trust in You.

Reflection 180: The Passion of Jesus

We who are familiar with the Gospels may suffer, at times, from a certain indifference to the sufferings of Christ. We hear the story read each year, have seen many images of the Passion, and as a result of this familiarity, we can fail to allow it to have the proper effect on our lives. But the Passion is real, it happened, and we should give it our full attention. Though it may not be pleasant, on one level, it is an act of love so mysterious that it requires much grace to enable us to penetrate its meaning and significance in our lives. Every scourge, ridicule, nail and thorn wounded not only our Lord's body, but it caused excruciating pain to His soul. But every pain that He endured He took into His Heart and redeemed it, offering it to the Father for the salvation of all. We must see this great mystery of our faith and gaze upon it in awe and holy wonder (See *Diary* #948).

Have you gazed upon the suffering Jesus? Have you allowed yourself to see His pain and His suffering? Have you seen Him endure all in silence and acceptance? Reflect upon this incredible mystery of our faith this day and allow yourself to grow in love and compassion for Him who endured so much for you. Know that His suffering destroyed the effects of sin and transformed suffering itself into the instrument of His Divine Mercy.

Precious Lord, I thank You for Your suffering. For in this act You took human suffering into Your glorious soul and redeemed it. You endured the effects of my sin and said not a word. Lord, You paid the price for my sins and You did so with perfect love and resolve. Give me the grace, dear Lord, to embrace all that I suffer and to unite it to the redeeming power of Your holy Cross. In that unity, free me from my sins and pour forth Your abundance of Mercy.

Reflection 181: Holy Indifference

Does it matter what the Will of God is for you? That may sound like a strange question at first. But think about it. Does it matter what God wills of you? What if He were to call you to constant work? Or what if He were to call you to a restful repose? Or what if He were to fill you with delight? Or remove all delight from your soul? Or call you to be extolled and honored in the sight of many? Or draw you into the desert of solitude and hiddenness? The truth is that it matters not *what* God's call is in our lives, it only matters *that* He calls. We must strive for a holy indifference in our lives. A "holy" indifference is not indifference to God and His Will; rather, a *holy* indifference is a detachment to all preferences regarding what the Lord asks of us. We must be ready for all but we must be willing to receive nothing. The goal is to be ready for God and His Will, whatever it may be (See *Diary* #952).

Reflect upon whether or not you are ready and willing to accept whatever God wills of you. *What* He wills is not as important as the fact *that* He wills. This may be a difficult subtlety to grasp at first. But it's important to understand. The simple truth is that we should be ready for anything God asks of us without clinging to our personal preference. If you can achieve this level of detachment, the Mercy of God will begin to flow in abundance in your life, and through you into the lives of many others.

Lord, I surrender to You all my selfish preferences in life. I give You complete freedom to do whatever You will in my life. No matter what You ask of me, I accept, and no matter what You take from me, I give to You. Give me, dear Lord, the grace of a holy indifference so that I may be free to love You and Your holy Will more than life itself. Jesus, I trust in You.

Reflection 182: Wisdom to Penetrate the Secrets of Pride

Pride can consume us. When it does, all we think about is ourselves and our own pain. Perhaps you can relate to this. Maybe you've encountered a wound and you sit and sulk over that wound. It creates bitterness in your heart and you seek to heal that wound. But when this happens, it is often our pride that leads us to remedy hurt through a form of revenge, anger or self-pity. We can even fool ourselves into thinking that our desire to solve our problem and rid ourselves of the hurt is justified by God. But if you are willing to let the Lord penetrate the inner secret of your soul, you will see that your motivation in many things is your wounded pride. This is not the solution. What is needed is Mercy. Mercy solves every problem. First, you must seek Mercy from God, then you must offer it unconditionally to others. There is no other way to resolve the hurt and confusion present in your soul. This is a hard lesson to learn, but necessary (See *Diary* #958).

What is it that motivates you? Perhaps you have some interior obsession that you can't seem to shake. Perhaps it lingers in your mind day and night. Be attentive to this and identify it as your own sin. Do not hesitate to humble yourself to the fullest extent and do not be afraid to take ownership of the pain you feel. Pointing the finger at another does not heal and does not remedy anything. We are solely responsible as a result of our pride. Seeing this is a grace of the Lord's mysterious and unfathomable Mercy.

Lord, I cannot shake the anger, the hurt and the pain I feel at times. It is overwhelming and all-consuming, subtle and deceptive. But it is my sin, lurking within me drawing me from You, keeping me from true repentance. Lord, I do repent and I beg You to humble me so that I may love You with my whole being. Jesus, I trust in You.

Reflection 183: Attentiveness to the Value of Suffering

When we suffer, we look for a way out. We seek relief. But from Heaven, we will be able to look back and see the immense power of freely chosen and embraced suffering. It's not that suffering is good in and of itself; rather, it's that suffering has been redeemed and endowed with a spiritual power by God as a result of the sufferings of Christ. Therefore, if you trust in the Lord, let Him reveal to you, here and now, the great value of your suffering freely embraced. By embracing every hardship that comes your way, you will be making an offering to God that can only be understood by grace. This will not make sense to the world, but it will become a powerful weapon of Mercy through which the Lord will do great things to you and through you, He will flood the world with His grace. Do not wait until Heaven to become aware of this sacred gift of the redemption of your inner suffering offered in confident prayer to God (See *Diary* #963).

Are you aware of the power of your suffering when you freely unite it to the sufferings of Christ? Does this make sense to you? This realization is only possible by grace and is only embraced by that same grace. Reflect, today, upon what you do suffer interiorly and do not shy away from it. Face it, embrace it and love it. For in that holy embrace, God will work wondrously in and through your life.

Lord, make me attentive to the value of all I suffer in my soul. Help me to see this as a gift of Your Divine Mercy. I recognize the fact that I do not recognize the power in this holy gift. Give me Your eyes to see my suffering as You see it, and Your Will to embrace it with a holy embrace. I make this offering to You, this day, dear Lord. Jesus, I trust in You.

Reflection 184: The Mercy of the Ministry of Priests

No, priests are not perfect. They sin day in and day out. They are in constant need of repentance and conversion in their daily lives just like all the rest of humanity. But they are priests. And because of their sacred ordination, the Lord speaks through them in a clear yet mysterious way. Some speak with the authority of Christ only when speaking the words of Consecration at Mass or the words of Absolution in the Sacrament of Reconciliation. Others embrace the charism of their ordination and are used by God in a multitude of other ways, through their preaching, their holy living, and their words of counsel offered to their flock. Seek out these holy priests. Listen to them and allow the Lord to guide you through them. For in listening to the voice of God, spoken through them, you will be blessed with an abundance of Mercy (See *Diary* #968).

Ponder today, with all charity, the priests that God has placed in your life. It may be your own parish priest, or a priest speaking through the written word, or a priest speaking through some other form of modern communication. God will point you to His holy priests and will speak to you directly through them. Listen to them, for in hearing their words you will be hearing the words of the Mercy of God.

Lord, I thank You for establishing the sacred priesthood as a sign of Your continued sacramental presence in the world. I pray for all priests, especially those You have entrusted with my pastoral care. May I always be open to You, speaking through them, in their sacred ministry. And may I respond with abandon and generosity at the sound of Your voice spoken from their lips. Give me humility, dear Lord, that I may always hear Your voice spoken through priests. Jesus, I trust in You.

Reflection 185: Generosity with Unlimited Resources

If you were aware of great famine in a far away land, and were also blessed with unlimited resources to address that famine, why would you withhold this gift from those in need? Hopefully you wouldn't. Hopefully you would see your responsibility and do what was necessary to satiate the thirst and satisfy the hunger of those in dire need. But there is a great famine, and you are blessed with unlimited resources to address this famine. The famine is the hunger and thirst for the Mercy of God. Yet most people who are starving for this Mercy are unaware that this is what they seek. The unlimited resources you have been given is the Mercy of God. He has entrusted you with the task of dispensing His Mercy and withholds nothing from you. Do you see the importance of your cooperation with this grace? Do not shy away from God's call to bring His limitless Mercy to others (See *Diary* #975).

In what way is God calling you to distribute His wealth. No one is deserving of the Mercy of God, that's why it's Mercy. But everyone is invited to feast on this grace. The Lord wants to use you as a dispenser of His Divine Mercy. All you need to do is to be ready and willing to allow Him to use You as He wills. You will not be acting on your own; rather, God will act through you. But He is only able to act if you let Him.

Lord, I thank You for the limitless gift of Your Divine Mercy. And I thank You that I am called to become a dispenser of this grace. Help me to say "Yes" to You in all things and to embrace the responsibility that You have given to me. Use me, dear Lord, however You will, and give me the wisdom and courage I need to be a generous dispenser of Your Divine Mercy to a world in dire need. Jesus, I trust in You.

Reflection 186: Transpierced by God

Has your soul been "transpierced" by God? Does He "pervade" you? Do you allow yourself to "dissolve" into His divinity and become "enveloped" by His Mercy? There are so many words we can use to describe our relationship with God. Though they all add to an articulation of who God is and what sort of relationship we should have with Him, none of them will ever fully be able to present the mystery of our union with Him. We are called to "oneness," to "transformative union." And this union is like a drop of water being placed into the mighty ocean. Slowly and surely, that drop of water is lost in the vastness of the ocean depths. So it is with God. We are called to a unity so deep and so profound that words will never suffice to speak what the soul is called to experience (See *Diary* #983-984).

What is your relationship with God like? Are the words above even a faint description of your life of prayer and communion with Him? Do you see and experience Him interiorly, calling you to His unfathomable depths of Mercy? Or is He distant to you, seen by you as someone you talk about and are aware of, but not living a "holy fusion" with? The words we use matter because they point to the deeper reality. Reflect upon how you would describe your relationship with God. And when you find that no words suffice, you are on the right track.

Most Holy Trinity, may my whole being become consumed by the brightness of Your radiance. May I become possessed by You in every way so that it will no longer be my life that is lived, but is Yours living within me, consuming me and transforming me. May I be like that one small drop of water, entering into the mighty Ocean of Mercy. Jesus, I trust in You.

Reflection 187: A Rainbow after the Storm

It's fascinating how Creation itself proclaims the glory of God and teaches us about matters of faith. Take a rainbow. It is bright and beautiful, colorful and awe-inspiring. Everyone rejoices on seeing a rainbow. But there would be no such thing as a rainbow without rain, or storms. Such is life. We will have good days followed by bad and bad days followed by good. We should not be surprised by one or the other. On a good day filled with joy we should thank God and be aware that the "rainbow" is a gift. We should savor it so that we will remember it on the bad days. When a bad day comes we should thank God. We should thank Him for the knowledge that this too shall pass if we wait patiently upon Him. Life is full of ups and downs but the Mercy of God is eternal and it will bring us through all things, enabling us to rejoice after the storm has passed (See *Diary* #992).

Reflect, today, upon the difference between a rainbow and a storm. Imagine a rainbow full of radiant color stretching across the sky from one end to the other. It is beautiful and inspiring, the cause for a smile and delight. Now compare that to the storm that preceded it. In the midst of the storm, the coming rainbow would not have been thought about. Instead, the primary focus is to seek shelter. Reflect upon how this may be similar to your personal life. When you feel pain or are bombarded with challenges do you run and hide? You should also remind yourself that every struggle is the precursor to a rainbow. Keep the blessings of God's Mercy alive in your mind so that they will daily carry you through the challenges of life.

Lord, keep my eyes on You at all times. May I retain hope and joy in the midst of every storm of life. Please remind me when I feel oppressed and bombarded that this too shall pass and that You will bring my struggles and my life to a full and joyous conclusion. Jesus, I trust in You.

Reflection 188: The Demands of the Lord

If the Lord asks you to do something, do you have an option? You do insofar as you can say no. And this is a sin. But if you have chosen to follow Christ and your goal is Heaven, then it's proper to say that we are *obliged* to do whatever the Lord asks of us. His requests are certain and immovable commands of Love. He will not budge. He will not change. This is only hard to accept if we are stubborn and unwilling to submit to Him. But if we understand the nature of His Will, as described above, then we should be overjoyed when we hear His crisp clear voice speaking to us with commands of Love. We should see His Will and His Law as the perfect answer to every problem and every need we have in life. The demands of the Lord are demands we must give into. And one of those demands is that He desires that we all enter into and distribute His abundant Mercy (See *Diary* #998).

Reflect upon the demand from our Lord that you dispense His Mercy. He not only invites you to do so, it is His immovable and irrevocable perfect Will. He will never change His Mind.

There is only one option you have. You must concede to be a missionary of His Divine Mercy if you choose His Will for your life. Are you willing to accept this calling? Are you willing to say "Yes?" Ponder this question today and make a choice that reflects the certainty of God's perfect Will. Say "Yes" to our Lord and you will not regret it.

Lord, Your Will is perfect and the delight of my soul. I thank You for inviting and obliging me to be an instrument of Your Divine Mercy in the world. May I embrace this calling with zeal, love and devotion. Use me, dear Lord, as You will. And I thank You for the incredible honor of serving You. Jesus, I trust in You.

4

Reflections on Notebook Three

We continue now to the third notebook that Saint Faustina filled with messages of Mercy from our Lord. As you enter into this notebook, pause and reflect upon all that you have read so far. Has it changed your perspective on life? Has it changed you? If it has, then continue down that same path and trust that the Lord will continue to do great things in your life. If it has not, reflect upon why!

Sometimes we need more than the words we read. We also need true prayer, deep prayer and what we may call "soaking prayer." Consider this as you read through the reflections flowing from this notebook and allow the words to not only enter your mind, but to also enter deeper. Read them prayerfully and carefully. Speak to our Lord as Saint Faustina did. Read some more of her actual diary in addition to these reflections and learn from her humble and childlike faith.

The Lord wants to do great things in your life! Open the door, through prayer and reflection, and let Him in!

Reflection 189: Overcoming Fear

Fear results from various causes. The perception of some immediate threat causes sudden fear as a sort of defense mechanism. In fact, this could save your life if, for example, the immediate threat is a car swerving into your lane. Sudden fear compels you to take action and avoid a collision. However, fear can also result from other more remote factors that we experience as threats to our well-being. For example, one may struggle with fear over an economic downturn or loss of profit in a business. The fear may be, "How will I support my family?" Or one may have health issues and this causes increasing fear about the future. And the list could go on. Though some forms of fear are healthy (swerving to avoid a car accident), most others are not. Specifically, when fear causes anxiety and worry, leading one to lose trust in God and His providence, this is a problem. But if God is alive in your heart, living and reigning there, His presence produces a supernatural confidence and trust in the midst of any and every struggle we face (See *Diary* #1001).

Reflect upon the specific fear you struggle with right now. What is it that causes excessive worry and anxiety? Whatever it may be, the Lord wants you to trust Him. Yes, a certain "holy" fear can help us evaluate all situations properly and act diligently and responsibly, but too often what we actually struggle with is a lack of trust in God. Reflect upon your fear and your trust and invite Christ more deeply into your heart so that His presence will cast out all useless fear, enabling you to fully trust in His care, providence and Mercy.

Lord, I do trust in You, help me to trust You all the more. I surrender to You all that tempts me to fear. I trust in Your perfect love and desire to rely completely on Your Mercy in my life. My life is Yours, dear Lord, do with me as You will and guide me always. Jesus, I trust in You.

Reflection 190: All Creation Gives Glory to God

All things are made for one ultimate purpose: to give praise and glory to the Most Holy Trinity. We are made for nothing more, nothing less and nothing other than this purpose. As people, we are called to give the unique praise and glory of our adoration to God through lives fully committed and surrendered to Him. This surrender and total submission of our mind and will to Him offers God the praise that is due His name. But all Creation shares in the glory of God in that all creation reflects His perfect order and, especially, His perfect Mercy. For example, the providence that God manifests in caring for the birds of the sky, creatures of the sea and all living things on Earth reveals His glory and gives Him glory by their very existence. We must see this, rejoice in it and give God glory for His Mercy that keeps all things in being (See *Diary* #1005).

Do you recognize the Mercy of God as manifested in all of Creation? It may be easier to recognize His Mercy when offered to us through the forgiveness of our sins and His invitation to us to share in His life. But we must also see the perfect order of Creation and, in that order, see His providential care for it as an act of great Mercy. Reflect, today, upon Creation. Think of the flowers, the bees, the animals and all the small details that make up the design of the physical world. It's truly amazing and mysterious and reveals a God of perfect wisdom and love. Creation is a powerful revelation of God's Mercy.

Lord, I thank You for all that You have done in this world. I thank You for designing it, creating it and keeping it all in existence in accord with Your providence. May I discover Your Heart of Mercy in all that You have made and grow in admiration of You through this gift. Jesus, I trust in You.

Reflection 191: The Talkative Soul

A true danger to the interior life of communion with God is an excessive need to talk. No, talking is not a sin and many times is an act of Mercy toward another. But there are times when being too talkative is a hindrance to the Mercy of God. Talking, in and of itself, is neither good nor evil. The goal is to form our words in accord with the Mind and Will of God. That's it. We must see the words we speak as a sacred tool to bring forth Truth and to manifest God's love. Excessive words, or words that do not flow from our love of God or others, can do more damage than we may realize. Therefore, consecrate your speech to the Lord and seek to let Him speak through you as He will, when He will and to the extent He wills (See *Diary* #1008).

Do you talk a lot? Do you talk too little? It's not about how many words we say, it's about saying the right words at the right time in the right way. Our words can cause much hurt, but they can also bring the healing balm of God's Mercy. Reflect upon the conversations you have had over this past week. Were they pleasing to God? Did they give God glory and edify yourself and others? Reflect, also, upon any ways that you neglected to say what the Lord wanted you to say. These omissions of silence can also be the cause of hurt and can be the reason for a loss of Mercy in our world. Give your speech to the Lord and let Him manifest Himself through you.

Lord, I love You and I offer You my love, this day, through a consecration of my words to You. You are the Eternal Word spoken from the Father. You are the Truth that sets all people free. Give me wisdom, temperance, and courage to speak only what You call me to speak and to listen only to that which You speak. May my tongue be a sword piercing through the darkness of this world and my ear be a sponge for Your Mercy. Jesus, I trust in You.

Reflection 192: Loving God in Good Times and Bad

It's easy to "love" God when all is well. But *when all is well,* our love is not tested. The testing that comes from human suffering clarifies our love of God. This can be very fruitful for our spiritual lives. It's easy to believe that difficulties in life are nothing other than sad and unfortunate burdens and should be avoided at all costs. Though we would be foolish to create difficulties intentionally, we will each have our share of them in this life. Therefore, every difficulty and suffering in life must be embraced as an opportunity for you to increase your trust in God and, in so doing, to increase your love of Him. How blessed is the soul who suffers greatly in this life while choosing to love God throughout, making that suffering the source of its increase in holiness (See *Diary* #1014).

What do you complain about each day? What is it that burdens you? Too often we run from these burdens or get angry. Try to look at your struggles in a new light. Try to see them as opportunities to deepen your trust and your love. Every suffering and every burden in life has the potential of being infused with the spiritual power of the Cross. By embracing them in love, we embrace the Cross. And by embracing the Cross, we love God all the more. Do not think that hardships deal you a poor quality of life. Recognize them for what they are as a result of grace. They are opportunities for holiness and for an increase in the reception of the Mercy of God.

Lord, when I get down, angry or despairing in life, on account of the difficulties I endure, help me to use that struggle as an opportunity for greater trust. Lord, I desire to run to the Cross and to receive the love that poured forth from Your Cross so that I may become more like You in all things. Increase my love, dear Lord, especially through every suffering in life that I surrender to You. Jesus, I trust in You

Reflection 193: Do Not Hesitate

If you won a million dollars you probably wouldn't say, "No, just give me $100, that's all I want." And yet that is what we often do with the Mercy of God. God offers an abundance of wealth and we choose to take only a small portion. Why is that? His Mercy is limitless. It is infinite. If we understood all that God wants to do in our souls, and then cooperated with Him and allowed Him to do it, we'd be in absolute awe and eternally grateful that we discovered this priceless treasure. Perhaps the problem that many face in accepting His Mercy more fully is that it's risky. It's risky in the sense that we must change. Would a million dollars change your life? Probably. It would most likely change a number of things in your life, and not necessarily for the good. But the Mercy of God is a treasure of infinitely more value. Don't hesitate! Take the risk to accept it and to allow it to change you for the good (See *Diary* #1017).

Do you hesitate in accepting God's Mercy? If you do it's important to realize this, admit to it and face the reason why. It's a rare soul who is completely open to all that God wishes to bestow. It's a rare soul who is not cowed by the risk of total abandonment to the Mercy of God. Choose to be one of those rare souls and embrace, without hesitation, all that God wants to pour out upon you and rejoice as you see His grace change your life.

Precious Lord, I thank You for Your abundance of Mercy. I thank You for loving me with such a perfect love that You burn with desire to lavish the riches of Your grace on my life in an endless way. May I cease all hesitation in the face of this glorious gift and willingly accept You and all that Your Mercy will do in my soul. I thank You, dear Lord. Jesus, I trust in You.

Reflection 194: Satisfaction in Life

What is it that satisfies you in life? The answers to this question could be quite varied from person to person. One may find satisfaction in work, another in family activities, another in community service, another in wealth and worldly rewards. There are many and varied responses people will give. But the answer shouldn't be varied. There should be one answer for us all. And that answer is that you find true satisfaction in life by being with your Lord, resting in His

Heart and being close to Him. This may make sense to most people in a theoretical way, but in a practical way it may not connect. What does it mean to be "resting in His Heart and being close to Him?" The only way to discover this real and practical meaning is to do it. All the books in the world will not teach you. You must discover His Heart, love His Heart, be alone in His presence, and only then will you discover what true satisfaction is all about (See *Diary* #1021).

Do you understand, practically and experientially, the total satisfaction in life that comes from living close to the Heart of Christ? When you hear this does it make sense to you? Reflect upon this question today and if you realize that you do not know what it is to know Him this way, then admit that to yourself and begin to seek Him out. If you seek, with your whole heart, you will find. And when you find, you will be eternally grateful you did.

Lord, I want to be one with You. I want to dwell in Your presence and bask in Your Divine Mercy. Help me in my weakness to turn to You with every power of my soul and to encounter Your Divine Essence. I reject all false "satisfactions" in Life and turn to You and You alone. My Jesus, My Lord, I trust in You.

Reflection 195: Our Sweet Delight

If you were an expert in the area of wine tasting, and you had a choice between an excellent bottle of wine and a cheap one, obviously you would choose the excellent one. You would know the difference and you would not find much delight in the cheap wine knowing that the good wine was available. So it is with our souls. When we've tasted of the Mercy of God, and taken a sweet delight in His presence, we will long for more. We will also begin to realize that all the other "delights" in life do not compare. They are poor "tastes" of the glory of God. Drink the good wine of God's Mercy and become accustomed to it. If you do, you will find that all the other delights in life pale in comparison (See *Diary* #1026).

Have you tasted of the sweetness of the Lord? Have you discovered the aroma of His Mercy and His presence in your life? If you have, then you know what it means to want more and you will find yourself seeking Him out every day. If you have not, you do not know what you are missing. And when you do not know what you are missing, it's hard to actually miss it. But know this, you do not want to miss out on the Mercy of God. Reflect, today, upon this question. Have I tasted of the sweetness of my Lord? God wants to flood You with the delight of His presence, let Him do so and you will never seek out the cheap wine of life again.

Lord, I do want to become inebriated with Your Mercy. I desire that this Mercy fill me with the aroma of Your abundant grace. May my love for You become an appetite so strong that I turn to You as the only delight of my life. Jesus, I trust in You.

Reflection 196: Loving Jesus in Others

We are quite familiar with the Gospel passage, "Whatever you do to the least of my brothers, you do unto me" (Matthew 25:40). But do you believe this? If you do, then you will discover that loving Jesus is easy and that you have an opportunity to do so all day long, every time you encounter another. It may be through a kind smile or word. It may be through an act of generosity, forgiveness or service. But whatever you do to another in love, you do to Jesus. This is true. And it's also true that when we treat another with harshness or a lack of Mercy we wound the Heart of our Lord. This basic truth is easily understood as a concept in our minds, but not so easily understood through our actions. It can be hard to actually see Jesus in another and to believe that we are loving our Lord by our service of them. But just because it's hard to believe doesn't mean we should not believe it and live it (See *Diary* #1029).

Think of the people that you encounter daily. When you look at them, do you see their presence as an invitation to love our Lord? Is it hard to do this? We must believe that Jesus is there, hidden within them, waiting to be loved. Reflect upon your hidden Lord waiting for you in the persons you encounter this day. Do not hesitate to love our Lord through them. For in them, the font of Divine Mercy waits to be opened.

Lord, You desire that I show an abundance of Mercy to those I encounter every day. Give me the grace to see You in them and to love You in each and every person I encounter. May I have the eyes to see You, dear Lord, and as I discover You in others, help me to open my heart to them, loving them with the Mercy You give to me. Jesus, I trust in You.

Reflection 197: I Thirst

"I thirst." These two simple words have so much meaning. They were spoken by our Lord from the Cross. A soldier tried to offer some comfort by offering Him a sponge soaked in wine-vinegar to satiate Him. The wine turned to vinegar is a symbol of the soul turned sour from sin. After taking this sour wine Jesus cried, "It is finished!" And then He died. What does Jesus thirst for? He thirsts for you, a sinner. He does not turn away from you on account of your sins and the effect that they have had on your soul, He thirsts for you anyway. He thirsts for your love. He wants you to satiate His thirst by loving Him as you are despite your sins. Pay no attention to foulness of your soul as a result of your sins. Our Lord was satisfied with the wine turned vinegar so as to say that He is satisfied with you coming to Him in your fallen condition (See *Diary* #1032).

Reflect upon the image of the Crucifixion. Ponder Jesus hanging there, broken and suffering. In this state of great humiliation, Jesus cries out to you to bring comfort to His suffering. He seeks your love. Will you give it to Him? Can you offer Him yourself so as to enable Him to cry out that it is finished? It is finished when you love Him and give your life to Him. Go to our Lord this day in prayer, and tell Him you love Him and desire to spend this life with Him and on through eternity. In that act, you will quench His thirst.

Lord, I thank You for thirsting for me in the midst of Your own suffering and pain. Thank You for giving Your life to me, without reserve, as You hung upon the Cross. Your love is the only thing that will ultimately satiate my thirsting soul. Give me the grace I need to come to You, in my brokenness and sin, so as to offer You all that I have for Your thirst. I love You, dear Lord, help me to love You more. Jesus, I trust in You.

Reflection 198: The Mercy of True Empathy

The lack of true heartfelt empathy is a clear sign of a certain psychological, emotional and even spiritual disorder. This is mentioned because the opposite is true also. The presence of true heartfelt empathy is a sign that one is psychologically, emotionally and spiritually healthy. Empathy means that you are aware of the other. You sense when someone is hurting or when they are joyful. Furthermore, you feel the pain they feel and experience the joy that they experience. This is an act of mercy in your heart flowing from the Mercy of God. (See *Diary* #1039).

Reflect, today, upon your empathy or lack thereof. What takes place within your mind, heart and emotions when you encounter either the joys or the sufferings of another. Do you walk right past them, not caring and not engaging them? Or do you see their humanity, recognize their dignity, and treat them with care, compassion and respect? Empathy is ultimately all about the dignity of each and every person and our ability to acknowledge that dignity through our thoughts, feelings, words and actions. Try to honestly look at your own empathy today and if you are surprised at a lacking in this area, look deeper at the reason way. Do not be afraid to admit to this lacking and do not be afraid to seek its remedy. But if you see yourself blessed with a heart of compassion, filled with an awareness of the other, then rejoice because your heart is sharing in and dispensing the Mercy of God.

Lord, I pray that my heart will become an instrument of Your own merciful Heart. In any way that I lack the empathy and compassion flowing from Your Heart, bring me healing. And in every way that I have been blessed to experience the struggles and joys of others on account of sharing in Your Mercy, I thank You. Lord, my deep desire is to share in Your life and love so that my heart may become like unto Yours. Jesus, I trust in You.

Reflection 199: Unity with Jesus is Unity with Others

The Church is glorious for many reasons. One glorious aspect of the Church is the unity found within it. It's true that there is, at times, much internal disunity, hurt and disorder of every kind. But these are not qualities of the Church. These are the effects of the sins of Her members. The Church Herself is the Spotless Bride of Christ. And the more we enter into union with Christ Jesus, the more fully we are a member of this glorious Church. By uniting ourselves to Christ we unite ourselves to the Holy Father. And by uniting ourselves to the Holy Father, we unite ourselves to St. Peter, all the Apostles and all the saints who are living and in Heaven. We become mystically united with Christians throughout the world and our prayer and adoration of God becomes one song of praise rising to the glory of Heaven. And as we unite ourselves, through our unity with Christ, we receive the overabundance of Mercy from God making us one (See *Diary* #1044).

Do you see yourself as a member of the one Body of Christ? Do you understand that you are called to share in the unity that comes from your union with Him? Loving Jesus with your whole mind, heart, soul and strength brings about a profound love for others. If it does not, then it is not authentic love of God. Reflect upon the effect that your love of God has on your relationship with others. Let your love of God affect you in such a way that you discover an outpouring of love for all people, especially those within the Church. And let that love reveal the deep bond of unity that is established as a result. Unity is glorious. It is a central blessing flowing from the Church and a sign of the Mercy of God.

Lord, help me to always live in union with You and with others. May my love for You overflow into my love for others, especially those who are members of Your Church. I love You, dear Lord, and I trust in You.

Reflection 200: The Unity of Love and Suffering

Are love and suffering opposed? In other words, if you feel much suffering can you also have great love? One question to consider is this: What is the source of your suffering? Is it your sin? Is it compassion for another? Is it a physical or psychological wound? The truth is that every suffering is able to be united with love in your heart. This is true even of the suffering you endure as a result of your sin. Sin is clearly not from God, but when you experience interior suffering as a result of your sin, it's a sign that your conscience is at work and that is good. The goal is to take every form of suffering you endure, be it from sin or any other source, and let it become an impetus for mercy. First, you must allow the Mercy of God to soothe the pain you feel, and then you must let that love coming from the Lord's Mercy transform your suffering into your own mercy. Suffering and Mercy must meet within your heart and from there, extend out to others (See *Diary* #1050).

What do you see in your heart? Specifically identify any suffering you endure. No matter what the cause, look at it and experience it. As you do this, allow the grace flowing from the Heart of Christ to enter in. And as you allow it to enter in, let Him transform your hurt into a heart full of mercy and compassion for all, starting with yourself. The Mercy of God is abundant and can overshadow everything we experience in life, even our pain. Let your pain meet Divine Mercy in your heart and you will be forever changed.

Lord, I invite You into my heart. Come and dwell there and transform everything within me through an abundant outpouring of Your Divine Mercy. May I love You, dear Lord, above all things and allow Your presence in my life to change me for Your glory. Jesus, I trust in You.

Reflection 201: The Night with Jesus, In Prison

Imagine what it would be like if you could somehow be mystically transported to the night of Holy Thursday. And imagine if you could somehow see and experience everything that Jesus went through. Imagine the Agony in the Garden, the ridicule and harsh treatment, the mockery, the night alone in prison, the trial, the scourging, the carrying of the Cross and the Crucifixion. This would be too much to bear. To face Jesus and all His interior and exterior sufferings would be overwhelming. But, if you could do it, and face every experience that He had, it would change your life. The sufferings of Christ should not be ignored. They should not be turned away from and they should not be shunned. His Passion must be faced, understood, loved and lived by each one of us. When we do this we will be changed forever (See *Diary* #1054).

Try to spend time today letting yourself be drawn in, deeply, to the mysterious and profound sufferings of Jesus. Let the Lord reveal to you a taste of what He endured. Facing His sufferings is not only facing a great evil; rather, it's facing love in its purest form.   To face the Cross and all that it encompassed is to face the greatest act of love ever known, revealed through the greatest scandal ever experienced. God is astonishing to us, in a holy way, when we discover His love in His suffering. Ponder it today, let it sit in your heart, seek to understand the mystery and allow God to transform you through it.

Lord, please give me the grace to turn toward You on the throne of Your Cross and to gaze upon You now and for all eternity.   Help me to discover Love in its most pure form as I fix my eyes on You and all that You endured. My Suffering Lord Jesus, I love You and I trust in You.

Reflection 202: A Daily Anniversary

Anniversaries are blessed opportunities for reflection and gratitude.   Some anniversaries are joyous, such as the anniversary of spouses celebrating a long and holy marriage. Other anniversaries are difficult, such as the anniversary of the death of a loved one. Yet even in the difficulty of reliving the loss, it is a yearly reminder of your love for that person. There are many annual celebrations within the Church that point us to a remembrance of a particular aspect of Christ's life. But there is one "anniversary" which is celebrated daily. It's the daily commemoration of the death of our Lord at three o'clock in the afternoon. This hour is a sacred hour and is an important time to stop and reflect upon all that Jesus did for us. It's a time of gratitude as well as a time to mourn His sufferings with a holy sorrow. This hour is especially honored on Good Friday, but it's important to commemorate it every day (See *Diary* #1055).

Do you remember the three o'clock hour? It's easy to forget this most sacred moment of the day. Our lives can become busy and hectic and we can fail to pause and recall our Lord's agony of love. But try to see it as your daily anniversary with the Lord. It is this hour that our prayers are most effective. There are special graces of Mercy bestowed upon those who pause and pray at this hour. Commit yourself to this holy devotion and our Lord will bless you abundantly.

My Jesus, You hung on the Cross from noon until three in the afternoon. And at that holy hour You uttered Your final word, breathed Your last and died. May I always remember to honor this hour. May it be my daily reminder of Your perfect love. Help me to grow in devotion to Your sacred Passion, dear Lord, and through this practice, pour forth the Mercy of Your wounded Heart. Jesus, I trust in You.

Reflection 203: The Depth and Breadth of Mercy

Imagine being given the task of counting every grain of sand in the world. It would obviously be an impossible task. In fact, all the people in the world could not accomplish such a task together. Some things are simply beyond us. Another task that would even be more difficult to accomplish is to fully fathom the Mercy of God. This is impossible. The Mercy of God is completely beyond us. Its depths and breadth are infinite. You could spend your whole life contemplating and experiencing the Mercy of God and you would only begin to penetrate the surface. In fact, if every person ever created spent eternity contemplating the Mercy of God, our combined effort would not even suffice to comprehend it. Understanding that the Mercy of God is infinite will enable us to turn to Him no matter our struggle and no matter our sin, trusting in Him with all the powers of our soul (See *Diary* #1059).

Have you tried to comprehend the Mercy of God? Do you even understand that you can never fully understand this infinite Gift? If you are to trust in our Lord, you must begin this impossible mission of Divine contemplation. It's what you will do eternally in Heaven. And your Heaven must begin now. Doing so will deepen your ability to trust, and your trust will enable you to surrender. Do not wait, begin this glorious task today.

Lord of Mercy, I thank You for the infinite nature of Your love and for calling me to begin my journey into this unfathomable mystery. Give me the grace to open my eyes so that I may begin to plunge into Your Mercy and in so doing, deepen my trust in You this day. Jesus, I trust in You.

Reflection 204: The Calyx of Your Soul

The calyx of a flower is the outer leaf surrounding the forming petals, keeping them safe as they develop. It forms a sort of "nursery" for the tender petals to grow. As they grow within this hidden place, the calyx keeps them safe. And once they become developed, the calyx opens and reveals the beauty within. So it is with your soul. The "calyx of your soul" is a gift from God protecting your inner virtues as the dew of His Mercy gently seeps in so as to nourish the budding virtues within. And when fully matured, the radiance of these virtues shine forth so that the fragrance of grace becomes visible to all who gaze upon this work of God (See *Diary* #1064).

Look into your own soul this day. What do you see? Do you see sin and corruption? If so, repent of this and allow the Mercy of God to heal it through your confession. From there, allow Mercy to also nourish your inner soul so as to create a hidden inner sanctuary of His splendor. God desires to make your soul beautiful and as He forms you from within, He will allow those virtues to shine forth at the proper time. Wait on Him, let the dew of His gentle care sink in, creating His masterpiece. Reflect upon this sanctuary within you, this day. Rejoice in the protective covering of your soul as God does His miraculous work and be comforted by what you see forming. Surrender all to grace and allow the Creator of all to transform you into His radiant and fragrant gift to the world.

Lord, I thank You for the safety of this inner sanctuary in my soul. I thank You for gently entering in so as to nourish me as You form Your new creation within. May the dew of Your Mercy bring healing and forgiveness to the corruption of my sin, and may it strengthen me so that You can form the virtues that You desire to create. I thank You for Your perfect wisdom and power and give myself to Your gentle care. Jesus, I trust in You.

Reflection 205: The Fortress of Peace

The peace of the Lord is like a fortress in which we must take refuge from all the outer attacks from the evil one. Outside of this fortress we are exposed to all of these malicious attacks. The darts of anger, oppression, deceit and envy can do us great damage without the sacred protection of the Peace of God. But within the walls of this fortress, the Lord protects us from all that seeks to do us harm. Seek refuge in the Lord's Mercy and allow it to form a barrier of peace, protecting you from the evils of the world. Do not allow these attacks to penetrate this barrier; rather, remain content with the Lord and allow Him to work on you within the safety of His place of refuge (See *Diary* #1067).

What is it that seeks to destroy your peace? What shakes you and disturbs you from within? Know that the Lord wants to protect you and to give you refuge. Seek His peace. Seek Him and He will give you His peace. Peace is a gift that is beyond description and human comprehension. It's a place of safety that will shield your soul from the daily vices and attacks of the evil one. Do you know the Lord's peace? Are your eyes firmly fixed on this gift of His Mercy? Seek Jesus with all your heart and you will, indeed, know His peace. And in the shelter of that peace, the Lord will do great things to you, if you let Him.

Lord, I entrust to You the protection of my soul. I give to You all of my inner longings, hopes, desires and weaknesses. Please come and form a barrier of protection around me so that I may meet You in this sanctuary within. I thank You for the love of Your Mercy that envelops me and produces sweetness and strength. I love You, my Lord, and entrust myself to Your perfect care. Jesus, I trust in You.

Reflection 206: Spiritual Hoarding

A real danger to the spiritual life could be termed "spiritual hoarding." This would be the person who attempts to make themselves the *end* of God's Mercy rather than become an *instrument* of God's Mercy. By attempting to be an end of God's Mercy, a person becomes spiritually greedy, seeking spiritual things for their own purpose. This is a form of pride. Praying becomes an act by which one seeks to "look" holy. Good works are performed so as to be seen. And one may seek to accumulate many spiritual books so as to give the appearance of being wise and learned. But an essential focus of the Mercy of God is not "spiritual hoarding;" rather, it's "spiritual generosity." If we want true Mercy to pour forth into our lives, we must give it away. We must see everything that God gives us as a gift given for the purpose of distribution to others. Therefore, when God gives you a certain grace, the first thing that should come to mind is how you can use this gift for the upbuilding of another. By giving the Mercy of God away, we become increasingly rich and find that this act of spiritual generosity continually increases God's Mercy in our own lives (See *Diary* #1069).

Do you seek holiness? If so, why? What is your motivation? Is it so that you look good? Or is it so that you become good, distributing the goodness of God to those in need? Reflect upon the end result of the Mercy of God in your life. Seek ways to make sure that the end of all God gives to you is the generous distribution of His Mercy to others. In this, you too will be richly blessed.

Lord of endless Mercy, help me to see that Your grace increases the more that grace is given away. Help me to always be a holy instrument of Your Mercy and, in this act of generosity, receive the abundance of Your generous Heart. Jesus, I trust in You.

Reflection 207: Taking Comfort in the Heart of Christ

Children often find great comfort in snuggling close to a loving and tender parent. There is great satisfaction in being held tight in these arms of love. Fear and worry are dispelled in these moments and peace and solace are restored when distress has been present. So it must be with our Lord. We must seek the spiritual comfort that comes from bringing our weary selves to the source of all comfort. Drawing close to the Heart of our Lord brings peace in the midst of any turmoil. Stress, frustration, hurt and confusion are dismissed and replaced with a sense of confidence and safety. The Heart of the Lord reverberates in such a way that it invites us to take refuge in its rhythm. His compassion and Mercy are distributed with every beat as His Precious Blood covers us as a blanket of grace. Run to this source of comfort and allow the merciful Heart of your God to be your place of rest (See *Diary* #1074).

In your prayer, are you able to take comfort and solace in the Merciful Heart of our Lord? Reflect upon the intimacy that you are invited to share. It is an intimacy beyond any human comfort and distributes a grace that floods your soul with Mercy and peace. Ponder the image of a small child taking comfort in the arms of a loving parent. This is but a glimpse of the care that our Lord desires to show to you.

Heavenly Father, draw me close to You and to the Heart of Your Son. May I turn to You in all things and in every moment of distress in my life. I entrust myself to You and cling to Your Heart which is filled with compassion and love. May Your Heart be a resting place for my weary soul. I love You my God and I take refuge in You and You alone. Jesus, I trust in You.

Reflection 208: A Spiritual Arrow of Mercy

Normally, an arrow wounds and kills. Arrows have been used throughout history for war and for hunting. But a *spiritual arrow of Mercy* is much different. Recall the words of Simeon the Prophet spoken to our Blessed Mother, "And you yourself a sword will pierce" (Luke 2:35). And at the Crucifixion, recall that, "One soldier thrust his lance into [Jesus'] side, and immediately blood and water flowed out" (John 19:34). A sword and a lance pierced the Hearts of our Blessed Mother and Jesus. So also must our hearts be pierced. But the sword, lance or arrow that we must receive will not wound in a negative way if accepted in love. Rather, it will call forth mercy and compassion from our hearts. Sorrow and pain are transformed within this "wound of love" and that wound pours forth God's Mercy from our lives (See *Diary* #1082).

Reflect, today, upon two things. First ponder the spiritual wounds in the Hearts of Jesus and Mary. Enter into the mystery of their pierced Hearts. Try to understand that grace comes forth as a result of these piercings in that they produce compassion and Mercy for those in need. Second, ponder your own heart. Reflect upon any wound you carry and allow yourself to understand that this wound can be transformed. It has potential to share in the Mercy flowing from the Hearts of Jesus and our Blessed Mother. Allow yourself to share in their holy sorrow over sin and foster compassion for the sinner. In this act, you will become wounded by a spiritual arrow of love.

Lord, help me to comprehend the great mystery of the suffering endured by Your most Sacred Heart. Allow me to see that You freely accepted that wound so as to pour forth Mercy. And help me to also accept the arrows of others so that Your Mercy can pour forth in return. Jesus, I trust in You.

Reflection 209: Overcoming the Habit of Sin

Overcoming sin requires the Mercy of God. Too often we attempt to overcome sin through our own effort. This is a futile exercise in that you will never overcome your own sin through your own effort. There is one way and one way only to rid yourself of the sin you struggle with, and that is done by turning to the transforming power of God poured out through the Mercy of the Cross of Christ. It's entirely possible that you have identified some habitual sin in your life, have confessed it, and then, within the next day, fell into that sin again, over and over. This is because you have attempted to rely upon your own strength and not the power of God. Jesus is the only means by which you can overcome your sin. Turning to Him for the Mercy to eliminate sin from your life requires commitment and focus. It requires total trust in Him and a complete surrender to Him. You cannot do this on your own (See *Diary* #1087).

What is it that you struggle with each and every day? Whatever your sin may be, you can overcome it, but only by relying on Mercy and the purifying power of the Cross. This is done by fixing your eyes on Jesus and relying on Him alone. Your responsibility is to turn to Christ. His action is one of purification. Do not doubt the power of our Lord and His ability to purge sin from your life. It may "hurt" to be purified, but it is obtainable. It requires sacrifice on your part and Mercy on His part. Reflect upon this internal struggle you encounter and resolve, deeply, to abandon yourself to Him. He will begin to lift this burden in your life when you do so.

Lord, I give You my sin and beg for the grace to overcome it. I know that I am weak, but that You are strong. Lift this heavy burden and bring purity and sanctity to my soul. I love You my Lord and I surrender my sin to You. Jesus, I trust in You.

Reflection 210: Good Works in the Light of Divine Love

Do you work hard? Do you strive to be good? Do you want to make a positive difference? It is certainly *good* to try to be *good*. But in so doing, we must never think that our "goodness" is truly good in the eyes of God, unless it is Divine Love that has become the source of all activity in our lives. Humility enables us to turn our eyes to the One and Only source of goodness in our lives. And that source is the abundant Mercy of God. We cannot decide, on our own, to do even one single act that is good or beneficial to others. We cannot please God by our own effort, and most certainly, cannot attain Heaven or any eternal reward by our works. All is a gift and all is grace. Only the humble soul sees this and believes it. But when it sees it and believes it, great things will happen for the Kingdom of God (See *Diary* #1092).

Reflect upon the good works you do. As you do, see them for what they are, nothing less and nothing more. If there is goodness in your life, humble honesty will enable you to understand that this goodness is 100% dependent upon the Goodness of God. Without Mercy, you cannot do any good work. With Mercy, you can do every good work. God, at work in your soul, produces abundant blessings in this world. Reflect upon your desire to be an instrument of the abundant blessings of God in this world and rejoice, humbly, that God has chosen to use you. Say "Yes" to Him and you will see beautiful fruits for all.

Lord, please give me a humble heart. Help me to see that all good things begin with You and are only accomplished by You and Your Mercy. I give myself to You so that You may use me for Your glory. And I thank You for the privilege of being used as an instrument of Your unfailing Love. Jesus, I trust in You.

Reflection 211: Close to the Mother of God

A mother's love could be described as "fierce" in the sense that she would willingly give her life for the protection of her children. A motherly instinct kicks in when her child is in danger, hurting, or in need, and she loses all sense of her own well-being in favor of the protection of her child. So it is with the Mother of God. You are her child by grace and by the will of Jesus her Son. As a result, she holds you close to her heart in times of need and shelters you in her mantle of protection. This motherly love is offered even when you are not in harm's way as a result of her unwavering motherly care. She is an advocate for you like none other. And she is not only your mother; she is also the Mother of God. And as the Mother of God, she obtains special graces for all her children from her Divine Son. He answers every request she makes on your behalf and will never abandon you. Stay close to her, nestled in her arms of Mercy (See *Diary* #1097).

Have you consecrated yourself to the love, care and protection of the Mother of God? If not, why not? What are you waiting for? Does it confuse you why you should trust in her maternal care? God deigned to create a spiritual family of love and He entrusted His mother with your care. Motherly care is central to the natural order of God's design for humanity. Therefore, it is only logical to conclude that it is also part of His supernatural plan for humanity. Turn to her as your spiritual mother and trust that the Lord wills to pour an abundance of Mercy upon you through her mediation.

Dearest mother, I love you and entrust myself to your motherly care and intercession. I believe that you are my mother in the order of grace and that you are "full of grace." Pour down upon me the motherly Mercy in your heart as I put my trust in you. Dearest Mother, I consecrate myself to you. Please pray for me. Jesus, I trust in You.

Reflection 212: Overcoming Doubt

What is "doubt?" To doubt is to lack faith, and to lack faith is to lack trust in the perfect revelation and plan of God's Will. First and foremost, a doubt, resulting from a lack of faith, means you are not listening. When we doubt God, His plan and all that He reveals to us, we are left on our own. But when we listen, hear, understand and believe, we are covered in the protection of His Mercy on account of the faith that we manifest. Faith means that we *know* with *certainty* all that God says and wills. Faith is not just believing in something we <u>hope</u> is true, it's knowing and believing all that <u>is</u> true (See *Diary* #1101).

Do you doubt at times? Or do you have faith? This is an exceptionally important question to ponder. Begin by asking yourself these questions: Do I listen to the Voice of God? Do I hear God speak to me and do I comprehend all that He says? Without these first steps, faith is impossible. Hearing Him speak can only come through prayer. And the form of prayer we need could be called "soaking prayer." Soaking prayer is a form of prayer by which we allow ourselves to daily become immersed in the Voice of God revealing His holy Will. He speaks to us all day, every day. Little by little we listen, comprehend and respond. This produces the gift of faith and that faith will lead your life. Reflect upon this process in your life and renew your commitment to start at the beginning so that the Lord will lead you one step at a time.

Dear Lord, I desire to hear You speak to me. Help me to open my ears to hear so that I may know You and discern Your perfect Will for my life. I desire to be led each day only by You and to trust in the gentle guidance of Your holy Will. Jesus, I trust in You.

Reflection 213: The Spiritual Gift of Understanding

Do you understand the mysteries of God? Imagine that you were a theologian who studied the faith of our Church for many years. Would knowledge of all the theological disciplines of our Church necessarily produce in you an authentic understanding of these mysteries that were studied? No, it wouldn't *necessarily* produce understanding. In fact, it is entirely possible that while knowing all *about* God and all that has been revealed through the ages, you still might lack an authentic understanding *of* God and the profound mysteries of our faith. Understanding ultimately comes as a gift from God. It's an infused gift which illumines and enlightens and is obtainable only by a direct and personal revelation from God. Yes, study of the faith and attentiveness to clear articulation of this same faith disposes one to understand, but the inspired gift of Understanding is still required to penetrate and grasp all mysteries of our faith. Understanding is a true gift of God's Mercy (See *Diary* #1107).

Reflect upon your own understanding of the infinite Mercy of God. How fully do you comprehend this Mercy? Reflect upon all that God has revealed to us throughout history. He has spoken definitively through Scripture and has also spoken definitively through His Church in numerous ways. Reflect upon how fully you grasp all the articles of our faith that have been revealed through the ages. God has spoken in a clear and public way. Now He desires to speak those same truths to you in the depths of your soul. If you are willing to listen, your understanding will open the floodgates of the Mercy of God.

Lord, there are so many truths that I do not fully grasp. Your life and Your workings are glorious and mysterious all at once. Give me the grace of Understanding so that I may penetrate the depths of Your Truth and Your Mercy. I open myself to You, dear Lord. Jesus, I trust in You.

Reflection 214: A Complete Pardon

Imagine that you were guilty of a serious crime and faced life in prison. You were sorry for what you had done and fully confessed to it. On the day of your sentencing you came in handcuffed from where you were being held knowing that you would soon return. Instead, the judge ordered that your shackles be removed, that you were to receive a full pardon and that you were being granted a complete restoration to your former life. Certainly you would be filled with gratitude. But we must realize that God has not only done this, He has done even more. He also elevates us the status as His sons and daughters, a new status that we do not deserve in the order of grace. The Mercy of God is amazing and beyond what we can comprehend. All we have to do is repent and entrust ourselves to the benevolence of this good Judge. This is especially done through Confession and trusting in the abundance of Mercy offered to those who specifically go to Confession in honor of Divine Mercy Sunday (See *Diary* #1109).

Can you admit to your sin? Are you aware of your sin? If so, then you are one step away from receiving a full pardon from the Most Merciful Judge. God longs to not only wipe away your sins, He also longs to elevate you to the glorious heights of Mercy. Do you want this? If so, do not hesitate in believing in the glorious Sacrament of Confession, and do not hesitate to trust in His Mercy poured out on Divine Mercy Sunday each year. Seek His pardon, especially on that glorious day.

Lord, give me the grace of knowing my sins and confessing them in the Sacrament of Reconciliation. May I have great courage to face Your

Mercy in that Sacrament so as to be elevated to the glorious status of Your sons and daughters. And may I especially trust in the Mercy You bestow on Divine Mercy Sunday. Thank You for the graces bestowed on this most holy day. Jesus, I trust in You.

Reflection 215: The Freedom to Choose

In one sense we can say that God imposes upon us an obligation to turn to Him with our whole being and receive His Mercy. He also imposes upon us the obligation to spread His Mercy to others. But we must understand that this is no ordinary "obligation." It's an obligation of love. This means that the "imposition" of this obligation is no imposition at all. It is something that God gives us complete freedom to choose or reject. There are no strings attached, no forms of force; rather, we are left in complete freedom to choose or not to choose to accept and bestow the Mercy of God. This freedom is essential to our lives and is essential to the gift of God's Mercy. Only by giving us this freedom can we fully cooperate with this gift because Mercy must be freely given and freely received. If it is not, then it is not Mercy. Be grateful for the freedom the Lord has given you and use it to make a glorious choice (See *Diary* #1115).

Reflect, today, upon these two gifts God has given you. First, reflect upon the gift of freedom. In having freewill, you are able to make your own choices in life. As a result, you also either reap the blessings of the choices you make, or suffer the consequences. Reflect, also, upon the fact that you are invited by God to accept and distribute His abundant gift of Mercy. By freely choosing this gift, you invite the God of the Universe to descend from His Throne of Grace and embrace you with an embrace of pure love, enabling you to offer that embrace to others.

193

Lord, I give You my life and freely choose to receive all the Mercy of Your most Sacred Heart. Help me to be open to all that You wish to bestow, and help me to be open to bestow all that You wish to offer others. I thank You, Lord, for these glorious gifts of freedom and Mercy and I choose Your Mercy with all my heart. Jesus, I trust in You.

Reflection 216: Clarity of Mind through Authentic Love

Our Church sets before us many teachings that can only be understood by grace. Some teachings are about morality, calling us to a life of great virtue. Some teachings are about God, His very being and essence. Some teachings are about humanity and bring clarity to who we are. What's important to understand is that nothing that the Church teaches can be fully understood without love. Love is like a window inserted into a brick wall surrounding the many truths revealed to us by God. Unless we find that window and peer through, we are left unaware of all that God wishes to teach us each day. Love of God and love of others enables us to *quickly* make sense of the greatest mysteries of life. Through love, our minds perceive and clarify life itself and all that God wishes to reveal to us in faith. Choose to love God and others with a spiritual, selfless and sacrificial love, and allow that love to become the source of your understanding in life (See *Diary* #1123).

What is it that causes you the greatest confusion? Is there some article of faith taught by the Church that you do not understand? Or perhaps there is confusion over a relationship you have, not knowing how to approach it or to resolve some underlying problem. Whatever it is that you find difficult to "solve," know that your answer will come only when you choose to love God and others with a pure love, the love of Mercy. This is not a selfish love based on your feelings, but is a sacrificial and selfless love that imitates Jesus and His Cross. Commit to this love and you will quickly and easily comprehend the mysteries of life.

Lord, please enlighten me. Help me to realize that pure and holy love opens the door to the mysteries of life. May I open that door through my love of You, and discover all that You wish to teach me. This is a Mercy for which I am eternally grateful. Jesus, I trust in You.

Reflection 217: The Lazy and Idle Soul

We please the evil one when we allow our souls to become lazy and idle in the things of God. An idol soul is one that does not seek to engage the life of God. An idle soul is one who is *passive* in spiritual things rather than *active*. Being "passive," means that the person is somewhat indifferent to matters of faith and morality. There is little interest in these areas and, as a result, very little effort is given to them. Do not delight the evil one by being idle in your spiritual life. Become zealous, passionate, hard working, diligent and committed to the path of holiness. Seek to meet our Lord, personally, through a life of generous self-surrender to Him. And never tire of doing so with all the powers of your soul (See *Diary* #1127).

What are you passionate about? For example, do you have some hobby or pastime? Do you have some activity that you love doing and spend much time with? Though a hobby can be healthy, your greatest "pastime" should be that of seeking God and serving His holy Will. Nothing in life should take up more time and focus than your love of God. Reflect upon how determined you are in your life of faith. How committed are you to building a relationship with your merciful Lord? Are you idle or lazy in this area? Renew your zeal for God and allow that zeal to guide you into an ever deepening relationship with your Lord. Give Him more than an hour a week and you will reap the blessings of your commitment.

Lord, I want to be holy. However, I realize that I do not desire holiness enough, preferring instead to be idle and lazy at times. Please increase my zeal and my desire to come to know You more. And as I grow in a deeper love for You, magnify that love and help it to continue growing in an exponential way. May I never tire of seeking You and loving You, dear Lord. I give you my life. Jesus, I trust in You.

Reflection 218: A Single Perception of God

It is important to understand God and His ways, but *understanding* is not the same as *knowing*. Knowing God means we encounter a Person. We do not only understand what this person says; rather, we engage, meet, experience and enter into a relationship with this Person. In fact, one of the greatest blessings we can ever receive in this life is to obtain even a single perception of God. Even one single perception of Him, one single encounter with Him, one single act of knowing Him is enough to change our lives forever. An act of authentic *knowing* of God is more important than any other act we can do in life (See *Diary* #1133).

If you were offered all the wealth and fame of the world, great success and prestige, would you take it? Most likely you would. Being successful or wealthy or well known or greatly honored is often desirable. In and of themselves, none of these qualities are bad. But there is a grave danger in these desires the moment that they become more important to us than our desire to know God, distracting us from that ultimate goal. The moment we find ourselves desiring worldly things more than a desire for the very Person of God is the moment that we have mixed up our priorities in life. Seek even one single act of encountering our merciful God and you will find that this knowledge of Him is worth more than anything this world can offer.

My Lord, I desire to know You. Please increase that desire in my soul so that it is more powerful than every other desire in my life. I pray that You give me even a single perception of You, a single knowledge of You, dear Lord, and in that knowledge please change my life. Jesus, I trust in You.

Reflection 219: Difficulties in Proclaiming Mercy

If you commit yourself to a full embrace of the Mercy of God in your life, you will be transformed beyond your wildest dreams. But you will also have another experience. You will encounter great difficulties in your attempts to live and proclaim Mercy to a fallen world. The world does not understand the Mercy of God. The world only knows harshness and judgment. It seeks revenge and honors pride and self-assertion. Mercy, however, it does not understand. And when you embrace Mercy and allow it to be made manifest through your life, it will not always be accepted. You may be misunderstood, labeled as weak and even ignored by many. Do not get discouraged at the rejection you will encounter as you seek to be an apostle of the Mercy of God. This is inevitable, but in that rejection and in every difficulty you encounter, you will discover a new level of holiness as you rest close to the Heart of Christ (See *Diary* #1142).

As you attempt to embrace Mercy in your life, what difficulties do you encounter? Do others fail to understand the path you are on? Do you feel misunderstood and even judged? Reflect upon your experience and try to surrender every difficulty you experience over to the Heart of Christ. His act of perfect Mercy, manifested through His death on the Cross, was seen by many as a pitiful and unfortunate consequence of His weakness. However, Jesus' love was not hampered by these false perceptions. He pressed on, offering His life for the salvation of the world. You must do the same.

Lord, Your Mercy is so profound and so mysterious that, at times, I question its wisdom. I question whether I am walking the road to sanctity or foolishness. Give me courage, clarity and strength to persevere down the

*road You have called me and help me to continually trust in Your
abundance of Mercy. Jesus, I trust in You.*

Reflection 220: The Tormented Soul

Some people feel deeply tormented in the depths of their
souls. Sometimes this is caused by sin, sometimes it is caused
by a special Mercy of God which enables the soul to
experience the sufferings Jesus went through. Whatever the
case may be, if you encounter any torment, whatsoever, in the
depths of your soul, know that you have a special right to the
Mercy of God. Why do you have this "right" to Mercy? Not
because you deserve it; rather, because God wishes to bestow
it. The greater your suffering the greater your right to the
Mercy of God. For that reason, do not be afraid to run to
God in your misery and pain. Do not be afraid of any form of
rejection from God. The soul that suffers is dearer to Him
than any other (See *Diary* #1146).

The term "tormented soul" is powerful language. But it's also
very honest language, describing the experience of many
people. So many people feel this deep interior torment,
especially on account of their sins. They feel dry, alone and
trapped in this cycle of pain. If this is you in any way, reflect
upon the truth that God offers you a right to His Mercy more
than any other. He chooses you as His special object of
compassion and lavishes upon you more than you could ever
ask for. Let yourself grow in confidence as you seek the
Mercy of God and allow it to penetrate every torment you feel,
no matter the cause, even if it comes from your sin.

*Lord of utmost compassion, please help me to know, with certainty, that
You love me and will never reject me. I believe in Your Mercy and I trust
that You desire to dispense it in abundance. When I feel lost, confused
and even tormented by my sin, help me to turn to You all the more, calling
upon You to fulfill Your promise of love. Jesus, I trust in You.*

Reflection 221: Glorying in Yourself

Sometimes, those who are quite "religious" speak of many "religious" things. They speak pious language and talk about holy things. But in the end, it may be that all they say and do is actually said and done as a way of glorifying themselves in the sight of others. This is the struggle of the Pharisees. Sadly, those who struggle with this, just like the Pharisees, may even be fooling themselves into thinking they are exceptionally close to God. But their pride has blinded them. The goal of our lives must be to humbly point to God and offer all glory to Him, not to ourselves. This can be very hard, but when done well, as an act of the utmost humility and truth, we realize that God actually does draw us into His glory and allows us to share in the honor that we owe to Him. Only in this way do we come to realize our true dignity as His sons and daughters. And in humbly pointing to God in all things, we are also lifted on high by God Himself (See *Diary* #1149).

Are you able to give all glory to God rather than trying to lift yourself up for others to see? Reflect upon this in all honesty and humility. The problem is that if you lift yourself on high, you will not be able to lift yourself very high and will actually find yourself in a more humiliated state than you could have imagined. Lift the Lord on high and point to Him as the source of all goodness and leave the elevation of your own life up to Him. He will raise you higher than you could ever do yourself.

Lord, I pray for the gift of humility. I pray that in my humility I will see the truth and proclaim only that truth. I especially pray that I will be able to see the truth that all good things come from You and are accomplished by You. All glory be to You my Lord! Jesus, I trust in You.

Reflection 222: Feeling Overwhelmed

There are days when you most likely feel overwhelmed on account of one thing or another. It may be that you find yourself with much responsibility and are anxious about being able to properly fulfill your duties well. Or you may feel overwhelmed for the opposite reason, finding that life seems to be at a standstill and you are not sure what to do next. In these moments, of feeling overwhelmed, we must make an act of trust in God. The truth is that God could enter any situation in an instant and transform it, enabling us to face what is before us with the ease of a child. But He doesn't always do that. Sometimes He allows us to wait on Him so that the situation we face will help to purify us and urge us toward greater surrender and love. Know that God loves you and could do anything to immediately lighten your struggle. Knowing that will help you also realize that, at times, He remains at an apparent distance as an act of hidden Mercy. It's a Mercy because His wisdom is perfect and He will always act in a way that is most fruitful for your soul (See *Diary* #1153).

Look at your life this day and identify that which has the appearance of being your greatest struggle. How does that make you feel? If you do feel overwhelmed then pause and try to see the wisdom of God. He will never abandon you and may actually be offering you a hidden gift of Mercy through which He is calling you to greater holiness than if He immediately made your burdens light and easy.

Lord, help me to trust in You especially when I feel overwhelmed by the hardships of life. May I never doubt Your perfect love and perfect wisdom in all things. Give me the grace to see beyond that which burdens me so as to discover the hidden Mercy You offer me to purify and strengthen my soul. I thank You for all things, dear Lord. Jesus, I trust in You.

Reflection 223: A Dreadful Day

Nothing in life has to be dreadful. Even the greatest struggle and suffering we endure can easily be transformed by God to become a source of His Mercy and our sanctification. But there is one thing that would be truly dreadful if it were to come upon us. And that one thing is the Day of Judgment if we were to remain closed to the Mercy of God through our obstinance and refusal to humbly repent and change our lives. This is a frightening reality to behold. When we stand before the Judgment Seat of God we will never be able to justify our stubborn adherence to sin. No amount of rationalization or self-justification will appease the Justice of God. Do not allow yourself to come to this point. Repent now. Honestly repent and confess your sin. Do not hold onto your self-righteousness. This will be easy to accomplish if you clearly understand the infinite Mercy of God offered you now and until the day of your judgment. After that, it will be too late. Do not wait (See *Diary* #1160).

What do you need to repent of? Seriously, what is it? Do not cling to your own self-righteousness acting as if you have no sin. You may fool others, you may even fool yourself, but you will never fool God. His love for you is greater than you'll ever fathom and knowing this should ease your worries about admitting your sin. Do it and watch the floodgates of Mercy open before you.

Lord, I am sorry and I do repent of my sin. I am so sorry, especially for the ways that I have failed to honestly admit my wrongs. Give me the grace, this day, to see my soul as You see it and to admit to the ways that I have turned from You, clinging to my own sin and especially my pride. Have Mercy on me, dear Lord. I give myself and all my sin to You. Jesus, I trust in You.

Reflection 224: To Speak or Not to Speak

One common human tendency is to talk excessively and to explain ourselves to others, especially to justify our actions in their minds. This is especially the case when we sense that others misunderstand us. But Jesus experienced this to the greatest degree as He stood before Herod and Pilate. In these cases, He remained silent. This is a lesson for us in that there are many times when our Lord calls us to remain silent in the face of misunderstanding. Sure, there are other times when He calls us to speak freely and openly to another about our soul and our inner thoughts, but we must strive to discern His Will in each situation and know that silence, in certain situations, is what He calls us to. Remaining silent, at times, will produce more good fruit than an excess of words. Seek to imitate the silence of our Lord in those moments, trusting that He sees your soul and is pleased with you as you endure false perceptions and misunderstandings (See *Diary* #1164).

Are there times when you sense that others do not understand you? This can be difficult and even painful. Notice that in these moments you may tend to look for ways to explain yourself to others and defend your honor. But silence in those moments may actually be what our Lord is calling you to embrace. Reflect upon Jesus, standing before Herod and Pilate, and ponder His silence in the face of judgment. Know that you will also be called to endure moments like this and, in accord with God's mysterious Will, this act of silence will win more grace for the salvation of souls than all the words you could speak.

Lord, give me wisdom so that I know when to speak and when to remain silent. I desire to imitate Your perfect silence and to endure the misunderstandings that You endured. In these moments, give me grace to imitate Your humility as I imitate You. Jesus, I trust in You.

Reflection 225: Spiritual Friendship Through Prayer

One powerful channel of the Mercy of God is friendship with another. But friendship can be lived on various levels. Sometimes this bond is based on superficial and unimportant things, and at other times it's deeply grounded in our Lord. A sign of a deep spiritual friendship is mutual prayer. If you have been blessed with a faith-filled friend, seal and deepen that friendship through a commitment to mutual prayer. Share your life and your needs with each other and commit to praying for those needs. Through the act of mutual prayer you will discover that the Mercy of God is poured forth in each of your lives, and that your mutual bond will be deepened in the Lord. This is a blessing of the Mercy of God as well as a source of its continued outpouring (See *Diary* #1171).

Reflect upon the friendships you have. What is the basis of each friendship? Perhaps each one will be varied. Some will be casual acquaintances, based on a shared interest. Others will be based on some deeper unifying bond. Spend time today especially reflecting upon those friendships that are based on your shared love of God. If you are blessed with one of these friendships, seek to deepen it through shared prayer. Reflect upon that which your friend is in need of the most and commit yourself to praying for this intention. And share your need with your friend. This mutual exchange of prayer will be a powerful source of the Mercy of God.

Lord, I especially thank You this day for the friendship of (mention a specific friend). I offer this friendship to You and ask for an abundance of grace to be poured out upon him/her. Lord, I especially offer this particular need in my friend's life (identify a need). I thank You for your unwavering love for each of us, dear Lord, and for Your own perfect gift of friendship in our lives. Jesus, I trust in You.

Reflection 226: The Good Fruit of Mercy

Our Lord had a Heart of perfect Mercy for others. It's important to note that His Mercy is not only a general concept; rather, it is lived out in concrete action. Specifically, there are many good fruits born of this Mercy such as concrete acts of compassion, kindness, understanding and consolation. This is important to understand. Mercy is not simply some general concept. It's concrete and practical. It is seen, lived and experienced in daily life. Those who were near Jesus while He lived on Earth would have experienced, first hand, His compassion, kindness, understanding and consolation. Jesus wants to continue offering these to others through you. Commit yourself to these concrete acts so that the Mercy of God will continue to take on flesh in our world (See *Diary* #1175).

When you look at your own life, and examine all your actions, what do you see? Do you see concrete acts of the Mercy of God shining through? Reflect, today, upon the particulars and specific acts you see or do not see. Know that God's Mercy shines through you in the smallest of ways. Look for those ways and seek their increase in your life. Do not wait.

Lord, please make me an instrument of Your Mercy in daily acts of kindness, compassion, consolation and understanding. May these good fruits of Your Mercy be alive in my life in small and great ways. I give myself to You for Your Mercy, dear Lord. Jesus, I trust in You.

Reflection 227: Human Plans are Thwarted

It's easy for us to come up with what we deem to be a great plan for our lives and for the glory of God. We can think, and plan, and develop and organize things in a certain way only to find out that what we have come up with is not what is in the Mind of God. The error some people find themselves in is that they have failed to sincerely listen to God speak and, therefore, have failed to allow Him to lay out His perfect plan for their lives and for their good work of giving Him glory. The fact remains that if something is not the Will of God, it will not happen. Our plans become thwarted by the Will of God. And this is good. The same is true if others attempt to inflict some idea upon us that is contrary to God's Will. The Lord always protects us from this when we trust in Him. It's true that, at times, He allows evils to befall us as part of His permissive Will, but this must be seen as a part of His plan for our holiness, permitting us to trust more deeply in His providential care (See *Diary* #1180).

Reflect upon whether you sincerely seek God's Will before you develop your own plan or idea. This takes patience and surrender. It requires that we deny our own impulses and preferences and allow the Lord to speak and act. Reflect, also, upon any plans you have had for your own life that have not come to fruition. Know that this is either the result of a lack of trust on your part, or because your plan did not align with the Will of God. Surrender any past "failure" you have experienced and renew your commitment to seek only the Will of God.

Lord, I trust that in Your perfect wisdom, You will direct my life and lead me to give You perfect glory. Help me to deny my own untamed impulses and preferences so that You and You alone will enter into my life and take charge. I give all to You, dear Lord. Jesus, I trust in You.

Reflection 228: The Unfailing Presence of God

Is God alive in your life? Does He live within you? Is He present to you in the inner depths of your heart day and night? There is only one thing that would ever cause God to leave you and that is mortal sin. Mortal sin is deadly sin. It's a freely chosen act that is in grave violation of the Will of God and a grave violation of your human dignity. When you obstinately persist in such a sin, God cannot be present. He waits for repentance and looks for an opportunity to return, but remains absent as long as the mortal sin remains. But with that said, this should give you hope because it reveals that as long as you avoid mortal sin, or repent of one you have committed, you can be *certain* of the presence of God in your life. You may not always sense His closeness, but He is there, living within you. Do not doubt this truth and have full confidence of this absolute and irrevocable pledge of our Lord (See *Diary* #1181).

Reflect, today, upon the presence of God alive in your life. And if you do not sense His presence, you only need to examine your conscience and discern whether you are in mortal sin. Most likely you are not. If you are, repent immediately and seek out the Sacrament of Confession. But if you are not, then make an act of faith in the presence of God in your soul. Thank Him for being there even if you do not sense Him. And if you do not sense Him, be certain that He is there, hidden and silent for good reason. God's closeness to you is greater than you will ever know.

Lord, I thank You for being alive in my life and for living within the depths of my soul. I thank You for being with me through all things and for never abandoning me. In those moments when I do not sense Your presence, give me faith to know You are there. And fill me with a confident trust in Your guiding Hand. Jesus, I trust in You.

Reflection 229: Day-to-Day Martyrdom

One early Church Father (Tertullian) said that "the blood of martyrs is the seed of the Church." This means that the shedding of one's blood for the faith is not ultimately a tragedy; rather, it's something that is transformed by Christ so as to nourish the faith of others. And although you are most likely not to become a martyr in fact (shedding your blood), you are called to be a martyr in spirit by the day-to-day willing sacrifice of your life for the good of the Church. Being a "day-to-day martyr" means that you offer each and every act of your day to our Lord as a sacrifice for His glory and for the salvation of souls. It means that even the small acts of your day, the monotonous and seemingly unimportant ones, have the potential of being used by God as an instrument of grace. Offer everything you do each day, all day, as a sacrifice for the Church and the Lord will use you as an instrument in ways you could never fathom so as to dispense His Divine Mercy (See *Diary* #1184).

Reflect upon both the great and small sacrifices you can offer to our Lord, this day. If there is some heavy burden you carry, then focus on that. But if your day seems filled with many small acts that all appear to be somewhat insignificant in the grand picture of life, know that you have a wonderful opportunity to offer these small acts to our Lord. The power in this daily offering is beyond what you could comprehend and may be the greatest gift you can offer, and the source of much grace in our world.

Lord, I place before You all my work this day. I give you every small act and every heavy burden. I surrender all to You, dear Lord, and make them my holy sacrifice to You. Use me as Your martyr of love this day and every day so as to become a greater instrument of Your glory and the upbuilding of Your Church. Jesus, I trust in You.

Reflection 230: The Contradiction of the Cross

We should never tire of pondering the wounds of Christ. Each and every wound He received was unjustified and caused by the sins of others. His perfect hands and feet, His brow and back and His Sacred Heart should have been treated with the utmost respect, adoration and care. But they weren't. Instead, they were treated with great malice and abuse. From a worldly point of view, this is tragic. But from the Divine perspective, each and every wound, be it from the scourging, thorns, nails or spear, opened up springs of grace flowing in abundance. This effect is only possible as a result of the Mercy of God. Think of each and every wound our Lord endured as an underground spring or the freshest water, gushing forth from the earth to provide nourishment for all. From the streams that flow on account of these springs of Mercy, we are invited to drink our fill so as to be refreshed and satiated by grace (See *Diary* #1190).

Ponder, this day, the very wounds of Jesus. Try to see them and to understand the pain that He endured. As you do this, see also beyond the fleshly scourge and trauma caused by the brutality of His persecutors. Ponder the spring of Mercy that is opened with each wound. Become aware of the streams of grace running forth from these wounds and allow yourself to taste of the refreshment that they provide. Mercy has come forth from the sufferings of Christ. Now He desires to flood you with Mercy and to pour forth Mercy from the wounds that you also endure.

Lord, I thank You for Your infinite power and for doing the unthinkable. You allowed Yourself to be beaten and scourged and produced from this malice the springs of new life. May I bathe in these waters, dear Lord, and may I also allow my wounds to become a source of Your grace for a world in such need. Jesus, I trust in You.

Reflection 231: Binding the Hands of Punishment

If you were a criminal, incarcerated for some crime, you would most likely see life from a perspective that is very different from others. You would daily long to have your punishment removed and your status of freedom restored. However, an act of mercy of this sort is rarely offered by secular society. Instead, harshness and judgment is the norm. But God is much different. God is perfectly aware of everything you have ever done in violation of His law. He sees even the minutest sin. And in the end, He will administer His strict justice upon all those who have not been bathed in the justice of His Mercy. So bathe in Mercy now and help others to do the same. God offers this Mercy in varied ways. One specific way God offers the Mercy which appeases His judgment is through your heart. By daily offering your heart to our Lord and by daily offering it for others, God's judgment is transformed. He sees your holy heart, enters it, and then allows you to offer it for the sanctification of others. In this way you are able to win many souls for God on account of His perfect justice of Mercy (See *Diary* #1193).

When you look at others, what do you see? Do you see a sinner who deserves punishment for their sins? If so, be careful because this is how God will in turn see you. Strive to see the sins of others as opportunities to pray for them and as opportunities to become an instrument of the Mercy of God. God invites your participation in this act of atonement and withholds nothing when you commit yourself to this act of love.

Lord, please transform the way I see others, especially the sinner. Help me to withhold my own judgment and, in turn, to offer my heart filled with love as an act of Your Divine Mercy. Cleanse every soul, dear Lord, and forgive every sin on account of my love for You. Jesus, I trust in You.

Reflection 232: Calming the Storm

Recall the story of Jesus calming the storm (Matthew 8:23-27). This miraculous act was done as a prophetic sign of Him bringing you peace during the particular challenges you face in life. Jesus did this on a practical level for the safety and well-being of His Apostles. However, by showing that He had absolute and immediate authority over the storm at sea, Jesus also made it clear that He has absolute and immediate authority over any storm within your life, pledging His closeness in your midst. It should be consoling to you to know that there is nothing too much for God's omnipotence. He can do all things and can bring peace to any and every situation. Knowing this should give you confidence as you surrender your "storms" to Him. And when the storm remains fierce, despite your prayers, you should be assured that it is for your good or the good of others. It's an opportunity to deepen your trust in Him and to know of His particular closeness in those moments (See *Diary* #1197).

Identify the storm in your life right now. And if things are relatively calm, be grateful but also call to mind that this will not always be the case. Life can "change on a dime" as has been said. We must be ready for anything and everything that befalls us. As you ponder a storm of life, ask yourself whether you believe Jesus is there, in the midst, by your side, keeping you safe. Do you know that He could solve any problem instantaneously? Reassure yourself of this fact and allow this faith to add confidence to your troubled heart. The Lord's love for you is perfect; He will never let you drown.

Lord, I trust in Your almighty power and unconditional love. I trust that You care about me and are present in every storm I face in life. Give me hope in the midst of every trial and enable me to turn to You as the source of my peace. I love You, dear Lord. Jesus, I trust in You.

Reflection 233: The Response of Silence

At times it can be helpful to speak openly and thoroughly to God about what we experience in life. You may feel compelled to talk and talk and talk. And God will listen. But there are other times when words seem quite insufficient. In fact, there are times when words appear to be counterproductive. In those moments the greatest blessings come through silence. We must realize that silence is a language. In fact, communication with God, in moments of silence, has potential to be far deeper than words can bring us. Do not be afraid of silent communication with God. Do not feel as though you must speak or even hear what He has to say. Simply being silent, in His presence, knowing that He is there may be exactly what your soul is in need of in those moments (See *Diary* #1200).

When you pray, do you feel as though you must speak continuously to our Lord? Do you feel as though you must talk continuously, saying this prayer or that one? Or are you content simply being in His presence in the silence? Ponder today your experience of being silent in the presence of God. Try to discern the unique and profound language God speaks this way. Try to commit yourself to these prolonged moments of silent communication with God and then look at the fruit they bear in your soul. If you discover that you are more at peace, gain a new level of clarity in life, or have grown in a certain confidence, then you can be assured that these good fruits in your life have come to you from God through the Mercy of His Heart, communicated to you in silence.

Lord, I desire to seek You and know You. Help me to hear You speak through the silence. Help me to understand this deep language of love and to allow You to transform me through this form of prayer. I love You, dear Lord, and I desire to rest in Your Heart. Jesus, I trust in You.

Reflection 234: The Obscurity of Deep Faith

Normally, when one begins a journey of faith, there are countless insights and revelations that are enjoyed. Various aspects of the life of faith come alive and understanding of the many mysteries in life is received. This gift of spiritual insight and understanding is a great gift and guide as one begins to walk down the path God has chosen. But as time goes on and a soul enters deeply into the mysteries of faith, a certain obscurity can begin to set in. If this is caused by sin or by a spiritual sloth, it should be remedied through Confession and a new resolve to seek the Lord. But this experience can also be the result of a deepening of one's faith. There comes a time when God's communication is one of darkness and obscurity. The soul begins to understand that it cannot understand. This is a gift in that the deeper mysteries of faith cannot be communicated through a concept or insight. The deepest communications from our Lord must be communicated through a darkening of the mind. Knowledge becomes dark, yet the certainty of God's voice remains (See *Diary* #1205).

Reflect upon your interior life of prayer. If you do not clearly have an "interior life," then it's time to start. Seek our Lord through meditation and conversation and allow Him to speak to you. If you do have an interior life of prayer and God is regularly present to you, seek to go deeper. And as you seek more, do not be afraid if you begin to sense that meditation and conversation give way to greater silence and obscurity in your soul. This may be a sign that God is speaking to you on a new level. Speak to a priest about this experience and remain faithful to our Lord in every way as He draws you more deeply into a new level of prayer.

Lord, I desire to be drawn in deeply to the silence and obscurity of a life of faith. Help me to commune with You on this deepest level and to be transformed in the depths of my soul. Jesus, I trust in You.

Reflection 235: The Simple Call to Mercy

As we grow deeper in our faith, it's easy to presume that life will become more complex. For example, when one begins to study mathematics, each course that is taken builds upon the previous, and the lessons become more challenging and difficult as time goes on. But in a certain sense the opposite is true with our life of faith. The deeper we plunge into the Ocean of Mercy, the more we realize the simplicity of our God. Though God is infinite and fully beyond our comprehension, He is also profoundly simple. In fact, the deeper we enter into His Mercy, the more we realize that the mysteries of life are not as complex as we once thought. We begin to realize that the mysteries of God bring us continually back to the simple truth that we are called to rest in the humble Heart of our Divine Lord (See *Diary* #1211).

Reflect upon the call you have been given to enter into the Mercy of God. Do you find life difficult, confusing or overwhelming? If so, it may be time to step back and reexamine your thinking. The call of God is exceptionally simple. To answer that call you may need to set aside the apparent complexity of life and plunge into the simplicity of His Will. It does not require a doctorate degree to comprehend this profound simplicity. But when you do embrace its simplicity, you will also discover its depth and beauty in a new way. Reflect, today, upon this simple call and dive in with the innocence and trust of a child and you will discover the deep wisdom of God.

Lord, I love You and desire to know You and Your holy Will. Give me the grace to plunge into the Ocean of Your Mercy and, in the simplicity of this act, to be fully committed to You. Jesus, I trust in You.

Reflection 236: Praying for Mercy for Everyone

Every person is unique and God wishes to lavish His Mercy upon each and every one of us according to our particular needs. When we pray for people, it's good to offer them individually as well as by groupings. Here are some groupings of people we ought to pray for: all sinners, priests, religious, the faithful, pagans, atheists, heretics, schismatics, children, those devoted to Mercy, those in Purgatory and the lukewarm.

This list is not exhaustive but each grouping needs prayer for a deepening of God's Mercy in a particular way in their lives. Do not be overwhelmed by the myriad of needs, but know that it is good to pray and offer sacrifice for a different group of people each day so as to slowly offer each and every person to the Mercy of God according to their particular needs (See *Diary* #1210-1230, Novena given by our Lord).

How attentive are you to the needs of those all around you? Some are strong in their faith and need continual encouragement as they seek to offer their lives fully to the service of God. Others are caught in sin and need to be freed from the burdens and attachments they struggle with. Others are lukewarm, going astray, or lost. Everyone is different and carries particular needs in their lives. You must remember that the Mercy of God is for everyone and will meet the needs of each person in the specific way they need it. The more clearly you see this fact the more you will love each individual as God loves. Your prayers will be one way that you are able to share in the distribution of God's grace to each person according to their needs.

Lord, give me the grace to be attentive to the needs of all people. Help me to be aware of the ways that Your Mercy is distributed and to share in that distribution through my prayers. May all people come to know and serve You with their whole heart. Jesus, I trust in You.

5

Reflections on Notebook Four

We continue to the fourth notebook that Saint Faustina filled with reflections and revelations from Jesus. As we enter into this notebook, allow yourself to seek God in the silence. This chapter begins with Saint Faustina revealing that she was experiencing a "dark night" (*Diary* #1235). She lacked the sensory feelings of closeness to God. By analogy, it would be as if you were in a dark room filled with treasures and someone told you that all the treasures of this room were yours. You could not see them but you trusted the person who spoke about all that was around you. Knowledge of these treasures filled your mind even though the darkness hid them from your eyes.

So it is with God. Saint Faustina loved our Lord with all her heart and with every beat of her heart. She knew His closeness and love. But it appears that she could not sense this through her human senses. This gift of darkness allowed her to enter into a relationship with God on a spiritual level far deeper.

Seek this depth of relationship with God as you read through this chapter. Move beyond a desire to *feel* close to God and allow yourself to *become* close to God. He wants to enter your heart on a much deeper level than you ever knew possible. Be open to the newness of a relationship shrouded in darkness and allow the Lord to communicate His Mercy to you on this new level of love.

Reflection 237: The Darkness of Faith Purifies our Love

Many of the great saints, including Saint Faustina, experienced an interior darkness in their relationship with God. This is quite a mysterious experience. As a soul grows intimately close to God there are numerous consolations and feelings of love along the way. However, there comes a point on the spiritual journey when God hides Himself. This is not on account of any sin on the part of the person; rather, it's God's way of entering much deeper into the person's life so as to sustain them without the help of emotional or even spiritual consolation. The soul is plunged into a darkness that can be quite painful. But in this darkness, the person is invited to know God with a new silence and surrender. The communication it receives on this new level is beyond words and beyond human experience. There is a knowledge of God and His Divine Will, but not an experience of Him. The soul is invited through this darkness to choose God and His Will despite the absence of any feelings or spiritual consolations (See *Diary* #1235).

Most likely your prayer life has not brought you to this experience of darkness. But even though few enter into this level of communion with God, it's good to be aware of it and to understand the experience that the great saints had. Knowing that this is the path of holiness will allow you to set aside desires to *feel* the love of God in exchange for a desire for God Himself. God is not a feeling; He is a Trinity of Divine Persons. Seek to love Him no matter what you feel and your relationship will grow deeper than you could ever imagine.

Lord, at times I do not understand Your perfect love for me. When I feel close to You I am so very grateful for this experience. However, I pray that you give me the grace to love You even when I do not sense Your presence. Please purify my faith, dear Lord. Jesus, I trust in You.

Reflection 238: Fidelity in Times of Darkness

Though Saint Faustina and many other great saints entered into a unique spiritual darkness, defined by St. John of the Cross as the "Dark Night of the Soul" and the "Dark Night of the Spirit," we all will experience a certain "darkness" of one form or another in our walk of faith. Our darkness may not be the result of the extraordinary purification of the soul that takes place on the journey toward perfection, but our response must be the same. No matter what we go through in life, when challenges arise we must speak the words spoken by the great saints, "Thy Will be done!" Holiness is all about doing the Will of God despite any confusion or apparent obstacle in our lives (See *Diary* #1237).

Reflect upon the level of conviction you pray that prayer, "Thy Will be done!" Do you mean this? Can you say it with all the powers of your mind, will and soul? Have you chosen the Will of God above everything else in life? Embracing the Will of God in times of trial is especially fruitful for a life of faith. When temptations set in, especially temptations toward despair, you must reaffirm your commitment to God's perfect Will. Reflect upon this holy act today. Say those words and mean them as completely as you can. Nothing in life should ever deter you from making this your daily prayer.

Lord, may Your Will be done on Earth as it is in Heaven! I make this my prayer today. I offer it to You with complete confidence and total surrender. I choose You above all things and make Your Will my own. I love You, my Lord. Jesus, I trust in You.

Reflection 239: The Seal of Mercy

Every great saint exemplifies some aspect of the goodness of God. Some live lives of exceptional detachment from worldly riches, some serve the poor with unwavering commitment, some live lives of deep prayer, some have mystical revelations, some write volumes of books revealing the depths of faith, but all are called to bring forth the Mercy of God in one way or another. The Mercy of God must be like a seal, stamped upon your heart. God's Mercy will shine forth from your life in the unique way that He has chosen for you. The "seal" of God's Mercy will become unique, shining forth as a gift given only through you. Be open to the ways that God has chosen to shine forth from your life. Allow that seal to become radiant and visible to all and you will witness great things take place by God through you (See *Diary* #1242).

Reflect upon your heart being sealed with the permanent and visible seal of the Mercy of God. In what ways do you discern that the Lord wishes to radiate His Mercy from your life? What are the concrete ways that His Mercy in Heaven is to come down to Earth through you? Seek the particular and concrete manifestations of God's Mercy offered through your life. Committing yourself to these visible and real manifestations will enable you to become a powerful instrument of His Heart in our world.

Lord, I love You and deeply desire to allow You to manifest Your Mercy through my life. I choose You as the source of all goodness in my life and give You my heart to seal with Your compassion and love. Shine through me, dear Lord. Jesus, I trust in You.

Reflection 240: Sweetness or Bitterness in Life?

Which do you prefer for your life? Daily sensory experiences of sweetness or bitterness? In other words, do you desire to take delight in the many aspects of your daily life or do you desire that the daily duty you fulfill leaves you with a certain bitterness within your senses? For most people the answer is simple. "Sweetness" is much better. But is it? Interestingly, the experience of sweetness or bitterness in life is not a good guide toward a life of holiness. At times, even sin can taste "sweet" to us while acts of holiness can be "bitter" at first. Understanding this will allow us to move deeper into our embrace of the Will of God. Our goal must be to seek His Will purely for the sake of His Will. We must have no preference regarding the delight or suffering that comes as a result of embracing His Will. If God's Will requires great sacrifice, leaving us with a sensory experience of suffering, then so be it. If His will draws us to an exchange of love that leaves us with a sweet delight, then so be it. Though it is hard to arrive at a level of total detachment, we must strive for it. His Will and His Will alone must be our focus. In His Will alone do we discover His abundance of Mercy (See *Diary* #1245).

Reflect upon the difference between God's Will and the delight or distaste you feel from embracing it. When His Will calls you to sacrifice, you will find it to be a sort of "bitter" experience. Bitter in the sense that it may challenge your senses. Do not worry about this. Seek His Will in all things and the joy in your heart will ultimately overshadow all other immediate experiences you have. His Will opens the door to His abundant Mercy.

Lord, I seek Your most holy Will about all things. Help me to choose Your Will no matter how difficult or how delightful it may be. Purify me, dear Lord, and give me a single focus in life so that my embrace of all You call me to do will bring forth Your perfect Mercy. Jesus, I trust in You.

Reflection 241: Remedying Your Particular Sins

How do you overcome your sins? Every sin is different and requires specific prayer and sacrifice so as to detach from them. Three common sins are: those of the flesh, those of anger and those of pride. Each one of these sins can be overcome but may require special attention. If you struggle with sins of the flesh, try to fast. Give up that which is delightful to you on a physical level by fasting from various kinds of food or drink. For sins of anger, try to do some good deed or speak some kind word to the person with whom you are angry. Pray for them and speak the words of Jesus on the Cross, "Father, forgive them, they know not what they do." And for sins of pride, try to bow down prostrate before our Lord in prayerful humility, emptying yourself before Him. Seek to offer these specific remedies for the sins you struggle with and the Mercy of God will be poured down in abundance (See *Diary* #1248).

What are the specific sins you struggle with? Make sure that you regularly do a thorough examination of conscience, focusing on each one of the Ten Commandments in detail or on the seven capital sins. Once you have identified the main sins you struggle with, especially those that are habitual, seek a holy remedy for them. Penance for sins is like medicine. You need the right medication for each illness. Be open to the ways that God reveals to you these "medicines" for your soul and take them without hesitation. Each penance you do will open up the door of Mercy in a new and profound way in your life.

Lord, I know that I am sick on account of my many sins. I am weak and in need of healing. Help me to see my sins and to face them with Your Mercy. Give me the means of overcoming them so that I may draw closer to You. I love You Lord, free me from all that keeps me from You. Jesus, I trust in You.

Reflection 242: True Beauty Uniquely Shining Through

It's been said that "beauty" is in the eye of the beholder. In other words, some say that the definition of beauty depends upon the subjective preference of one person or another. Though there may be some truth to this on a more superficial level, on a deeper level true beauty comes from God and is objective in every way. It's not dependent upon our personal preference; rather, it depends upon God. The more something or someone resembles God and His Mercy, the more beautiful it is. This is important to know in regard to our souls. We all want to be perceived as "beautiful" by others. But we must also understand that this is only possible through a life of holiness. And what's amazing is that the beauty of each person is unique. In Heaven, we will not all be the same; rather, the uniqueness of each person will shine forth the radiance of God in a special way, unique only to that person. Seek to allow the beauty and splendor of God to shine forth through your life so that you will be an instrument of His glory (See *Diary* #1251).

Do you desire to be beautiful? Perhaps this is a question more easily answered by women than men, since it is a word more common to women. But reflect upon the question. As you do, try to look at beauty from a different perspective. On the deepest level, it's not a natural physical attractiveness. True beauty is a sharing in the glory of God and allowing that glory to shine through your soul as light shines through a prism. Seek to let God shine through you so that the beauty of God will bless others with His Mercy in a unique and profound way.

Lord, You are the glory and splendor of my soul. Your beauty is awe-inspiring and radiant in every way. Come live in me and shine through me so that others will see Your transforming beauty in my life. I offer myself to You, dear Lord, as an instrument of Your glory. Jesus, I trust in You.

Reflection 243: Jesus' Special Gift to Those He Loves

How would you treat someone you love? Typically, with family or very close friends we desire that which is best for them and that which makes them happy. God desires the same for each one of us, but we may be surprised at what God sees as the source of our happiness and what He deems to be best for us. Furthermore, though God's love is perfect for every soul, it's also accurate to say that God's love deepens for those who draw close to Him. It's not that His love changes, it's that His love is received and encountered on a deeper level. When this happens, God is able to manifest His love in a profound way. And when God's love is received by a soul on the deepest level, it's often a love that calls that soul into suffering. If that surprises you just think about the Father's perfect love for Jesus. The Father, in His perfect love for the Son, called Him to the Cross. But in that Cross, Jesus' human soul was able to manifest the love of the Father in the most profound way. This is a mystery hard to understand, so if it's difficult to immediately grasp do not worry. Just know that God often allows great spiritual suffering in the lives of those who have been drawn into a deep intimacy with Him (See *Diary* #1253).

Reflect upon the perfect love of the Father calling His Son to the Cross. Sit with that and seek to penetrate its meaning. If you can understand how the love of the Father could call the Son to this sacrifice, then you will begin to understand God's perfect love for you as He calls you to a life of sacrifice. Do not think that God's love will make your life "easy." His love will make your life glorious, but most likely through suffering.

Father, the mystery of the sufferings of Jesus, Your Son, is beyond my comprehension. Help me to understand Your mysterious Will more fully and to see that suffering in this life is often a sign of Your love. Keep my eyes on the Cross in all things, dear Lord. Jesus, I trust in You.

Reflection 244: Working Until the End of the World

If you labor, day and night, spreading the works of God, this is good. Good fruit will come from your commitment to serve the Will of God and to spread His Divine Mercy. But we should also realize that God is able to use us to spread His Mercy until the end of the world. How? Only God knows. But He does desire to use you for this purpose. Some, like Saint Faustina, were used to set in motion devotion to Divine Mercy and that devotion will continue until Jesus returns. Others, and perhaps most of us, are called to contribute to the perpetual work of Mercy in various other ways. For example, one act of charity will bring about a good in another's life that could change them in such a way that it will set in motion an eternal work of Mercy. Or consider your prayer for those entrusted with special responsibility such as praying for the Pope, bishops or priests. Or consider the fact that your holiness achieved here and now will be magnified in Heaven and will enable you to intercede for the Church for all time. Be diligent now in your work of spreading the Mercy of God but also be aware that this work must continue on into eternity. Focus on this as your goal and God will use your present labors in unimaginable ways throughout time (See *Diary* #1256).

When you think about the work that God has entrusted to you, do you see it as something that can have eternal consequences? Do you see yourself as a "link in a chain" by which God desires to strengthen the Church throughout time? Be open to this goal and allow the Lord to use you in ways you could never dream up yourself.

Lord, my life is Yours. I give myself to You for the purpose of spreading Your Mercy now and for eternity. Use me as You will, dear Lord. I offer myself as a willing instrument of Your Mercy in our world. Jesus, I trust in You.

Reflection 245: Severity Postponed

It's important to know that Jesus has every right to bring forth His justice here and now. He has every right to be severe with us on account of our sins and to bring eternal judgment upon us. This truth is often forgotten on account of His Mercy. But we should never forget this fact. It's important to remember this because unless we understand the absolute right that God has to execute swift and irrevocable judgment on the world, we will never understand that His restraint is an act of immeasurable Mercy. The Mother of God is especially entrusted with the responsibility of praying for His Mercy and pleading on our behalf that her Son's wrath be withheld. God gave to her this responsibility of intercession for us and He listens to those prayers. He also calls each one of us to pray for Mercy in the world and, though our prayers are not as powerful as the Mother of God, they can be if we place them in her Immaculate Heart. Giving our Blessed Mother our prayers magnifies their power and transforms them into an instrument of unfathomable grace, holding back the hand of the Justice of God (See *Diary* #1261).

Do you understand the <u>right</u> that God has to bring sudden and severe judgment upon you? That may not be pleasant to think about but it's important to understand. Ponder this fact today. Believe it and know that He withholds His judgment on account of His Mercy. Seek the prayers of our Blessed Mother, this day, and offer her your own prayers. Through your prayers, offered through her intercession, God's justice is withheld and His Mercy will be bestowed in our time.

Dearest Mother, I offer you, this day, all my prayers, works and sacrifices so that you may in turn offer them to Your Son. Please pray for me and for all your children that the justice of Your Son will be withheld as His Mercy is poured forth. Jesus, I trust in You.

Reflection 246: Upon Receiving Holy Communion

What do you do after receiving Holy Communion? Do you go back to your pew in a distracted way, with your mind wandering, paying attention to others around you, and failing to encounter our Lord on an authentic spiritual level? Or do you allow that moment to be a moment of true prayer and communion with God? If the truth is the former, just be honest with yourself and with God and use this realization for an opportunity to reexamine your approach to this most sacred Gift! The moment after Holy Communion is a treasured moment in which each soul is invited to be consumed by Him who was just consumed. In other words, the act of receiving Holy Communion is not just the physical act we do, it must also become something God does to us. We must choose to not only consume our Lord, we must also allow Him to consume us with His Mercy. There is no better time to do this than the moments after receiving this priceless Gift. This is accomplished by making your life an oblation to God. An "oblation" is an offering, and the reception of Holy Communion must become a moment in which we completely offer ourselves to our Divine Lord (See *Diary* #1264).

Reflect upon the last time you received Holy Communion. What was that experience like? Did you have a complete focus on what you were doing? Did you offer yourself to our Lord as an oblation of love? Did you place yourself into the hands of our Lord in a sacrificial way? Did you allow our Lord to consume you with His merciful love? Ponder these questions and commit yourself to this depth of offering. If you do, Holy Communion will become the greatest act of Mercy in your life.

My Lord and my God, I give myself to You with total abandon and surrender. My life is Yours, dear Lord. I give myself to You without reserve as an oblation of love. Jesus, I trust in You.

Reflection 247: The Blessing of Those with Needs

If someone in your family were seriously ill, or in prison, or in some form of grave need, would that be a burden to you or a blessing? Think about it. Do those with special needs make your life more difficult? If this question were answered on a purely practical level the answer may be, "Yes." But if it is answered on a more spiritual level, the answer is that those who "burden" us with their particular needs offer us an opportunity for great holiness. This is the case because those with special needs call forth from us a response of charity, compassion and the service of Mercy. If we see them as a burden, we are missing an extraordinary opportunity for grace. God often allows others to suffer and impose a holy burden upon us so as to allow us to manifest His Mercy. Seek out these special souls and offer them the love, care and Mercy present in the Heart of Jesus (See *Diary* #1268).

Who has God placed in your life? More specifically, who is it that carries a special suffering, illness, weakness or difficulty that requires extra care from you? It could be a sick child, a depressed spouse, an elderly parent, a manifest sinner or a friend in need. Whoever it is that comes to mind, try to see them and their needs as a graced invitation from our Lord to manifest His love and Mercy. They are a far greater blessing to you than you will ever realize. Allow their needs to evoke the compassion and care in the Heart of Christ through you.

Lord, please give me a heart like unto Yours. Give me Your perfect Heart of Mercy and compassion so that I may manifest Your perfect love for others. Help me to see all people as a gift and to recognize their infinite dignity. And as I seek to love them, I thank You for the blessings I receive in this selfless act. Jesus, I trust in You.

Reflection 248: Unlimited Resources

Imagine if you found a source of unlimited natural resources by creating a machine that transforms only a small amount of oxygen into an unlimited amount of energy. All you had to do is turn on the machine you created and the energy is generated endlessly. That would be quite an invention. But something like this does exist on a spiritual level. The "oxygen" it runs on is our misery and sin. And the "generator" is the Heart of Jesus. The "energy" it produces is God's endless Mercy. If we could only understand this then our world would be flooded with this supernatural resource to an infinite degree. We must realize that God transforms our misery in life when we offer it to Him. In fact, this is His burning desire. His Heart longs to transform your misery into His Mercy so that your own life will be filled to abundance and so that, through you, the world will be filled to abundance. Give to God your misery and sin and let Him endlessly transform it (See *Diary* #1273).

What do you think about your own misery and sin? Do you hide it, cover it up, ignore it and pretend it doesn't exist? Do you go through life presenting the illusion of a sin-free and misery-free life? Some do this and others go to the opposite extreme, wallowing in self-pity and manifesting their misery for all to see as if their misery were a badge of honor. Neither approach is helpful. The only helpful approach is to surrender your sin and all misery to the Heart of Jesus. You can do this. You simply need to make the choice to do so. Do it today. Begin to make this act of total surrender and you will discover the miraculous power in the Heart of Jesus to transform everything into Mercy.

Oh Heart of Jesus, I run to You with my misery and pain and I surrender my sin to You, dear Lord. Please transform it into Your Mercy, enabling this gift to become a source of endless grace. Jesus, I trust in You.

Reflection 249: The Fruit of Suffering

Only after someone has suffered greatly do they begin to understand the good fruits that can come forth from such suffering. In and of itself, suffering is the result of our fallen human condition. But because Jesus entered our human condition, embracing all suffering and redeeming it, suffering now has great power when freely embraced by us and united to the sufferings of Jesus. One good fruit that can come from suffering is spiritual knowledge. When suffering is embraced in Christ and offered to Him as a sacrifice in union with His own Sacrifice, we will find that our suffering clarifies life, puts it in perspective and may even give us the spiritual gift of insight into the souls of others we encounter. This gift of knowledge of other souls will enable us to see their needs and offer the Mercy of God to them in the particular way they need it. Do not be afraid to allow your sufferings to transform you and bestow this gift of knowledge upon you along with the many other gifts God wishes to bestow (See *Diary* #1277).

Reflect upon how you deal with your own sufferings. Whether it is a small discomfort you feel or an intense interior pain, everything we experience in life can be redeemed and transformed so as to transform us. If you believe this then try to consciously embrace every discomfort and every suffering you endure as a sacrifice to God. Offer it to Him and then allow the purifying effects of this free embrace to produce an abundance of good fruit in your life.

Lord, so often I run from my suffering and deny the redeeming effects that the free embrace of my sufferings can have upon me. Give me courage to say "Yes" to the crosses I am given and to be open to the spiritual fruits that they can produce in my life. I give all to You, dear Lord. Jesus, I trust in You.

Reflection 250: Praying Face Down to the Ground

When you pray, how do you go to our Lord? It's certainly good to offer Him your entire day in loving devotion and to speak to Him throughout the day as to your closest friend. But there are other times when our prayer must be intense and should be expressed with intensity. One way to do this is to *literally* fall down prostrate before our Lord. In the silence of your room or in an empty church, look for an opportunity to pray in such a way. The "intensity" must be one of complete submission to our Lord. It must be prolonged and self-emptying. To pray in such a way is a beautiful act of love and is a way of worshipping God as He deserves. Though we could never offer perfect worship of Him, our attempts at doing so as completely as possible pleases Him and enables Him to draw us close to His Heart which is filled with an abundance of Mercy (See *Diary* #1279).

Have you ever prayed in a position of prostration before our Lord? If you have, keep doing it. Look for an opportunity to do so every day. If you have not, then this is a good time to start. Do not worry about what you are to say and do not worry if it feels uncomfortable at first. Just get down on your knees, bow down to the ground, and express your love for our Lord. Stay there and try to make an act of total surrender. The Lord will receive your act of worship and draw you closer to His Sacred Heart of Mercy.

Lord, I do fall down prostrate before You and offer You my entire life as a selfless gift for Your glory. I give all to You, dear Lord, and I pray that I will hold nothing back. You are my God and my all. I love you and surrender my life to You. Jesus, I trust in You.

Reflection 251: The Inner Dwelling of Your Heart

The Lord desires to come to you and make His dwelling within your heart. But when He comes to you, what does He find? What is the condition of your heart? Some hearts are like a fragrant rose garden. There is light, beauty, magnificence and radiance. It's a place of peaceful repose and a place made holy by the presence of our Lord. Other hearts are like a dark prison cell, cold, isolated and dreary. These are the souls who are trapped in a cycle of sin and have failed, over and over, to allow the Lord to enter in. But He does choose to enter your heart, no matter the condition. Be it a fragrant field of roses or the darkness and isolation of a prison, the Lord wants to enter (See *Diary* #1280).

Ponder the inner chamber of your heart. What does this dwelling place look like? Be honest and reveal this hidden place to our Lord. If your heart is more like a dreary dungeon, cold, dark and isolated, then know that you, more than any other, are invited to receive the Mercy of God. He desires to come to you and open the door to that prison in which you feel trapped and isolated. He does not shy away from you in this darkness and will enter in. But when He enters, He does so to break you free. He desires to transform your soul into a place of sweet delight. This takes work, surrender, honesty, humility and trust. But God can do all things and can transform the most wretched soul into a garden of beauty and love. His Mercy produces the soil, the Sun, the seed, the water and everything needed to recreate the inner chamber of your soul. Ponder this fact and begin your transformation today.

Precious Lord, I give to You the inner chamber of my soul. Come and rest within me, transforming my heart into Your holy dwelling place. I give to You, dear Lord, all that I am and all that I have. Recreate me and make me new. Jesus, I trust in You.

Reflection 252: The Apostolate of Mercy and Acceptance

Some people are deeply troubled in life and cannot seem to sort out their difficulties. They are "needy" in the sense that they are constantly seeking something to offer them consolation. They may believe that riches or other forms of earthly consolations are what they want but what they do not realize is that the Lord is the answer to all their needs. These wandering souls must become the focus of our mercy. One way we offer the Mercy of God to them is through our gentle presence, offering an accepting heart and listening ear. When those with heavy burdens in life discover that we care for them and wish to listen to them, they will often seize the opportunity to open up their hearts to us, revealing their wounds and troubles. It is not so much our responsibility to do the healing or to solve their problems. Our responsibility is most often to simply let them know we care and understand. This act of love and acceptance is an act of extraordinary Mercy flowing from the Heart of Jesus through us (See *Diary* #1282).

When you encounter others who are troubled and heavily burdened in life, how do you treat them? Do you treat them with judgment and disgust? Or do you listen to them, seek to understand them, and offer an accepting and compassionate heart? Reflect upon this question and think about those whom God has placed in your life who need to know God's love and acceptance through you. Do not neglect this act for you are called to be an apostle of the Mercy of God.

Lord, I offer myself to You as an apostle of Your merciful Heart. Give me a true compassion and acceptance for those souls in most need of Your Divine Mercy. Help me to listen to them, seek to understand them and be there for them as a representative of Your Sacred Heart. I give myself to You, dear Lord. Use me as You will. Jesus, I trust in You.

Reflection 253: The Response of Total Gratitude

What should our response be to God? Often times we become self-consumed in our relationship with God. We focus in on our troubles and needs. These must be given over to God and let go of. When we do this we will discover that we begin to see the glory and goodness of God at work in our lives and we will begin to be filled with the utmost gratitude toward God. Gratitude must consume us and fill our minds and prayers. We must allow gratitude to take over our passions and feelings and every part of our being. This is what we will do for eternity. Heaven will be one eternal act of thanksgiving to God for His goodness and Mercy. When we can turn our eyes away from ourselves and focus in on God, this gift of gratitude will begin to direct our lives (See *Diary* #1285-1286).

Are you grateful? You will be grateful only if you allow yourself to see the countless gifts that God lavishes upon you every day. It's easy to allow self-absorption to cloud our vision of these countless blessings from God. But if you can turn your eyes toward Heaven and see the truth, you will be amazed at God's infinite goodness. Do not let yourself miss out on this glorious discovery of all that God does for you day and night. Do not close your eyes to the abundance of His Mercy. Reflect, today, upon whether or not you allow yourself to see His merciful love lavished upon you and upon others. Fix your gaze upon this Mercy and allow this realization to foster within you a profoundly grateful heart.

My Lord, I thank You for all that You have done in my life and I thank You for all that You will continue to do in me. Help me to become increasingly aware of Your merciful love and the countless blessings You bestow upon me and upon all Your children. As I see Your handiwork all around, fill my heart with sincere gratitude. Jesus, I trust in You.

Reflection 254: Divinization

Our calling in life can be described as a call to divinization. What does this mean? It means that God came to Earth and took on our human nature so as to draw us into His very life. We are, in a sense, called to become God. This idea of "divinization" was common among the early Church fathers such as Irenaeus, Justin Martyr, Athanasius, Clement of Alexandria and St. Augustine. It's not that we are to become God in the sense that our nature becomes divine, this would be a heresy. Rather, we are called to become God in the sense that we are to share in His divine life, becoming one with Him in perfect unity. It would be as if God were an Ocean and we were a drop of water plunged into that Ocean. Though the specific particles of the drop of water representing us remain that one drop, it is absorbed by the waters of the Ocean representing God. Our union with Him must become so complete that God lives in us as we live in God (See *Diary* #1289).

Reflect upon your calling to become divinized. This concept goes to the heart of our Christian vocation in that it expresses the powerful unity we are called to have with our merciful God. He wants you to share in His life and to become one with Him in every way. Though this may be hard to comprehend, you must accept it as your calling in faith. Reflect upon this concept today and tell our Lord that you give yourself to Him so as to become one with Him and to share in His very life.

Lord, please come to me and divinize me in accord with Your perfect Will and abundant Mercy. I thank You for calling me to such a glorious and high calling in life and I accept this invitation from You. My life is Yours, dear Lord, transform me, consume me and do with me as You will. Jesus, I trust in You.

Reflection 255: The "Blessing" of Sin

This may seem like an unusual title. How can sin be a "blessing?" True, strictly speaking sin is an offense against God and has the effect of separating us from God. Thus, sin is not a blessing in the strict sense. But God is All-Powerful and can use everything for His glory, even our sin. Sin could be spoken of as a blessing only in the sense that when we see our sins, acknowledge them, humble ourselves before God and beg for His Mercy, He bestows it in superabundance. In the end, the effects of the humility of repentance do far greater good than the damage done through sin. God can repair the damage immediately, and when He does so, He offers a Mercy that not only heals but also elevates us closer to His Heart. Allow your sin to be turned into a blessing by the power of God and you will be amazed at His endless Mercy (See *Diary* #1293).

Reflect upon the attitude you have in regard to your sin. Too often you may deny your sin, justify it or turn a blind eye to it. This is a profound mistake for two reasons. First, doing this keeps you from repenting. Second, a failure to humbly repent leaves you without the abundant Mercy of God. Foster within your heart a burning desire to see every sin you commit. Seek to become aware of every sin, even the smallest imperfections. Attentiveness even to your spiritual imperfections will enable you to humble yourself before God in such a way that your honesty and thoroughness will bring countless blessings to your life.

Lord Jesus, Son of God, have Mercy on me a sinner. Lord, I do see my sin but I also realize that I do not see it clearly enough. Please give me the grace to see my every sin, even the slightest imperfection, and then give me the grace to humbly repent with a sincere and contrite heart. I trust in Your abundance of Mercy, dear Lord. Jesus, I trust in You.

Reflection 256: Doing Your Best

Blessed Mother Teresa is often quoted as saying that God asks us to be faithful, not successful. In other words, we are called to offer our best to the Lord, striving to be faithful to His holy Will, and then leave the rest to Him. At times it may appear that our "best" does not produce the desired good fruit that we desire. Perhaps an attempt you make at reconciling with another failed. Or perhaps you put your heart and soul into some apostolic work and it never appeared to take off in the way you had hoped. There is great freedom in the realization that all we are called to do is be faithful, not successful. "Success" is measured by God, not by human standards. We are truly "successful" only when we are faithful to the Will of God and diligent in committing ourselves to His divine work. If we are faithful in this way, nothing else matters. Do your best and leave the rest to God (See *Diary* #1295).

Reflect upon your level of commitment to the Will of God. Committing yourself to God's holy Will is not the same as committing yourself to perfect success in all you do. Even if everything you do appears to end in failure, you please God when you are faithful to Him without worrying about the results. God sees your heart and wants your good works to be offered to Him and done in accordance with His Will. Nothing else in life matters. Seek fidelity above success and you will delight the merciful Heart of our Lord.

Lord, I give myself to You for Your service and glory. I commit myself to all that You call me to do and pray that I may serve Your Will in fidelity and diligence. Use me, dear Lord, as You will and help me to leave the rest to You. Jesus, I trust in You.

Reflection 257: The Long Term Plan of God

When you seek to serve our Lord with your whole heart, you may find that He speaks to you about His daily Will. It may not be completely clear, but you may have a sense that He wants this or that from you. God does not typically present you with the entire plan He has for your life all at once. Rather, He offers bits and pieces as needed. Believing what He calls you to do each day requires faith and trust in His gentle voice. The truth is that God does have a perfect plan for your life if you will only listen and respond one step at a time. In the end, from Heaven, this will all make sense and you will see the incredible wisdom of our Lord. However, for now the big and full picture may not be as clear. This is God's way of drawing you into a relationship of daily dependence and daily surrender. The key is to be faithful each and every day to what you sense our Lord saying. If you do this, little by little, His glorious Will unfolds in your life, and through you His Mercy is bestowed upon the world (See *Diary* #1300).

What do you sense our Lord calling you to do this day? Whatever it is it may not make perfect sense right now. Trust His gentle Voice and inspirations today and follow His promptings. Do what you hear Him command you. If your sense of His Will seems unusual, speak to another about it so as to make sure it is from Him. But in the end, if you seek to fulfill His daily Will you will discover that the road He takes you down is glorious and achieves His glorious purpose for your life.

Lord, I desire to serve You with all my heart. Give me the grace of an open mind and heart so that I may discern Your gentle Voice calling me into Your perfect Will. My life is Yours, dear Lord, do with me what You will. Jesus, I trust in You.

Reflection 258: The Closeness of God

Where is God? It's easy to think of God being in Heaven or some far off place, looking down upon us and guiding all of creation in accord with His holy Will. This is true, but it's not the full picture. God is perfectly "transcendent" in that He is way beyond us and beyond the created world. But He is also perfectly "immanent" in that He lives within us. When you pray, seek Him especially within your own soul. Remember that when you receive Holy Communion, God makes your soul a tabernacle. He enters in and remains within unless He is excluded on account of sin. Seek His divine presence within your soul and you will discover the intimacy of His abundant Mercy (See *Diary* #1302).

Reflect upon the image of a tabernacle. Within that sacred dwelling the full glory of God exists in veiled form. But He is there, alive, radiant and glorious. Now see your soul as this tabernacle. See Him coming to you to make His dwelling within you. God desires to fully live within you, making your heart the place of His gentle repose. Spend time today seeking our Lord within. Talk to Him, listen to Him, and commune with Him. Let your heart become alive and radiant with His holy presence. For within your heart is the presence of God.

Lord, I thank You for coming to me and making my heart Your dwelling place. I thank You for Your perfect love and care and I pray that I may discover Your divine presence in my life more fully each and every day. I am Yours, dear Lord, make my soul radiant with Your eternal glory. Jesus, I trust in You.

Reflection 259: The Beauty of the Humble Soul

What is it that makes someone beautiful? More than anything else it is the virtue of humility. Humility is exceptionally attractive. Though some may not be that impressed with the humble soul at first, over time, humility will draw even the most arrogant and self-centered person to itself. It's hard to ignore the deep attractiveness of a humble soul because God is intimately present in that person. In fact, it could almost be said that God would do anything that a humble soul asks. It's as if humility imposes an obligation upon God to bestow extraordinary graces through their lowly heart. Humility is a complete self-emptying of oneself before God and others. The result is that the person "disappears" and all that is left is God. God shines through the humble more radiantly than the person filled with the greatest talents. Humble yourself before God. The lower you go, the more God shines through and the more His Mercy is bestowed (See *Diary* #1306).

Do you seek to be humble? Or do you tend to exert yourself and make yourself the center of attention? The irony is that, as the Scripture says, "For everyone who exalts himself will be humbled, but the one who humbles himself will be exalted" (Lk. 14:11). So many of the great saints are perfect examples of this in that their focus was love of God and love of others, but in the end these great saints were often lifted high for others to see. Seek to be one of those great saints by humbling yourself this day. Ponder humility and convince yourself of its value. Through it the beauty and Mercy of God will shine forth.

Lord, I know I am full of pride at times and that pride keeps me from admitting this fact. Please humble me and help me to lower myself before Your infinite majesty. Give me the grace to seek you above all things and to give You all the glory and honor. Jesus, I trust in You.

Reflection 260: The Enormity of Small Acts of Love

Do you want to do amazing things in this world? Do you sometimes have grandiose ideas and dreams? Sometimes we have more secular dreams of wealth and fame, and sometimes we may have dreams of doing extraordinary things for God and for the Church. But these do not have to be dreams because each and every one of us is called to extraordinary things. The problem is that we often misunderstand what "extraordinary" is all about. So what is it about? It's especially about doing small things with extraordinary love. Every one of us can do this every day all day. Our lives are filled with opportunities to do "small things." It may be cooking or cleaning, shuttling kids here or there, caring for the yard, completing tasks at work, or daily casual conversation with others. Every one of these tasks offers us an opportunity to love with extraordinary love. And if you do every small act with great love, then your love will be great and God will do extraordinary things through your life, bestowing His Mercy on many (See *Diary* #1310).

Think about the small things you have to do today. How can you do these simple tasks with exceptional love? Many things we do are done with distaste or indifference. We can fail to see value in the small monotonous activities of our day. This is a mistake. Look for ways to do everything as an act of love and as an offering to God. Be devout and intentional in each opportunity you have and your dreams of greatness will become a reality on account of the Mercy of God shining through your life.

Lord, I give to You, this day, every small act I perform. Help me to find value and meaning in even the smallest service. I pray that my love for You will increase in countless small ways so that I may be a holy instrument of Your abundant Mercy. Jesus, I trust in You.

Reflection 261: Jesus Hidden in Others

Imagine if Jesus came to you in poverty, hunger and cold and He asked you to care for Him. This experience might startle you and cause you to question if this person really was Jesus.

But it is Jesus. Jesus comes to us every day in the person who is in need. It may be that we encounter someone who is homeless, hungry and in need of clothing. If this is the case then this is Jesus. But there are many whom we encounter every day who have a different form of hunger and thirst. Many are starving for love, understanding, compassion and attention. They may present an exterior that is unwelcoming, but inside they are our Lord, seeking to receive mercy from your heart. Do not hesitate to see our Lord present in every person you encounter. Lavish the mercy of your heart on them, especially the most pitiable soul, and you will have lavished your love on Jesus Himself (See *Diary* #1312).

How do you treat the poor and the beggar? Start by thinking about those with physical needs but move deeper to consider all those who carry other needs. Think about the hard of heart, the sinner, the proud, the arrogant, the person filled with anger, etc. Every person you call to mind is our Lord coming to you for a taste of the mercy of your heart. Whatever you do to the *least* of these, you do to Christ. Do you believe this? If you do then this belief must have the practical consequences of you showing mercy to everyone, especially those whom you find most difficult to love. Ponder this practical question today and make a commitment to seek out our Lord in the next "beggar" that you meet, no matter how undesirable they appear.

Lord, I love You and I realize that I must seek You out in each person I encounter. Give me the eyes to see You and a heart to love You. As I love You in others, dear Lord, allow the mercy in my heart to give you a sweet delight. Jesus, I trust in You.

Reflection 262: The Rule of Love or Justice

We cannot escape the Hand of God. He is the one who sustains the Universe and keeps all things in being. Without

His constant care we would cease to exist. But we remain under His providential Hand in one of two ways. Either we are guided by the "rule of love" or by the "rule of justice." The rule of justice is God's way of guiding our lives when we turn away from Him. We cannot escape His justice here or at the time of death. When we sin, especially in a serious way, we become slaves to our sin on account of the justice of God. He leaves us to experience the imprisonment of sin on account of His great Mercy. It is Mercy in that the ill effects of His justice are imposed so as to call us to repentance. But those who live under the rule of love are blessed to live on a whole new level. These holy souls bask in the Mercy of God and are freed from the effects of sin. They experience the numerous fruits of the Spirit and act in accord with the holy Will of God (See *Diary* #1315).

Which rule do you live by? Are you regularly falling from grace and encountering the justice of God in your life? Or are you striving to live by His rule of love? Wherever you find yourself today, know that it is a gift of God's Mercy. Allow His justice to redirect your life when you fall, and seek to embrace the full outpouring of His Mercy. The Lord will never leave you, but it's up to you how you will experience His Mercy.

My Lord, I desire to be filled with Your merciful presence in my life. I pray that I will daily turn from my sin and experience the freedom and joy that comes from living by Your rule of love. Help me, dear Lord, to always make the right choices in my life so as to be drawn into the abundant life You have in store for me. Jesus, I trust in You.

6

Reflections on Notebook Five

As we begin Notebook Five, Saint Faustina's understanding of the Mercy of God should be more alive to you. Hopefully you have a deeper understanding of the infinite love of God and His burning desire to embrace you, free you from the burden of sin, and shower you with His grace.

It should also be clear that God is silent at times so as to strengthen you, purify you and deepen your trust in Him. God's wisdom and His ways are beyond what we could ever imagine. He is perfect in His love and you must have full confidence in the direction He gives to your life.

As we enter into this notebook, try to believe and live all that you have read so far. It's one thing to believe it intellectually, it's quite another thing to believe it with your actions. You must believe in the Mercy of God with your actions. You must let all that you have read take hold of you and direct the way you live. One way to do this is to go back to any reflections that have stood out so far. If something has stood out, be it a particular reflection or a general theme, pay attention to that. The Message of Mercy is broad and all encompassing, but it's also particular to you. Let the Lord speak directly to you revealing the specific truths that you need to embrace the most.

Reflection 263: God as Your Helmsman in the Storm

Imagine being a small child on a small boat in the middle of the sea. A storm sets in and you cannot see land in any direction. You are tossed and turned in the waves as they cover the bow with each crash and you wonder how you will survive. Now imagine that your dad is also on the boat with you. He tells you to sit and hold on and that all will be well. He is confident and in charge and shows no fear. The confidence that your father exudes calms you and you trust that he will keep you safe. This is an image of our lives. When we face a crisis we must realize that we are but a child in the midst of the stormy sea in need of our Merciful Lord. It would be foolish for a child to try to take charge of the boat. It would also be foolish for us to try to direct our own lives. We need the steady confidence of Jesus to put our hearts at rest. The Lord must be your Helmsman whenever the waves begin to rise. Do not doubt His ability to handle everything in life (See *Diary* #1322).

What do you do when the storms of life set in? Do you panic? Do you try to take control and handle things on your own? Or do you turn your eyes to the strength and confidence of our Lord and let Him take control of the situation? Turning to Jesus is not simply a matter of sitting back and doing nothing. Rather, turning to Him in abandon is an act of the greatest trust. That trust, when all seems chaotic and overwhelming, opens the door to His peace and keeps you safe and still no matter what comes your way. Reflect upon the way you handle difficulties in life and make the conscious choice to turn to the Divine Helmsman to direct your life through the storm.

Lord, I turn to You in confidence and choose to put my full trust in You. I know that You can handle all things and that Your love and care will keep me safe. Increase my confidence in You, dear Lord, and help my heart to always remain at peace. Jesus, I trust in You.

Reflection 264: A Retreat With Jesus

Have you ever made a retreat? Some are privileged to take time away from the busyness of life so as to spend an extended time listening to our Lord and being in His merciful presence. Others find it hard to find even a day to enter such a retreat. Regardless of whether you have or have not had this opportunity, know that you need time alone with Jesus. It is not possible to speak to Him only during your busy day and maintain a proper relationship with Him. The depth of the relationship desired by Jesus requires time set aside solely for Him. Seek these opportunities and do not neglect them. It is through moments of extended prayer and reflection that life is clarified and the Will of God is made manifest (See *Diary* #1326-1327).

When is the last time you spent an extended amount of time alone with our Lord? Perhaps it was only an hour in the chapel or in your room, or perhaps it was longer. Think about how much time you give to Him. We often can find plenty of time to watch a movie, go shopping, or engage in some other recreational activity. The truth is that if we make time alone with our Lord a priority in life, it will happen. We will find the time and our time with Him will be abundantly fruitful. Ponder the level of priority that you give to these moments of quiet reflection with our Lord and recommit yourself to making them the most important part of your life. If you do so, all else will fall into place as His Mercy is poured forth.

Lord, I desire to make You the number one priority in my life. I desire to make time for You on a daily basis and to find an extended period of time for You regularly. Help me to have the will to do this so that I may bask in Your presence and allow You to sort through the difficulties I face in life. Jesus, I trust in You.

Reflection 265: The Danger and Blessing of Passions

God created us with passions. These can be either great blessings in our Christian walk or they can become great snares. It all depends on what controls each passion. Passions of anger, for example, can either be used for good or ill. When anger takes over and the source of this anger is a wound or lack of mercy toward another, then we become bound by this sin. But holy anger is a gift from God in that the Lord may inspire us to be "fierce" in one act or another. A parent protecting an innocent child from danger or the direct confrontation with evil may require a certain holy anger as a supporting force. Sexual passions are the same way. When they are used for marital union in accord with God's design, they are holy. When they are the source of adultery, self-gratification, or any other form of lust, they do us great damage. Seek to be free from unruly passions and allow the Mercy of God to so consume them that these natural gifts are given over to the service of love and the Will of God (See *Diary* #1331).

Are your passions under the control of the powerful Mercy of God or do your passions control you? This is an important question to honestly answer. Passions, when they become strong and untamed, can be hard to control. But when properly surrendered to God, they become a great motivating source of love. Reflect honestly upon your struggle with your passions. Know that God wants to turn them into a great blessing and a source of much mercy in your life. Turn them over to Him, over and over, through prayer, fasting and Confession and the Lord will bring order and stability to these natural gifts.

Lord, I offer You my heart, my soul, my body, my mind and my passions. Please bring order and stability to me in every way and use me as an instrument of Your holy and passionate Love. Jesus, I trust in You.

Reflection 266: Discouragement in the Face of Sanctity

Do you want to be a saint? Hopefully the answer is "Yes." But what about this question: Do you think you *can* become a saint? This may be more difficult to answer. It's easy to dream of sanctity and to desire it, but when faced with the task of achieving it, discouragement can easily set in. Discouragement comes when you see the high call of holiness and conclude that you will never be able to achieve it. You may become fixated upon a certain fault and give up, thinking that you are destined to remain lukewarm and that's it. You may feel as though you are a nice person and that will have to suffice. But God has great plans for you! He not only calls you to be a saint, He knows you can become one. The key is to allow His Mercy to become so clear to you that you begin to realize sanctity is possible. Holiness, or sanctity, is not achieved because we are good; rather, it's achieved because God is merciful and we have chosen to fix our gaze upon that Mercy. Never doubt the truth that you are both *called* to be a saint and that you *can* become a saint (See *Diary* #1333).

Reflect upon these two questions today. Do I *want* to become a saint and *can* this be achieved in my life? Look for ways that you get discouraged at the thought of holiness. Whatever it is that is causing discouragement in you is false. It's not the truth. Let the Mercy of God appear before your eyes and realize that His Mercy is able to be received by you. And when you are open to receiving the Mercy of God, you will begin your journey to true sanctity.

Lord, I do desire to become holy as a result of Your abundant Mercy. Remove my struggles with discouragement and help me to have hope in Your power to change me. I give myself to You, dear Lord, and I trust that You will make me a saint. Jesus, I trust in You.

Reflection 267: Justice or Mercy?

It is proper to speak of both the Justice of God as well as His Mercy. They are not opposed to each other. His Justice will be dealt to those who refuse to repent just as it was dealt to the angels who refused to serve God. But, for now, is it more proper to say that God is Merciful. In fact, the evil one would love for us to become consumed with the idea that God is only Just and that He imposes His judgment upon us continually. When this idea is accepted, it is hard to understand that God actually withholds His Justice as long as we are open to His Mercy. Seek His Mercy, believe in it and run to it. Do not doubt it for a moment. Know that God offers it day and night and never tires of lavishing it upon you. When you are faced with the fear that comes with facing His Justice, turn your eyes to His Mercy and you will be able to easily turn from all sin as you bask in the rays shining forth from His Heart (See *Diary* #1338).

Which of these two images of God do you reflect upon more often? Are you frightened by God's Justice? Or are you consoled by His Mercy? Both can be useful but never at the expense of the other. We should never presume on God's Mercy and we should never become fixated on His Justice without immediately remembering His Mercy. Ponder His Mercy today more than anything and you will have no need to fear His Justice. Let your heart experience His love and turn to Him with full confidence and trust.

Lord, I am aware that You are Just and will issue Your Justice upon me if I fail to turn to Your Mercy. Therefore, I do turn to Your Mercy. I seek it with all my heart. I love You, Lord, and I desire to love You more. Give me the grace to open my eyes to Your radiant Heart and to be open to all that You wish to bestow. Jesus, I trust in You.

Reflection 268: Pondering Death

Perhaps thinking about your death is frightening. It may not be something that you actually consider very often. But it is a grace to be able to look at one's death directly and with full confidence. And this is only possible to do with full confidence if your life is in order and given completely to God. If you can honestly look into your soul and see that you have made holiness your ultimate goal, then you can also look directly at death with peace and calm. What is there to fear in that case? What is there to fear if you have dealt with the sin and regrets you have? There is nothing to fear in this case. Death, to the holy soul, is a reward and a journey to look forward to with delight and anticipation (See *Diary* #1343).

Try to do this simple exercise today of imagining this as being your last day on Earth. Perhaps you immediately think about family or other tasks that you need to complete first to prepare. Or perhaps you are filled with fear because you are aware of your sin. First, try to set aside the practical tasks that would be left unfinished and even try to set aside your concern for your family and friends. Though these are good and holy concerns, it is helpful to look at death only in regard to the condition of your soul. If you were to die today, would you be able to look at the merciful Heart of our Lord and tell Him, honestly, that you die with Him as your greatest love? Could you say to Him that His Will is your primary goal in life? If not, reflect upon any obstacle you see and use this meditation to take an honest inventory of your life.

Lord, I know that Heaven must be my goal and my focus in life. Help me to put my eyes upon You and all that awaits. Help me to also look honestly at the condition of my soul and to identify any obstacle in the way of my holiness. I love You, dear Lord, help me to make You the central focus of my life. Jesus, I trust in You.

Reflection 269: A Twofold Gaze at Mercy and Misery

If you could pick two things to gaze at, what would they be? Ideally, the two greatest things to gaze at are the Mercy of God and your own misery. Most likely, it immediately makes sense that the Mercy of God would be one of the most important things to gaze at, but the wisdom of gazing at your own misery may not be immediately apparent. What we need to understand is that there is danger in seeing only one or the other. If you were to focus in on the Mercy of God without also seeing your misery, then you would not be in a position to invite that Mercy into the parts of your life that need it the most. And if you were to gaze at your misery without also seeing the Mercy of God, you would be led into despair. The Mercy of God is given so that every sin, hurt, confusion, struggle and the like will have a remedy. Our Lord longs to heal us and lift our burdens. Allow His Mercy to meet all that burdens you and His Mercy will achieve its end (See *Diary* #1345).

Try to take some time to quietly and reflectively gaze at both God's Mercy and your own inner burdens. As you look at both, try to imagine them meeting within the sanctuary of your soul. Let the Mercy of God fuse with any misery you experience in life and, in that act, you will be allowing God to do what He longs to do.

Lord, please have Mercy on me and heal me. Help me to see the areas of my life that are in grave need of Your Mercy. As I see them, help me to also fix my eyes upon Your Sacred Heart from which Mercy and grace flow. In this gaze, may I discover Your unending compassion and love and so be healed of all that burdens me. Jesus, I trust in You.

Reflection 270: The Details of the Will of God

Are you willing to accept the Will of God in your life? If so, you must be open to all the details. God's Will is not some grandiose generalization. Choosing His Will is not simply a matter of saying that you choose to follow Him with broad strokes. Rather, choosing His Will is saying "Yes" over and over to every little prompting and every inspiration that the Lord gives. It's about building a habit of attentiveness to the small ways that God speaks to you. Mercy is also in the details since Mercy and the Will of God are one and the same. Being open to the Mercy of God means that you come to realize that God wants to enter into the most "insignificant" parts of your life. The truth is that nothing in your life is insignificant to our Lord. Therefore, you must realize that those parts that you perceive as insignificant are very dear to Him. His care and concern reaches far and wide and is offered at every moment to every detail that makes up the apparent complexity of your life. When you realize this, you will, in turn, want to seek the fine details of His holy Will. You will want to serve Him in every way possible and, in so doing, you will be living in His merciful Will (See *Diary* #1356).

Reflect today on the small things in your life. What is it that, at first thought, seems far from the Will of God? Knowing that every little detail of your life is important to our Lord and is always in His sight will give you a new perspective. As you reflect upon the small things that make up your life, turn them over to the Will of God and invite His Mercy into those details. Doing so will lead you down the path of true happiness.

Lord, I offer You, this day, every part of my life. Thank You for Your perfect love and concern. Help me to love You in the details, embracing Your perfect Will in all things. May I never tire of allowing Your Mercy to enter so as to produce the smallest acts of love. Jesus, I trust in You.

Reflection 271: Looking Past the Obstacles in Life

One very common tendency and temptation most people struggle with is to become fixated upon sufferings, humiliations and the false opinions of others. When we experience one or more of these burdens, we can be tempted to make them the central focus of our life. For example, if you are unjustly humiliated and others have an erroneous opinion of you, it can be exceptionally hard to keep this from dominating your thoughts. Similarly, whatever it is that causes you grief or suffering can easily become the focal point of your life. These tendencies must be overcome by a commitment to look beyond these obstacles and to gaze only on the Truth. What is the Truth? It's that which is in the Mind of God. Nothing less, nothing more, nothing other. As you seek to look beyond the struggles of life and focus only on the Truth, you will discover God's glorious Will. His Will always offers us hope, confidence and joy as we move forward in life (See *Diary* #1360).

What is it that dominates your attention? What is it that you are most aware of day after day? If you tend to let yourself become drawn into the confusions of life, work to change the focus of your attention. Instead, look only at the Will of God. His Will is glorious, inspiring, hopeful and renewing. Pay no attention to anything that is not contained within His Divine Will and the confusion, hurt and humiliation that you struggle with will slowly disappear as it is overwhelmed by the Mercy of God.

Lord, help me to remain focused on the Truth as it is seen by Your watchful eye and known by Your perfect Mind. Help me to discover Your Will as the only Truth that I must know and help me to embrace Your Will with my whole being. Jesus, I trust in You.

Reflection 272: The External Manifestation of the Heart

No one can see your heart except you and God. God is aware of every detail of your interior life to a perfect degree; you see the details of your interior life to an imperfect degree. Nonetheless, it is important to become increasingly aware of the reality of your inner life. See your soul as a hidden and secret world in which the Mercy of God resides. Allow the inner chambers of your heart to become consumed with the love of God. This holy and pure love of God must direct all things within you. And although others will not see that which takes place within you, they will see the good fruits that come forth from your life and these good fruits will become an exterior witness to the Mercy of God alive within you. Though the inner life is hidden, it must become manifest so that the secret workings of God will produce Mercy in a visible and radiant way (See *Diary* #1363).

Are you aware of the powerful work of God within your soul? Are you attentive to His merciful hand, leading you and guiding you within this secret sanctuary of your interior life? Fix your interior gaze upon the pure love of God and allow this hidden place to bring forth an abundance of good fruit. As the good fruit of your life is produced, allow it to be made manifest for the world to see and to be inspired and changed by the Mercy of God coming forth from you. Ponder today this direct connection between your interior and exterior and allow your heart to shine forth.

Lord, I love You with a burning love. Please continually purify my heart so that Your grace may become active and alive within my soul. As You work Your miracles of grace in my life, bring forth the good fruit of Mercy in my exterior actions so that Your works will become a public testimony to the pure love that is alive in my heart. Jesus, I trust in You.

Reflection 273: No Earthly Ties, Only Love of God

The pinnacle of our relationship with God includes being stripped of every other earthly tie so that nothing holds us back from running toward God with great passion and purpose. We must be freed of every attachment in this life so that our one attachment is God and His holy Will. This does not mean we ought to neglect our love for others. This is especially true with family love. Love for those in your family must take on a special focus and become total and irrevocable. However, there is a difference between loving your family with a perfect love and being attached to them in an earthly way. In fact, holy detachment is necessary if you are to love with the Heart of Christ. Loving Jesus as your one desire in life will direct you to Him through others. You will love Christ in your family and in all aspects of your earthly vocation. But your love for all will be a love for Christ when you love Him with this perfect love. When this happens, every other attachment will be transformed into your love of God (See *Diary* #1365).

What do you love in this world? What is it that you are attached to? Think about your greatest earthly loves. Hopefully these loves include family members and others whom God has put in your life. Now examine those loves and ponder whether they are centered in Christ. By loving them are you actually loving God? Or do these earthly loves remain ends in themselves? Reflect upon the goal of making love of God the one and only focus of your life and try to discover how you love God in and through every other person and every aspect of your life.

My Lord, I love You and desire to love You above all else and in all else. May You become the one and only goal of my love. As I love You in all Your creatures may I be drawn closer to You and lavish Your perfect mercy upon their lives. Jesus, I trust in You.

Reflection 274: Renewing Your Vows

It is a common practice for those who are married to renew their vows from time to time, especially on significant anniversaries. The renewal of vows and promises also takes place by priests and religious. This practice is a good and holy one in that we must constantly renew our total dedication to God in our vocation. But the renewal of vows and promises to God should go beyond our particular vocations and enter every universal vocation to holiness. Through Baptism, Confirmation and Holy Communion you have been given over to God for His service. You are His and He is yours and this mutual exchange of your hearts must be renewed daily. In fact, the reception of Holy Communion has this renewal as one of its goals. Not only do you receive our Lord into your soul in this precious gift, you also renew your total self-giving to God through its reception. As you daily renew your total commitment to our Lord, allow Him to consume every part of your life as if a blazing fire were consuming a log. Allow your renewal to consume your sin, weakness, sufferings and even joys. Let everything in your life be for the glory of God and the manifestation of His Divine Mercy (See *Diary* #1369).

Ponder today how often you renew your total commitment to our Lord and His holy Will. Reflect upon the image of a blazing fire consuming a log. See this as an image of what happens when you renew your love of God and your commitment to Him through your vocation to holiness. Hold nothing back, surrendering all each and every day. Let God consume you completely, transforming you into His Mercy.

Lord, I renew, today, the vows of my Baptism, Confirmation and Holy Eucharist. I renew the total dedication of my life to You and surrender all for Your service. Receive me, Lord, and do with me as You will. I am Yours, Lord, given without reserve. Jesus, I trust in You.

Reflection 275: The Glory of Humdrum Days

At first thought, "humdrum" and "glory" may not appear to go together unless they were used in contrast. But these two words are married together in the Mind of God. They are "married" in the sense that we are able to glorify God and obtain holiness through our day-to-day humdrum duties. Though this may not be immediately apparent, understanding this unlocks a door to the treasures of Heaven in countless ways. By discovering this deep spiritual truth you are able to offer every moment of every day to God and win His abundant Mercy through every action of your life. For example, even your breathing can become a source of the Mercy of God when you offer it to Him for His glory. If that doesn't make immediate sense to you don't dismiss it. Seek to offer and sanctify every action and you will begin to discover that every action of every day can become a source of the continual outpouring of the Mercy of God (See *Diary* #1373).

Try a simple exercise today. As you breath in, pray interiorly that the Will of God enters your soul, and as you breathe out, offer your own selfishness to God. Try to think about this as often as you can throughout the day. Pretty soon you will discover that you are glorifying God even through this most basic human act. Discovering this will help you realize that every act of your day, no matter how small, can become a source of the outpouring of the Mercy of God.

Lord, as I breathe in I invite Your perfect Will and Mercy into my life. And as I breathe out, I submit to Your Mercy all my sin and self-will. Jesus, please consume every act I do this day. May even the smallest act be done for You and for Your glory. Nothing is too small for You, dear Lord. May I discover Your abundant Mercy in all things throughout my day so that my life may become a continual offering to You and a constant instrument of Your Mercy. Jesus, I trust in You.

Reflection 276: Seeing Without Accomplishing

Does God get angry with you when you do not accomplish a certain task for His glory? It depends. He may issue forth His holy wrath if the failure is on account of your sin. This wrath is an act of His Mercy calling you to repentance. But at other times your work and service of God may be hindered by things beyond your control. The Lord knows this and sees it. You may wonder at times why God does not "fix" this or that problem. You may wish you had it in your power to move someone to act when they appear to be a hindrance to your work of mercy. But this is not your concern. Your concern must be to do all that is in your power to accomplish the Will of God, leaving the rest to Him. God is pleased by your efforts, not by your successes. He does not measure the objective success; rather, He measures the subjective success. In fact, sometimes God allows many obstacles to arise as a way of purifying your work and sanctifying your soul through patience and deepening resolve. Do your duty and that will suffice for the work of His Mercy our Lord has given you (See *Diary* #1374).

Think about that which you believe God has given you as a duty to perform. It may be some ordinary activity or it may be something that appears to be grander in nature. Reflect, also, upon apparent obstacles you encounter in fulfilling your duty. Try not to look at these "obstacles" as obstacles at all. Rather, see them as opportunities to deepen your resolve to fulfill the mission of Divine Mercy God has given to you.

Lord, help me to be faithful to You in all that I do. Help me to refrain from focusing on the results of my efforts and, instead, to offer my effort to You for Your glory. I know You are pleased by my total dedication to You, dear Lord. Help me to daily resolve to deepen that dedication so as to become a better instrument of Your Mercy. Jesus, I trust in You.

Reflection 277: Mercy to Dispel Tension

Tension is often a part of life. Some deal with much tension, frustration and even extreme anger in their daily lives. At first, the anger of another can set you on guard and tempt you to fear. This is a normal reaction. The anger of another can also push you to react and to fight back with anger, spite and bitterness of your own. You may get defensive and even lash out. But the Mercy of God is able to bring peace to any situation. His Mercy is bestowed when you turn a blind eye to the anger you face from another and speak as sweetly to them as you would to Jesus. Leave the wrath of God to God. If He inspires you to bring forth His holy wrath, you will know what to say and how to say it and this will be an act of His Mercy. But don't be surprised if God inspires you to act with extraordinary kindness in such a situation. This takes great resolve and a tremendous amount of patience. Do not allow yourself to become engaged by or tangled in the irrational wrath of another. Instead, let the peace of God's Mercy so flood your soul that, through you, His grace dispels all vice (See *Diary* #1377).

Reflect upon any regular situations of tension and anger you deal with. Perhaps you are the cause or perhaps you are the target. Whatever the case may be, know that God's peace can reign. Seek His peace, keep your eyes upon it and allow this firm focus to become a source of His abundant Mercy. He loves you and wants to free you from these burdens.

Lord, I invite You into the tension in my life. First, I surrender my own frustrations and anger to You. Please free me from these unruly passions and replace them with Your peace. Help me also, dear Lord, when I face the unjust wrath of another. Keep me calm and focused upon Your Heart. Help me to react as You will and to be an instrument of Your peace. Jesus, I trust in You.

Reflection 278: Windows to the Mysteries of God's Mercy

Saint Faustina was asked to have an image of Jesus painted with rays of Mercy flowing from His Heart. She did so and Jesus affirmed to her that many souls would be drawn to Him through this image. It's interesting to think about the importance that Jesus and Saint Faustina gave to this image. Indeed it speaks volumes regarding the Mercy flowing radiantly from His wounded Heart. It's also insightful to think about this in a more general way, namely, that a sacred image of any sort can become a source of Mercy. But the reason for this is that sacred art speaks a language. It communicates the Gospel message and meditating upon a sacred image opens your heart to hear God speak in a new way (See *Diary* #1379).

Reflect upon the Gospel images that you have in your home. Do you have many or very few? Do not shy away from filling your home with sacred images reflecting the message of the Gospel. Additionally, it is important to spend time in prayer with these images. Take a moment today to find the image of Divine Mercy that our Lord asked Saint Faustina to have painted. Spend quiet time looking at it and "listening" to it. What does God say to you through this image? He will certainly speak the fundamental message of His Mercy in that the rays of blood and water shine forth from His wounded Heart in a radiant way. These rays cover the Earth and shine on you day and night. But what else does God say to you through this image? Spending time prayerfully gazing upon this image and others will allow you to hear God speak of the mysteries of His love.

Lord, I know that any representation of You is but a drop of water compared to the reality. Help me in my prayer to be drawn into the reality of Your perfect love and Mercy as I meditate upon the sacredness that holy images represent. May I meet You, dear Lord, through these treasures of art and grace. Jesus, I trust in You.

Reflection 279: Your Inner Conviction

You must seek to hear God speak to you through an inner conviction within your soul. At times you may sense that God's Voice is loud and clear, and at other times it may seem faint and confusing. There are many things that can compete with the Voice of God but if you are open, you will come to know His Voice with familiarity. This is important for your spiritual life. Learning to hear Him speak and coming to recognize His Voice allows you to more easily walk in His ways throughout your life. Seek to know this inner conviction that His Voice presents to you. And as you learn to discern it, grow in confidence at His commands of love. Daily obedience to Him in this way must become the foundation of all that you do in life and it will become an abundant source of His outpoured Mercy (See *Diary* #1383).

How familiar are you with the Voice of God? You most likely will not hear Him speak to you in an audible way. His Voice often comes as a strong sense that we ought to do this or avoid that. He speaks by influencing our will even more than our mind. We may be attentive in our mind to what we sense, but the conviction God gives us is a spiritual sense. Though God may speak to each person in a unique way, this inner conviction is a common experience of God's communication. Reflect, today, upon God speaking in this way and if you struggle with this goal, recommit yourself to listen. Through this habit you will discover the abundant Mercy that God has in store for you as He guides you day by day.

Lord, I desire to hear Your Voice speaking to me in the depths of my conscience. Please do speak and fill my will with a sense and a conviction of Your holy and perfect Will. May I learn to be attentive to You every day and follow Your gentle commands as the guiding light of my life. Jesus, I trust in You.

Reflection 280: Ignoring God

Do you ignore God? It's far too easy to do and, therefore, all too common. Very often, God is ignored after receiving Holy Communion. Many people get in the habit of coming forward to receive Him and do so with many distractions and little attention to the sacredness of this encounter. Do not allow yourself to fall into this habit. Receiving our Lord in Holy Communion must become a profoundly intimate encounter. Our souls are fused as one in this moment and we must be attentive to this reality. Though Holy Communion is the most profound encounter we can have with our Lord, we must be deeply aware of His presence all the time. When we pray to Him, we must allow ourselves to not only say prayers, but to be drawn into His glorious presence and consumed by His Mercy. As we go throughout our day, we must be constantly aware of Him walking with us, leading us and speaking to us. Do not ignore our Lord. If you find that you do this at times, or if it has become a regular habit, know that the opposite habit can be formed. Making regular choices to be aware of Him within you and all around you will open the door to you walking in His Mercy every day (See *Diary* #1385).

Reflect upon your attentiveness to our Lord as honestly as you can. Reflect, especially, upon your attentiveness to Him as He comes to you in Holy Communion. Seek Him, listen to Him and receive Him and your life will take on a new direction.

Lord, I know that I ignore You at times and that I fail to be attentive to Your gentle and holy Voice speaking in the depths of my conscience. I know that I do not properly reverence You and adore You in the countless ways that You come to me. Give me the grace to form a holy habit of always knowing that You are near. As I form this habit, give me the grace to love You with all my heart. Jesus, I trust in You.

Reflection 281: The Immovable Will of God

At times, when we love God with a profound love, we may find that we have strong impulsions to do great things for God. And yet, despite our desire and firm resolve, it can seem as if God is not permitting our work to move forward. This may be because the Lord is not ready to act. Though it's good to have a strong desire to do great things for God, we must always remember that our desires must align with the perfect timing and wisdom of the Will of God. He knows best and He will allow the work He inspires to come to fruition when He wills it, not before. Surrendering your impulsions to God is a way of letting God purify the work He calls you to do so that it is ultimately His work in us and not our own work done in accord with our own idea of what is good. God's Will is immovable and all the longings and desire in the world will not move Him to act contrary to His perfect plan set forth at the perfect time. Humble yourself before God so that He will bless the world with His Mercy through You in the way He desires (See *Diary* #1389).

Do you have a heart filled with the desire to serve our Lord? Hopefully you do. Reflect upon these desires and know that they please our Lord. But also reflect upon the fact that, if they are to come to perfection, even the most pure desire must be submitted to the Will of God. Make that prayerful resolution today and God will use your heartfelt desire to manifest His Heart of Mercy to the world.

Lord, I do desire to serve You with all my heart. Please increase that desire and purify it so that my will dissolves into Yours. Help me to let go of even my "good" ideas as I submit to Your wisdom and love. I do love You, dear Lord, and desire to be used by You in accord with Your perfect Will. Jesus, I trust in You.

Reflection 282: Suffering, Persecution, Abuse & Disgrace

This heading may not seem immediately attractive to you. Who would want to endure these things? But we ought to remember that Jesus endured them all to the greatest degree. Was Jesus happy? Was His soul at peace? Most certainly. This reveals to us that these crosses in life cannot ultimately do us harm if we are immersed in the presence of God. Remember Jesus agonizing in the Garden, or the mockery He endured, or the rejection that many directed at Him, yet in all of this He remained in a peaceful repose. Nothing in this world can steal us away from a profound peace if we remain immersed in the presence of God. All the suffering, persecution, abuse and disgrace in the world cannot ultimately have victory over a soul given to God (See *Diary* #1394).

Reflect upon that which has the effect of stealing your peace away. If you were perfect, this would not happen. That may be hard to accept but it's true. We easily point to this or that as the source of our unrest when the source is always within. It's either a sin we have clung to, such as anger, or a sin of omission, such as a lack of trust. Whatever your experience is, do not get caught up on your sin. Simply turn your eyes to our merciful Lord and know that He can keep you in His peace through anything if you let Him.

Lord, I invite You to take control of all my inner thoughts, feelings and emotions. Bring stillness and peace to my heart as I continue through this life filled with struggle. When I experience the harshness of others, help me to use that as an opportunity for greater trust in Your Mercy. I know that in all things I can remain wrapped in Your arms of grace. I give myself to You, dear Lord, please protect me and keep me close to Your Heart. Jesus, I trust in You.

Reflection 283: Overcoming Sin

The message of God's Mercy is so simple that we can easily miss it, even after reflecting upon the many pages of this book or upon the *Diary* of Saint Faustina. The simple truth that the message of God's Mercy must convey is that we should have no fear, whatsoever, of admitting our sins and trusting in God's perfect forgiveness. Fear easily paralyzes us and keeps us from being honest in regard to our sins. But if you understand the Mercy of God and realize how all-consuming it is, fear will have no power over you. And though this may be easier to understand in theory, it can be very hard to embrace in your actions. The only way to fully enter into the Mercy of God is to give Him that which properly belongs to you, namely, your sins. Do not hesitate in doing this. Have full confidence in your loving Father and allow the light of His Mercy to replace the darkness of your sin (See *Diary* #1396).

How easily can you admit your sins to God? And when you do so, are you able to admit them with full confidence and hope? Are you able to admit them in the Sacrament of Reconciliation, the greatest source of God's Mercy? You do not need to carry guilt and shame in regard to your sins no matter what they are. Trust in the omnipotent love of God and let go of your hesitation and fear. If you do this, you will discover that joy will begin to permeate your soul and lift the heavy burden that sin imposes.

Lord, please remove all fear from my life. Cleanse me of my sin and free me from the burdens they impose. Give me full confidence in the abundance of Your Mercy and open my heart to receive all that You wish me to receive. I love You, dear Lord, may I allow that love to dispel all that is not of You. Jesus, I trust in You.

Reflection 284: Living in the Moment

One common temptation that many face is that of living either in the past or in the future, and failing to live in the present moment. You live in the past when you remain controlled by past events, sins, hurts, etc. The past must be healed and your sins of the past must be forgiven. Once that is done, you must let go of the past and not allow it to affect you in a negative way. The past can affect you for good when 1) you learn from the mistakes you have made, 2) you are strengthened by the healing of past hurts, 3) you continue to rejoice in all that God has done for you. You are affected negatively by the past when you dwell on your past sins and hurts, failing to seek forgiveness and healing. You live in the future when your mind is constantly obsessed with that which is out of your control. It's easy to fear the future or to be anxious about it, but you must remember that the future is not yet here and you ought not allow fears or worries about it to cause undue stress. All we have is the present moment. Therefore, it must be your constant goal to live each moment, day by day, hour by hour and minute by minute. Be present to the present moment. Embrace it, live it and encounter the love and Mercy of God as He is present to you here and now (See *Diary* #1400).

Do you struggle letting go of the past or trying to control the future? Seek to embrace this present moment and all will be well. Reflect upon this tendency and especially look at what God wants of you today. Keep your focus upon this present moment and seek to meet our Lord in it. His Mercy awaits you here and now.

Lord, I offer to You all the events of my past and entrust to Your care all that will happen in the future. Free me from past hurts and sins, and alleviate my worries about the future. Help me to meet You and Your abundant Mercy in this present moment alone. Jesus, I trust in You.

Reflection 285: Deception as an "Angel of Light"

The evil one hates you with a profound hate. And the closer you draw to God, fulfilling His Divine Will, the more he will seek to attack you. Do not fear the bark of this little dog. One of the most common ways the evil one attempts to deceive you is by presenting himself as an angel of light. He does this by using his natural angelic powers of influence, speaking lies that have a faint resemblance to the truth. He rarely speaks outright with obvious lies since he knows we would immediately identify him as the source. Instead, he seeks to manipulate the truth and lead you into confusion, tempting you to doubt the truths that God has spoken and to doubt the holy Will of God. He may subtly remind you of your past sins and weaknesses while trying to mask the infinite Mercy of God which eliminates those sins and manifests its power through your weakness. He may tempt you to discouragement and despair, removing from your heart the hope you have been given in Christ Jesus. He may tempt you to anger and resentment leading you to believe that you are justified in holding on to these feelings. Whatever the case may be, the evil one is a slippery liar and you must overcome his deceit by turning constantly to the truth of the Mercy of God (See *Diary* #1405).

Reflect upon the subtle lies that you have allowed yourself to believe. Whatever they are, you will know them by their fruits: sadness, anger, hurt, confusion and the like. Identify these and dismiss them through prayer. Allow the Mercy of the Lord's Truth to permeate your soul and set you free.

Lord, help me to know the truth and to be set free through this knowledge. Please protect me from the subtle lies and deceptions of the evil one. I rebuke him in Your holy Name and entrust myself to Your protecting Hand. Jesus, I trust in You.

Reflection 286: Humility, Purity & the Love of God

What is it that is most dear to the heart of our Blessed Mother? If she were to appear to you and offer you her greatest desire for you, what would it be? Perhaps there would be some specific need that she has been made aware of by God for your life, but in addition to this she would most certainly call you to the virtues of humility, purity and love of God. We especially see these holy virtues alive in her life. Our Blessed Mother was humble in many ways. She was The Immaculate Conception, freed from all sin and the most glorious creation of God, yet while on Earth she was hidden and even thought to be a sinner on account of Jesus being conceived before she was married. However, she lived perfect purity in her life which was the source of her most perfect love for Jesus, Joseph and everyone else she encountered. Her purity enabled her to love others with the utmost dignity and respect. Her love of God was also perfect in every way and was made manifest by her total submission to His holy Will. She said, "Let it be done to me according to Your Will." She meant that and lived it. Allow this witness of our Blessed Mother to call you to embrace these holy virtues so as to imitate and share in her glory and holiness (See *Diary* #1415).

Reflect upon these three virtues in your life. How well do you manifest them? Think about how they would have been lived in the life of our Blessed Mother and seek her powerful intercession so that you may imitate these virtues which she lived to perfection.

Dearest Mother, I gaze upon your beauty and upon the virtues that radiate from your life. I especially rejoice in your humility, purity and love of God. Help me to imitate these virtues in my own life so that I may imitate your beauty and holiness. Mother Mary, pray for me. Jesus, I trust in You.

Reflection 287: The Cloak of Ignominy

"Ignominy" could mean public shame, disgrace, humiliation and embarrassment. But it takes on special meaning when applied to Jesus. The "cloak of ignominy" refers to the public humiliation that Jesus endured as a result of His Cross. He was condemned as a sinner and liar. He was charged with deceiving the people and attempting to undermine the civil authorities. He was the object of extreme hate and ultimate persecution by the religious leaders of His day. This was a brutal blow. If Jesus would have had the sin of pride He would clearly not have been able to endure their scorn and mistreatment. He would have brought forth a myriad of angels to destroy His persecutors. But He didn't. Instead, He endured every humiliation with confidence and integrity. The sufferings Jesus endured never evoked in Him even a single feeling of hatred or revenge. In fact, from the Cross itself He cried out, "Father, forgive them, they know not what they do." This powerful witness must influence you and strengthen you to pay no attention whatsoever to the false judgment of others. God has no concern about false judgments and the public humiliation that these judgments impose. Embracing the "cloak of ignominy" means you ultimately allow every worldly humiliation to dissipate before the Mercy and truth of God (See *Diary* 1418).

Reflect upon this struggle within you. It requires great humility to ignore false opinions. Seek to embrace that humility and allow the truth to make you free. Jesus' "cloak" must cover you since it is ultimately a cloak of His grace and Mercy.

Lord, I take upon myself Your cloak of ignominy. I wear it with confidence and trust. Help my only care to be Your truth and to shed all other opinions that are contrary. My happiness rests in You alone, dear Lord, and all my hope is in You. Jesus, I trust in You.

Reflection 288: Silence in the Face of Ridicule

If you are given the glorious gift of a deep faith, many will see this and rejoice in it. But it may be the occasion for some to have jealousy. This is a sad and painful experience. Know that the jealousy of another is not caused by you or by your faith, it is caused by their sin. Therefore, if you experience the jealousy or ridicule of another stemming from their jealousy, do not be alarmed. Certainly it is appropriate to feel holy sorrow over their action, but that sorrow must not turn into a wound. Instead, pay no attention to the mistreatment of another other than this holy sorrow that leads to silent surrender to God. Pray for this person and have great hope that their sin will be realized by them and that they will repent. Your hope, your silent suffering, and your holy sorrow will become an act of Mercy to them allowing them to see the effects of their sin (See *Diary* #1422).

Accepting the darts of another's sins can be difficult. Reflect upon how you react when one of these arrows is sent your way. Though it is easy to react with vengeance, your mistreatment by another offers you an opportunity for much grace. Mercy, silence and holy sorrow provide you with the tools you need to help bring conversion to those who mistreat you. This is difficult to do and can only be done when you have fully surrendered to the Mercy of God. God loves you and He loves every sinner with a burning love. Reflect upon that love God has for those who have hurt you and reflect upon the fact that you are in a unique situation to help them experience God's love. Do not shy away from this duty and the Lord will bless you more than you could ever imagine.

Lord, I pray that Your Mercy floods my heart, especially for those who have hurt me. May I love them with Your Heart and become a source of grace in their lives. I love You, dear Lord. Jesus, I trust in You.

Reflection 289: The Desire for Souls

When you look at the desire in your heart, what stands out the most? Certainly there are many things that draw you. Many worldly rewards and pleasures can easily occupy your longings. A desire for physical pleasure, money and worldly success are among the strongest desires for many. The single desire you should have is a desire to Love God. From that desire you will also love others and you will find that your love of God is fulfilled by a deep longing to bring other souls to God's Mercy. Do you desire this? Do you long to help others experience the tender Heart of our Lord, to know His compassion and to experience His Mercy? If you have completely given yourself to the love of God then God will accept you and send you forth as His missionary of Mercy, searching for souls who are hungry for His love. Allow yourself to be consumed with this passion and the Lord will use you in marvelous ways (See *Diary* #1426).

Reflect upon the desires of your heart this day. Do not be afraid to admit to what is there. Whatever you see you must confront and place in the hands of God. His Mercy must become a consuming fire in your soul, burning away all that is not of Him. When this happens, you will find a new desire placed in your heart by God. It will be a desire for the salvation of many souls. Let yourself receive this desire from our Lord and allow this desire to direct you in the Lord's work of Divine Mercy.

Lord, I burn with a desire for many things. Most of them I must humbly admit are not from You. Please purify my heart, dear Lord, and make me holy. Help me to love You with a perfect passion and from that love may I have a great desire for the souls of others. I love You, dear Lord, please increase that love. Jesus, I trust in You.

Reflection 290: Bodily Sufferings Redeemed

Many people enjoy excellent health while others do not. Some experience great physical discomfort in life due to infirmity or old age. Though many look for ways to alleviate this physical discomfort, it must be said that these pains offer an opportunity for grace. First, much grace is won in the life of the person suffering when that suffering is freely embraced. Grace can also be won for the lives of others when physical suffering is offered as a prayer for their good. The way this grace is won is not so much by the suffering itself; rather, it is won through the free choice to embrace that suffering as a sacrifice. This denial of one's own will becomes an open door to the storehouse of Mercy in Heaven. God smiles upon these physical sacrifices and especially upon the free choice of their embrace. Do not hesitate to allow your physical pains and discomfort to be turned into the Mercy of God for you and for others (See *Diary* #1428).

Do you have physical pain or discomfort in your life? If so, it is normal to look for ways to alleviate it. But reflect upon this deep spiritual truth that your suffering can be transformed into grace. If you doubt this, just look at the Cross. The physical pain our Lord endured may not have matched His interior suffering, but it was part of His perfect Will to offer His physical pain to the Father for the redemption of the world. Do not doubt the value of your free embrace of every pain and discomfort. Give it to God and you will be blessed as others are blessed through this offering.

Lord, I do offer to You, this day, all the pain and discomfort I feel now and will feel in the future. Help me to embrace this suffering with a free embrace. I choose it, dear Lord, and make it my offering to You so that You can transform it into Your Mercy. Jesus, I trust in You.

Reflection 291: The Value of Silent and Hidden Suffering

When something burdens us we often seek consolation from others regarding our suffering by speaking about them openly. Though it may be beneficial to share our burdens with another to an extent, there is also great value in embracing them silently in a hidden way. It may always be wise to share your burdens with a certain person such as a spouse, confidant, spiritual director or confessor, but be aware of the value of hidden sufferings. The danger of speaking of your suffering openly to everyone is that it tempts you toward self-pity, lessening the opportunity to offer your sacrifice to God. Keeping your sufferings hidden enables you to offer them to God in a more pure fashion. Offering them in silence will win much Mercy from the Heart of Christ. He alone sees all you endure and will be your greatest confidant through it all (See *Diary* #1430).

Reflect upon those burdens you carry that you can reasonably keep silent about and offer to God. If you are overwhelmed, do not hesitate to speak to another for their assistance. But if it is something that you can silently suffer with, try to make it a holy offering to our Lord. Suffering and sacrifice do not always make sense to us immediately. But if you seek to understand the value of your silent sacrifices, you will most likely obtain insight into the blessings they can become. Silent sufferings, offered to God, become a source of Mercy for your good and for the good of others. They make you more like Christ in that the greatest suffering He endured was known only by the Father in Heaven.

Lord, there are many things in my life that are difficult at times. Some seem small and trivial and others can be quite heavy. Help me to always sort through the burdens of life and to rely upon the help and consolation of others when needed. Help me to also discern when I can offer these sufferings to You as a silent source of Your Mercy. Jesus, I trust in You.

Reflection 292: The Value of Special Vocations

Some people are called to a unique life of prayer and solitude within the context of religious life. In particular, there are those called to the eremitical life or the cloister. These holy souls are separated from the world and spend their days in quiet prayer and work. But what value does this life have to the world? This is an important question to understand. From a worldly point of view, they add little to society. They may be looked upon with curiosity and intrigue, offering inspiration and admiration, but little more is rarely understood of their life. Never underestimate the incredible value of these holy vocations. Their life of hidden prayer and sacrifice brings delight to the Heart of our Lord and is a constant source of His Mercy in the world. In fact, without these holy souls, the world would be in grave danger. Through their lives of prayer and sacrifice the Lord withholds much of His judgment and issues Mercy in its place (See *Diary* #1434).

What is your understanding of the value of the hidden vocation of religious? Seek to understand the great value of their vocation. Look to them for a deepening understanding of the spiritual life and trust that their prayers are a source of much Mercy in your life. Additionally, reflect upon the fact that you are called to imitate their lives of prayer to one extent or another. Though you may not be called to the cloister or to live as a hermit, you are called to a deep interior life of prayer. Allow these holy souls to teach you by their writings, their witness and their unique vocation. They are an abundant source of Mercy in our world; seek God's Mercy through them.

Lord, I thank you for the gift of those holy souls called to lives of solitude and prayer. Please sanctify them in their vocation and help them to win many souls for Your Kingdom. I pray that their witness and vocation will inspire many in an interior life of prayer. Jesus, I trust in You.

Reflection 293: Reduced to Nothingness

Do you see value in being reduced to nothingness in your own eyes? Perhaps not. The reason this language is difficult to accept is that humility is only fully understood by a special gift of God's grace. Some ancient philosophers even hold up pride as a great virtue, discounting humility as weakness. Sadly, there are few souls that obtain the actual virtue of humility. Some may obtain a certain semblance of this virtue, but few actually become humble to a great degree. Again, humility can only be understood and embraced by a special grace of God. Naturally speaking, we are drawn to those things we deem to be beneficial to us. Therefore, the first step in growing in humility is to see it for what it is and to discover its true value. When we understand humility, we will desire it. And when we desire it, we will be drawn to it. And when drawn to it, we will more easily embrace it (See *Diary* #1436).

Do you understand humility? Do you understand the value of being reduced to nothingness in your own eyes? If not, ponder this idea for some time. Don't give up on it thinking it is out of date, weak or misguided. You must become reduced to nothingness in your eyes if you are to discover grace in the Heart of Christ. Only by the discovery of your nothingness will you understand that God is everything and provides everything you need. You will find, in this discovery, that you begin to choose God over yourself and, thus, you become transformed into God's grace rather than living by your own strength. God must possess you completely, live within you and live through you. In this way, your humble soul becomes Christ to the world.

Lord, make me humble. Help me to see my nothingness and to see Your greatness. I choose You, dear Lord, over myself and invite You to possess me completely, transforming me into Your grace. Jesus, I trust in You.

Reflection 294: Never Tire of Contemplating the Trinity

Do you understand what you will be doing for all eternity? Heaven, if we are blessed to obtain it, will be an existence of eternal contemplation of the Most Holy Trinity. Though there is no time in Heaven, imagine if there were. And then imagine contemplating the Trinity for a million years in a row. Would you eventually become tired of this life and find boredom in it? Never in a million years and beyond! It's essential that you regularly remind yourself of the life you will live in Heaven in this perpetual contemplation of God. Though there is no way you can understand what this life will be like, you must try to comprehend it nonetheless. At very least, understanding that you can never understand and comprehending that you will never comprehend is at least a good start. The Trinity is a mystery that we will never solve; rather, it's a mystery that we must enter into. Begin your eternal contemplation of the Trinity today and allow this contemplation to draw you into the infinite Mercy of God (See *Diary* #1439).

Ponder today this great mystery. It may seem beyond you, and it most certainly is. But try anyway to spend some time trying to comprehend the unfathomable mystery of God. In truth, this is not something you can do on your own. Only God can draw you into this holy contemplation, but you must accept His invitation. Say "Yes" today and allow the merciful hand of our Lord to begin drawing you into the immense depths of His love.

Oh Most Holy Trinity, I adore You with profound adoration and love. Please take hold of my soul and draw me into the mystery of Your very life. Reveal to me the secrets of Your inner heart and help me to begin my journey into eternity with You today. I love You, my God. Help me to love You with all my heart. Father, Son and Holy Spirit, I trust in You.

Reflection 295: The Embrace of the Infant Jesus

It is most appropriate to prayerfully reflect upon being held in the holy arms of our God. Understanding the Merciful love of the Father in Heaven through the holy embrace of love reveals to us His fatherly care. Running to the arms of Jesus opens our hearts to His merciful love. But one image that will also be helpful and holy to reflect upon is that of the infant Jesus. Imagine if you were privileged to be present when Jesus was an infant. And imagine if this infant looked at you, reached out His arms and sought to be held by you. And imagine if this infant held you tightly as He rested on your heart. This holy exchange of love will most certainly be understood by parents as they hold their children. Contemplate the profound love and infinite Mercy of God coming to you through this warm and unconditional embrace of a little child. Jesus is reaching out to you, embrace Him and hold Him tightly (See *Diary* #1442).

Ponder today this beautiful and holy image. But do so by imagining that this infant burns with a holy and pure love for you and longs to be held close to your heart. Resting in your arms you feel the love of this sweet embrace. This is an image of the Love of God and a holy image. Allow your own experiences of holding a child to teach you about the Mercy of God. And express your own love for God through this holy image of a child's embrace.

My dear Lord, so small and innocent, may I hold You in my heart with an embrace of pure love. May I feel Your Heart beat with mine and Your love poured forth in this sweet embrace. I thank You, Lord, for coming into our world as an infant. May I always treasure this image and be drawn more deeply into love of You every time I hold one of Your precious children. Jesus, I trust in You.

Reflection 296: A Parent's Love

Imagine the parent who loves a child with burning love. They are committed in every way to the care and well-being of their child. Their love is steady and irrevocable from the time of birth on into adulthood. Now imagine the pain in this parent's heart if at some point their child walks out on them and fully rejects their love. This loving parent will not give up but will think about their child day and night, aching inside with love, hoping to be able to receive their child back. This is but a faint image of the love of the Heart of Jesus. As a "faint image," we must realize that when we reject the love of our Lord, the wound of love in His Heart produces the deepest suffering. But this is a suffering of love. And instead of this wound of love causing Him to reject us, it does the opposite. The more we turn from God, the deeper His wound of love, and the deeper His wound of love, the more He pours out His Mercy upon us. Never doubt for a single moment the irrevocable love God has for you. Believing in this love will give you courage to always return to our Lord (See *Diary* #1447).

Reflect upon the love that your parent has for you. No, it may not be perfect, and some may have experienced great hurt from a parent, but try to imagine what it would be like to have a parent who loves you with an unconditional love. The knowledge of this love would become a constant invitation to let them into your life. Reflect also on this being a faint image of the love of God for you. Do not doubt this love. Turn to it and trust in this irrevocable love of our merciful Lord.

Lord, help me to understand Your irrevocable love. And as I understand this love, give me courage to never turn from You, but when I do, give me courage to always return to You. Your love is perfect and constant. It never fails and never gives up. Thank You, dear Lord, for loving me to this perfect degree. Help me to love You in return. Jesus, I trust in You.

Reflection 297: Lessons from Nature

All of creation is capable of reflecting the glory and workings of God. God is the wisdom behind the Universe, setting all its laws in order and guiding all things perfectly. We only need to spend time meditating upon the laws of nature to perceive the laws of grace which they reflect. For example, take the morning dew. It arrives silently and without notice of its coming. It sinks in and soaks the earth leaving all things covered by its presence. So it is with the countless graces of God's Mercy. It's as if every grace God gives us is like one drop of the morning dew. He bestows it in abundance, and we often do not see it coming. It is given to soak in and to nourish our souls. Let the message of the morning dew speak to you this day and allow it to reveal the outpouring of the Mercy of God (See *Diary* #1449).

Do you ever spend time reflecting upon creation? There are so many lessons to learn about God through that which He created. Ponder the morning dew this day. Spend time on it and seek the countless messages that God can reveal through it. Consider, also, the many other messages that reveal the wisdom and Mercy of God within creation. We can grow in our faith and knowledge of God by pondering the birds, the grass, the fish, or any other creature God made. Reflect upon creation this day and you will find that you are reflecting upon the Mercy of God.

Lord, I thank You for the gift of creation and the countless ways that You speak through that which You created. May my life be like the soil that soaks in the morning dew each day, being covered with Your grace. I love You, dear Lord. Help me to be more open to Your love each new da, and to see Your hand at work in all things You have Made. Jesus, I trust in You.

Reflection 298: The Virus of Senseless Murmuring

One unfortunate tendency within our fallen human nature is to "murmur" about another. It's like a virus in that once someone starts, it passes to others quickly. Before you know it, many can be spreading rumors and gossip not based in truth, or truths not spoken in charity. This can be very painful to the person who the murmuring is about. We see this commonly among teens, but it is not exclusively a teenage phenomena. The two questions to ponder in this regard are: 1) Do I murmur about others? 2) How do I react when others murmur about me? First of all, the virus of murmuring will only be cured if people of integrity cease to speak unnecessary words or calumny or detraction. We have no right to spread errors about another, and we have no right to spread truths that do not need to be shared. Second, if you find yourself to be the object of the murmuring of others, it's understandable that this will hurt. Allow yourself to feel the hurt, unite it to the Heart of our Lord, and then move on without returning the mistreatment. A peaceful resolve to pay no attention to these actions helps to dispel their effects and it keeps us from being drawn into the foolishness (See *Diary* 1453).

Ponder today both of these experiences. If you are the cause of senseless murmuring then see the seriousness of this sin. It is a sin and a serious violation of charity as a result of the hurt it can cause. Confess it and resolve to silence your tongue. If you are the object of such murmuring, know that Jesus was first. Turn to Him and allow Him to console you, and try to rejoice that you have been treated like our Lord.

Lord, please guard my tongue and help me to speak only the words You wish me to speak and to only listen to those words inspired by You. If I am the object of hurt from another, give me the grace to receive healing and strength and to rejoice that I am treated like You. Jesus, I trust in You.

Reflection 299: The Weariness of Human Wisdom

The words of truth, spoken from the Heart of our Lord, bring joy to our lives and rejuvenate our spirits. When you hear these words of truth, take them in and act on them, you are set free from the burden of error and may experience a certain lightness of spirit and refreshment. However, the opposite is true also. When you listen to an error, take it in and believe it, the fruit of this error is one of sadness and burden. The truth sets you free and an error weighs you down. This is good to be attentive to when you offer advice to another. If your words appear to lift them up and strengthen them, then you have an indication that you are speaking from the Heart of Christ. The same is true when you take the counsel of another. If their words immediately connect with you, filling you with a sense of inspiration and clarity, then listen and receive this word because they are most likely speaking the words our Lord has inspired them to speak to you (See *Diary* #1461).

Reflect today upon the conversations you have had this past week. How did you feel afterwards? Did you feel inspired and renewed? Or did you feel dry and down. And how have your words affected others over this past week? Did you notice a healthy difference in them and a lightening of their spirits? Do a practical and concrete examination of your conversations and recommit yourself to listening to and speaking that which comes from the merciful Heart of Jesus.

Lord, I desire to be an instrument of Your Mercy in every way. I pray, today, that I may especially do so through the words I offer to others. May my words be Your Word, dear Lord. And may I seek refreshment from Your Heart as I open myself to Your Word spoken through others. I love You, dear Lord, help me to love You more and to be an instrument of that love to all with whom I converse. Jesus, I trust in You.

Reflection 300: Revealing the Secrets of Your Soul

It is actually quite consoling to have someone with whom you can reveal the depths of your soul. This sort of confidant is a great blessing when absolute confidentiality, mercy and understanding are offered. Speaking even of your sins without hesitation can bring much healing when the person with whom we share these things responds with perfect love and is able to offer you the Mercy of God. We all need such a confidant. But in truth we do! We have the priest, waiting for us in the glorious Sacrament of Reconciliation. His confidentiality is certain, his compassion and mercy is offered and the forgiveness and Mercy of God is poured forth upon the deepest and darkest secrets in your heart. Do not hesitate and do not delay in going to Confession. You need this gift from our Lord and He will bless you with an abundance of His Mercy through it (See *Diary* #1464).

Reflect honestly upon the deepest and "darkest" sin in your heart. What is it that you fear revealing the most? The Lord desperately desires to enter into that darkness and bring the healing balm of His light and Mercy. Do let Him in through the Sacrament of Reconciliation. The power of this Sacrament is unmatched and is exactly what you need to begin your healing and to be set free from your burdens. Do not fear it and do not put it off. Make an act of faith today in this glorious Sacrament and you will be amazed at the effect that it has on your life.

Lord, please give me courage to confess my sins in the Sacrament of Reconciliation. Please also give me the wisdom to know that this is among Your greatest gifts. In this Sacrament I encounter Your Mercy to the greatest degree. Thank You, dear Lord, for this priceless gift. Jesus, I trust in You.

Reflection 301: The Communion of Saints

One motivation we should have for working diligently at spreading the Mercy of God is the reality of the Communion of Saints. Understanding this eternal communion will enable us to realize that what we do now we will rejoice in forever in Heaven. For example, if you go out of your way to share the Mercy of God with another and this Mercy is received and affects that soul for the good, this fact will be known and proclaimed for all eternity as you share Heaven with this person. Imagine spending your whole life on Earth spreading the Mercy of God as your greatest passion. And then imagine spending eternity glorying in the effects of this Mercy in the lives of countless other saints who are in perfect communion with you in Heaven, some on account of your holy efforts. Pondering eternity in this way will motivate you to fervently make it your most central mission in life to spread God's Mercy to all whom you meet and in the way our Lord inspires you (See *Diary* #1471).

Do you ever think of Heaven? Spend some time today thinking about this glorious reality that awaits us. What will you delight in once in Heaven? Certainly you will delight in God, but reflect today upon the delight you will have when you see clearly the effects of the love you have shared with others. These merits of grace will live on forever. Think about these treasures that await and try to allow them to become an inspiration to you and a motive for your work of Mercy.

Lord, I pray that You will inspire me continually to work diligently at spreading Your works of Mercy. Use me, dear Lord, and touch many lives through my efforts. Keep my eyes on Heaven and help me to make this goal the guiding force and motivation of my love for others. I give myself to You, dear Lord. Use me to save souls. Jesus, I trust in You.

Reflection 302: A Great, Powerful & Keen Intellect

Our minds are a gift from God and one of the two primary ways we are made in His image and likeness. The other way is through the gift of our free will. But the intellect is an incredible gift that must be given to the work of God. It is good to pray that our Lord make our minds great, powerful and keen so that we may know Him, understand Him and comprehend all the rich mysteries that He desires to reveal to us. Our minds grasp the truths of God in two primary ways. First, we must strive to engage all the many truths revealed by God through His Church. This includes the truths contained in Holy Scripture, the teachings offered by the Magisterium, the revelations from the lives of the saints and the theological discourses that seek to clarify and deepen our understanding. These precious gifts, given through the Church, reveal to us the mysteries of God. But the mind is also capable of receiving direct infusion from God. When we allow our minds to be given to God, He imparts a knowledge and wisdom directly from His own Mind. This gift offers us immediate clarity in life and discernment of His holy Will (See *Diary* #1474).

Reflect today upon how fully you have given your mind over to the teachings of our Lord. Reflect, first, upon whether you seek God's Truth through the Church. Do you study the Scripture and all that has been revealed through the Church? Reflect, also, upon the direct infusion of Truth that our Lord wishes to impart to you. This precious gift comes on account of His abundant Mercy so as to lead you into knowledge of His very essence and His holy Will.

Lord, my life is Yours. Today I especially surrender my intellect to You to use as You will. Teach me Your ways and reveal to me the very essence of Your eternal being. As I come to know You, dear Lord, give me the grace to follow You with all my mind and heart. Jesus, I trust in You.

Reflection 303: Silence

One of the dangers many encounter in our modern technological world is that of constant noise. We are easily bombarded with chatter all day long. It could be through the radio, TV, Internet, or the ceaseless conversation of another. Rarely do we find times of great silence. As a result, when silence is offered us, we often look to fill that silence immediately. But is this wise? Is it good to occupy our minds day and night with noise? Though every person will be different, especially depending upon their vocation, every person does need times of regular silence and solitude. Without this it is hard to be recollected and to hear the Voice of God. God speaks in the silence and He desires to communicate to you through this sacred language. Do not run from silence for, if you do, you will be running from the Voice of God (See *Diary* #1476).

Try to take some time today alone in silence. If you find that it is difficult to do even for five minutes, then this is a sign that there is too much noise in your life. Entering silence can bring on a form of "withdrawal" from noise. We tend to be comfortable with it as we are entertained all day long. But try to take time in silence today. Resolve to do so as long as you can. Turn off the radio in the car, go for a walk, or sit and pray without thinking or speaking, just being quiet in the presence of God. The gift of silent communication with God is a gift that you need and you will learn more from silence than from hours of the noise of the world.

Lord, I desire to seek You in the silence. I choose to listen to Your quiet promptings of love spoken in this way. Give me the wisdom and strength I need to dedicate myself to moments of quiet every day. May these moments bring clarity to my soul and understanding to my life. Jesus, I trust in You.

Reflection 304: The Truth in All Things

Should we fear the truth? On one hand the truth can get us in trouble. Look, for example, at the Martyrs. They are witnesses to the truth with the shedding of their blood. They "got in trouble" only in the sense that their testimony to the truth brought forth their persecution. But in the eyes of God this is no trouble at all. It is an act of great love and honesty, courage and resolve. They chose the truth over life itself. Though you most likely will not be called to be a witness to the truth to the point of literally shedding your blood, the resolve in your mind and heart must be the same as the great martyrs. We must have an unwavering adherence to that which is in the Mind of God and must never hesitate to speak that truth with conviction. Of course, prudence is a guiding virtue that will enable us to discern what to say when. But we must, nonetheless, always be ready to adhere to and proclaim the truth with all the powers of our soul (See *Diary* #1482).

Reflect upon how firmly you attach yourself to Him who is the Eternal Truth. Do you submit your mind to all that God speaks and believe it with every fiber of your being? This must be your firm resolve. Reflect, also, upon how you speak the truth to others. At times we can be tempted to speak without prudence which is ultimately a lack of charity. But at other times we can give into fear in the face of some opposition to the truth which is also a lack of charity. Seek to live in the Truth of God and to proclaim it with His merciful Heart and the Lord will accept this resolve of yours as a sacrifice of holy martyrdom.

Lord, I pray for courage and prudence as I go through life seeking to live and to proclaim all that You speak. May I never give into fear or cowardice when opposed or challenged. Instead, give me a peaceful resolve to be a great witness to You in all things. Jesus, I trust in You.

Reflection 305: The Depths of God's Love

Imagine if someone gave their life for you because they loved you. They were put into a situation where they knew you would lose your life if they did not freely give theirs. As a result, they chose to step forward in confidence, giving their life in exchange for yours. In order for someone to do this they would have to have an incredible depth of love for you, so much so that they valued your life over their own. This depth of love may be rare but it does exist and we haven't far to look to find it. We only need to look at a crucifix to be made aware of this reality. We easily become so familiar with the Crucifixion of our Lord that we overlook the fundamental fact of His perfect love. He valued your life more than His own. He did not hesitate to die a horrible death so that you could live. This fact should not escape your daily notice. It is not some far away sublime idea; it's a practical reality that has absolute consequences in your life. Jesus' death is the only reason that you can live eternally in Heaven. This is an act of Mercy that should leave us with eternal gratitude (See *Diary* #1485).

Spend time today pondering the Crucifixion of our Lord. Try to see it not as some far away event that has only an inspirational influence on your life. See it instead for what it is. Without the free gift of Jesus on the Cross you would be lost for eternity. It's as simple as that. His act of love was an exchange of His life for yours. The depth of His love for you is more than you will ever fathom. Ponder this truth today and rejoice that you are loved to such an absolute extent.

Lord, I will never fully understand the depth of Your perfect love. In my small way I thank You with all my heart and choose to accept the total gift of Your death on the Cross. Help me to never doubt Your love for me, dear Lord, and help me to love You in return. Jesus, I trust in You.

Reflection 306: God is Relentless

Do you doubt the Love of God? The truth is that God is relentless in His pursuit of you. Though much of our holiness depends upon us, most of it depends upon God. While here on Earth, God never ceases to pursue you and to seek your conversion. He sends His Mercy to you constantly in every way imaginable. The problem is that if your heart is "deaf and blind" it will not perceive the tireless ways that God pursues you. But even in your deafness and blindness, God speaks and pursues and seeks and attempts everything possible so as to win you for Himself. In the end, if a soul remains obstinate and closed, God can do little more. He only needs a very small opening in order to begin His good work in you but if there is not even a small opening, then even God's active pursuit will not change your life. Open your heart to Him. Even if you are in the depths of despair, allow Him to come to you with one drop of His perfect Mercy. Never close the door completely and if you have, do not hold it shut. He will find a way if you let Him (See *Diary* #1486).

Hopefully you daily seek to open your heart wide to the Mercy of God. But if you find that you have been bound by the chains of sin, realize that your greatest advocate is our merciful Lord. He can do wonders for those who are trapped and imprisoned by sin, or have become deaf and blind to His grace. Reflect upon how open you are to His Mercy today and resolve to let Him come to you so as to begin pouring His Mercy into your weary soul.

Lord, when I feel trapped or confused in life I know that You will pursue me with Your unlimited passion and Mercy. Your relentless love gives me hope when I am tempted to despair. Help me to open myself to You and to allow You to do Your perfect work of Mercy on my life. I thank You, dear Lord, with profound gratitude. Jesus, I trust in You.

Reflection 307: Conversing with a Divine Friend

How do you pray? There are many good ways to pray. Here are some common ways: attending the Holy Mass or another Liturgy, praying the rosary or other chaplets, reading the Scripture meditatively, reciting beautifully written prayers, sitting in silence before our Lord, falling prostrate before Him especially in the Holy Eucharist, etc. One additional way to pray is to have a conversation with our Lord, speaking everything on your mind. It's true that He knows all your needs, He knows all your thoughts and He knows you far better than you know yourself. But, at times, you will find it a blessing to converse with Him anyway. You may choose to go through your life, all of your concerns, all of your questions and confusions, and speak them directly to our Lord. This form of prayer helps to clarify life, as long as you seek to listen while you speak. But speaking all of your concerns is a wonderful act and will be most useful as you invite God into every part of your life (See *Diary* #1485-1489).

So how do you pray? Reflect today upon the various methods you use and ponder whether there are other ways that you might add. Especially consider sitting down and conversing with our Lord as you would a friend. Think about even the psychological benefit that comes by speaking everything on your heart, expressing every concern, and presenting every question you have to God. There is value in the conversation. You may not have perfect understanding of His answers, but God knows what you need and by coming to Him with everything, you can be assured that He will listen and respond.

Lord, teach me to pray. Help me to know how much You love me and desire to hear from me about every burden of my soul. I desire to bring all to You, dear Lord, to lay it at Your feet and to abandon myself into Your gentle Hands. Thank You for always listening. Jesus, I trust in You.

Reflection 308: A Mother's Love

It's true that no earthly image can fully reveal the perfect love of God. God is transcendent and His love is beyond what this world can contain. But nonetheless, there are many things in this world that do reveal aspects of the love of God. One such image is that of a mother's love. Though God has been revealed to us as the Father in Heaven and the Son of God came as a man, we can discover much about the love of God from a mother's love. In fact, it is even appropriate to understand that God is like the tenderest mother to us. Motherhood is sacred because it is part of the natural design of God for humanity. He puts into a mother's heart a powerful love for her child, offering unwavering commitment. Though no mother is perfect except our Blessed Mother, it's good to look at the beauty of a mother's love when using it to understand God. The tenderness and unconditional acceptance of a mother stand out as two aspects that reveal the love of God. God does love you with a perfect motherly love. Though this may not be the most common way to speak of His love, it is of great benefit to ponder this beautiful revelation from creation (See *Diary* #1490).

How do you see God? Reflect upon your image of God and rely first upon the various images in Scripture. But also ponder the many natural means through which God communicates His love. Ponder, today, especially the love that a mother has for her newborn infant. Reflect upon the unique and powerful draw she has and her unwavering commitment. The Lord loves you infinitely more. Always find comfort in this love.

Lord, I thank You for loving me with a perfect love. I thank You for the gift of motherhood and for the way that You reveal Your unconditional and tender love for me through this gift. Help me to always know of this love and to seek You as an infant seeks a mother. Jesus, I trust in You.

Reflection 309: Conversing with Others

When we engage in a conversation with another, it is always an opportunity to share the love of God. Even casual conversation has such potential. For example, listening intently to the details of another's life expresses care and concern for them and reveals the fact that you see their dignity and are acknowledging it by listening. Sometimes conversations can go astray and become dominated by things that are not of God. In these moments the love and Mercy of God can also be shared by gently bringing the conversation back to where it should be, in gentleness and respect. It's important to remember that every conversation should be consecrated to our Lord. It's good to do so intentionally but this can also be done when one builds a habit of speaking of the good things of God. Praying for another while speaking will also open the door to a holy and healthy conversation. Do not underestimate the value of a holy conversation with another. It always has the potential of being a source of the Mercy of God for both of you (See *Diary* #1494-1495).

Reflect upon the conversations you have had this week. Did they glorify God? Were you attentive to the opportunity to use your speech and your listening to bring Mercy and comfort to another? Try to say an interior prayer this day each time you have a conversation. Invite the Lord to enter and consecrate the person and yourself to our Lord. He will act through you in wonderful ways.

Lord, I do consecrate my speech to You. I pray that every conversation I have may give You glory and bring peace to others. Give me wisdom and charity and help me to speak only what You desire. Give me also a listening ear so that I may act with Your Heart of compassion, hearing the needs and concerns of others. Jesus, I trust in You.

Reflection 310: The Foolishness of the evil one

The devil is real and his temptations are real. He hates you with a pure hate and desires your destruction. This is good to know. But the evil one is also quite shrewd and manipulative and will rarely speak blatant lies to you since he knows this temptation will most likely not convince you. Instead, he seeks to speak confusion to you, identifying things that are partly true and mixing them with subtle lies so as to lead you astray. You may find that you begin to obsess about this thing or that. And you may find that your reasoning might make some sense, but you begin to experience a sadness and confusion as you think. Stop thinking in those moments and run to the Mercy of God. When your thinking is immersed in God, you are left refreshed and light. You begin to have new joy and clarity. But when the evil one begins to have his way with you, the opposite effects are felt in your soul. Be attentive to his sneaky deceptions and pay no attention to them (See *Diary* 1497-1499).

Reflect, today, upon your thinking process. It is here that the tempter works his worst work. Reflect also upon how you feel as you have tried to figure out this situation or another. Commit yourself to a discernment of spirits by especially looking at the effects of your thinking. The Lord invites you to run to His Mercy every time you find yourself confused or misled. Be attentive to these moments and know that they may be the temptations of the evil one. Trust in the Lord always and continually submit your thoughts to His holy Mercy.

Lord, please always protect me from the lies and snares of the evil one. I rebuke him and his works in Your most holy Name and entrust all my thoughts to You. Come pour forth Your Mercy and truth into my life and dispel all darkness and gloom. I love You, dear Lord. Jesus, I trust in You.

Reflection 311: The Truth of Humility

The glorious virtue of humility must be understood, continually pondered and continually embraced. What is humility? It is nothing other than knowing the truth about yourself, believing that truth and living in accord with that truth. Only you and God know the depths of your conscience. Human opinion matters little. Some may offer false judgments of you presuming your pride or another sin. And at other times some may speak words of flattery, exaggerating your virtue from impure motives. Neither false criticism nor words of flattery foster humility because they both have as their intention something other than the truth. Some holy souls may even seek to misrepresent the truth of who they are by either exaggerating their holiness or by misrepresenting their misery so as to gain the praise or sympathy of others. But, again, humility has as its goal the truth of who we are. Seek to know and believe the full truth of your life, and then seek to live that truth openly and honestly. This purity of intention will allow your true self to emerge, and through this humble act the Lord will shine forth from your soul (See *Diary* #1502-1503).

Ponder today the truth of who you are. Seek complete honesty in regard to your actions and your intentions. Understand yourself and seek to know yourself as God knows you. Doing this will foster great humility. As you grow in humility, see also the truth of God and His greatness. Humbly acknowledge all that God does for you. Seeing God at work within you and honestly expressing this with gratitude will allow Him to shine forth beautifully for all to see. This is truth and this is humility.

Lord, I desire to know the truth of who I am. I seek this truth and desire to allow it to shine forth with honesty and integrity. I pray also that I see Your greatness and acknowledge Your workings in my life. You are glorious, dear Lord. May this truth shine forth. Jesus, I trust in You.

Reflection 312: True and Faithful Friends

It is difficult to stay friends with one who is suffering, especially when that suffering endures. Often, at first, when a soul is suffering from some illness or other difficulty, many friends come to help. But as time goes on, fewer friends maintain their love and support. This offers a test of their love and mercy. But there is one Friend who will be there through it all. This is our Divine Lord. He endured the greatest sufferings in life and, as a result, He does not shy away from the friendship that enters into a relationship of long suffering. Jesus' love remains steadfast and immovable. This witness of perfect love must also inspire you in your love for others. When you see someone suffering it takes great resolve to remain faithful to them and to your friendship over time. But the longer the suffering endures, the greater the opportunity to love. Time purifies and strengthens love and when you are aware of the long suffering of another, see it as one of the greatest opportunities to manifest the unwavering love of our Lord (See *Diary* #1508-1509).

Reflect upon those with whom you have shared friendship. Are there people in your life that have carried a heavy burden for many years? If so, how firm have you remained in your dedication and love toward them? They offer you an opportunity to manifest the unfailing love of our Lord. Reflect upon how easy it is to love another when they are popular, healthy and praised by many. And then reflect upon the strength and commitment that is needed to remain steadfast to those in the opposite condition. Renew your love and friendship and you will manifest the great Mercy of God.

Lord, make me a true friend. Help me to see the sufferings of others as an opportunity to love with Your Heart. May I become as faithful as You, dear Lord. I love You. Help me to love as You do. Jesus, I trust in You.

Reflection 313: Sleepless Nights

There are some who easily fall asleep each night and remain asleep until morning. There are others who struggle greatly with sleep and this becomes a great burden and a source of discouragement. If you are one who struggles with sleep on a regular basis, or even on rare occasions, see this cross as an opportunity rather than as a burden. A sleepless night offers one particular opportunity to you. It can be seen as an invitation to spend the night with our Lord. Though it is healthy to work to deal with the cause of sleeplessness so as to remedy it, it is also good to embrace it in the moment if it happens. Even something as seemingly insignificant as this can become a source of holiness. Seek to use a sleepless night as an opportunity to pray and meditate upon the life of our Lord. One good reflection on such an occasion is to prayerfully meditate upon the night of Jesus' arrest and imprisonment. His night that night in prison would have most certainly been one of constant prayer to His Father. Recall also that there were many nights when our Lord chose not to sleep. Scripture reveals that Jesus regularly "spent the night in prayer" (e.g., Luke 6:12). Thus, in this act, Jesus gives great power to pulling an "all-nighter" with Him in meditation and prayer. By embracing this Cross with our Lord you will see an abundance of Mercy pour forth on your life (See *Diary* #1515).

If this is a struggle that you face, try to look at it from a new perspective. Seek the Lord in your sleepless night and enter into communion with Him in His. Much Mercy awaits you as you seek to transform this cross into grace.

Lord, I pray that every cross I carry will be transformed by Your Mercy into an opportunity for holiness. I especially offer my nights to You, dear Lord. Whether I sleep in Your arms or remain awake in Your presence I give each and every night to You. Jesus, I trust in You.

Reflection 314: Mercy as a Strong Defense

When an army is under siege, it seeks a place in which it can defend itself. Seeking higher ground or a place that gives it shelter and protection is immediately sought out. So it must be in your spiritual life. When you experience the darts of the evil one, or when life becomes burdensome to you, especially on account of your sin, seek the higher ground and the greatest place of refuge. This place is the merciful Heart of our Lord. Do not doubt that His Heart is a place of refuge for you. Within His Heart you will find safety from the weary battle and you will discover that you are in a fortified fortress of Mercy. This specific aspect of Mercy, that of being a place of protection, must be understood and welcomed. We cannot endure the hardships of life on our own. We cannot fight the battles of life if we rely upon our own strength and skills. No one is talented enough to fight off the raging enemy. Seek refuge in the Mercy of God and He will protect you from all harm (See *Diary* #1516).

Reflect upon your need for protection. By yourself, alone in this world, you will never survive. The temptations, attacks and evil that pervade this world will ruin you. But if you have a fortress of protection, nothing will do you harm. That protection is the Mercy of God. Spend time today thinking about God and His Mercy as such a fortress. See Him as your defender in all things and run to this place of safety. The Lord will surround you with His grace and will keep you at peace within the dwelling of His Heart.

Lord, when I feel the weight, attacks and temptations of the world come upon me, give me the wisdom to seek refuge. May I run to You and hide in Your merciful Heart. May I never doubt Your perfect protection and always find shelter in You. Jesus, I trust in You.

Reflection 315: Mercy, Mercy and More Mercy

Do you tire of speaking of the Mercy of God? Do you find that it becomes repetitive and unimpressive? If so, speak of Mercy all the more and ponder it with new zeal. You must never tire of the Mercy of God. The Mercy of God is so great and abundant that, in Heaven, you will see clearly how vast and wide it is. You will comprehend that it is incomprehensible and will never tire of contemplating its beauty. On Earth, you may find yourself tempted to dismiss Mercy as impractical and unimportant. It may be perceived as something old and outdated. When this happens, be reminded that this is foolishness and irrational. Understanding God's Mercy must become your daily goal and daily mission. You must seek it day and night and never relent in your pursuit of this unending and unfathomable gift of God (See *Diary* #1521).

Ponder, today, these three simple words: Lord, have Mercy. Say them often and intentionally. Remind yourself that if you grow weary thinking about and speaking about the Mercy of God then you are failing to understand its depth and beauty. God's Mercy must engage your mind and will so forcefully that it is ever present and ever new. Its newness, especially, will help to keep you engaged in this gift and it will enable you to continually probe its depths. Lord, have Mercy, Christ, have Mercy, Lord, have Mercy. Say this over and over and realize that you can never exhaust this glorious mystery of love.

Lord, you are never changing but always new. Help me to never tire of the simple yet profound truth of your Divine Mercy. Help me to always see the beauty and splendor of Your Divine Love. I do love You, dear Lord, and I pray that I may love You more every day. Lord, have Mercy on me. Christ, have Mercy on me. Lord, have mercy on me. Your Mercy, Lord, is great and glorious. Jesus, I trust in You.

Reflection 316: The Burning Flame of Love

There are many images we use to describe the Love of God. One such image is a "Burning Flame of Love." This is seen in the spiritual classic, "Living Flame of Love," written by St. John of the Cross:

> O living flame of love
> That tenderly wounds my soul
> In its deepest center! Since
> Now you are not oppressive,
> Now consummate! if it be your will:
> Tear through the veil of this sweet encounter!

Why do we speak of God and His love as a fire burning within us? This is a powerful image worth spending much time meditating on. A flame does many things. It brings light, it purifies, it consumes, it emits heat and energy, it draws us close, it is ever changing and ever new, and so much more. God's love must become not only a spark or a flame within you, it must become a raging fire of love, consuming your soul and producing, in its place, the radiance and divine presence of God (See *Diary* #1523).

Reflect, today, upon this image of the Love of God. Meditate upon this all-consuming fire raging within you. What are the effects of such a living flame? What does it do to your life? What will others notice when this flame is blazing? Ponder this holy image and invite the Living Flame of Love to consume you from within.

Lord, come to me and consume me with the burning fire of Your Love. Purify every sin and transform me into the light of Your grace and Mercy for all to see. You are a powerful Flame ever burning yet never harming. You renew me and radiate Your presence from within. I love You, dear Lord. Set me on fire with Your sweet Love. Jesus, I trust in You.

Reflection 317: Passing Judgment

It is very easy to pass judgment on another, but it is very difficult to withhold judgment. Why is that so? Why might you find yourself easily passing judgment on others when you truly do not know their heart? There certainly can be many reasons for this sin; one of them is that some people do not even know themselves well enough to judge their own conscience. When this is the case, the person will be in no position to try to judge another. Judging another often comes from a heart that has little interior knowledge, understanding or personal insight. They feel this disorder within and project it out on others. This is helpful to understand for two reasons. First, if you tend to judge, stop and look into your heart. There is a very good chance that you do not know who you are, what your sins are, or how God sees your soul. Second, if you become the object of another's judgment, do not be offended. Instead, use it as an opportunity to have a holy sympathy for them. Chances are that their judgment of you is a sign of their own interior confusion. This should evoke compassion toward them, not judgment in return (See *Diary* #1528).

Reflect today upon these two experiences of judgment. First reflect upon whether you judge and why. Also spend time reflecting upon the way you react when others judge you. Seek the truth in both of these experiences and surrender your own judgments and your experience of others' judgments to the Mercy of God.

Lord, please free me from having a judgmental heart. You and You alone probe the minds and hearts of all Your children. Give me insight into my own soul so that I may continually examine my life in the light of Your Truth, and give me a heart of mercy that I may love others with the Mercy of Your Divine Heart. Jesus, I trust in You.

Reflection 318: Indifference and Forgetfulness

If you were married and you were regularly indifferent to your spouse, this would be a problem. Indifference means there is a lack of sincere care for the good of the other. Forgetfulness is a symptom of indifference in that when one cares little, it's easy to forget. For example, if you forgot an important anniversary in your marriage this could be a sign of either a very poor memory or an uncaring and indifferent heart. If it is the latter, this brings much hurt to that relationship. One reason this brings much hurt is that the cause of the hurt is subtle. If one were to *actively* do something hurtful, it's easier to point it out. Indifference is a *passive* action in that something is missing. But this passive action can be just as hurtful, if not more hurtful, than a more obvious action. So it is with God. When we are passively indifferent to Him and His Mercy, and when we "forget" to turn to Him day and night, we are bringing much pain to His Sacred Heart (See *Diary* #1537).

Examine your conscience today and try to honestly identify any struggle you have with indifference. It may not be manifestly clear to you. You may not even realize this is a sin and the cause of much hurt to others. But this form of neglect causes deep wounds over time. Try to make an honest examen and if you realize that this is your sin, do not hesitate to do something about it. Renew your care for those whom God has put in your life, and especially renew your caring heart toward God and the Mercy He wishes to bestow. If you are indifferent to the Mercy of God, this wounds His Heart and does even more damage to you over time.

Lord, I desire to care to the greatest degree. Help me to be continually aware of others in my life and to anticipate their needs, lavishing love upon them. Help me to also be continually aware of Your Mercy and to never be indifferent to this most sacred gift. Jesus, I trust in You.

Reflection 319: Dealing with Loneliness

Loneliness is a deep suffering that many endure. One reason it is so painful is that the lonely person obviously suffers alone with few people, if any, to help ease their hurt. If this were not the case, they would not be lonely. Interestingly, even those who are surrounded by others all day every day can be lonely. Even the most popular and outgoing person in the community can sometimes struggle with great loneliness. This may not be easily noticed because they often "wear a mask" covering the loneliness they experience. Loneliness is real and comes as a result of one particularly deep need we all have. And this is the need to be known by another. We want to be known and understood. We need people who will listen to us, care, understand and love us at our deepest core. Simply being popular or being surrounded by many people does not meet this need since the "popular" person may not truly have revealed what is inside to anyone. The best answer to loneliness is the intimate presence of God in your life. An authentic and deeply personal relationship with your Lord enables you to be at peace, knowing that God knows you, understands you and loves you. This gift also opens the door for you to find people to whom you can share your joys and struggles. Seek intimacy with the Lord. This is the greatest help to a lonely heart (See *Diary* #1542).

Be honest today and ponder the question of loneliness in your own life. No matter if you are the life of the party or a quiet bystander, loneliness can affect everyone. Reflect, also, upon the fact that intimacy with our Lord is the primary cure. Look at your relationship with Him and open your heart to His love.

Lord, I invite You into my heart. Come dwell there and reveal Your tender love. Help me to understand that You know and love me through and through. I give my heart to You, dear Lord. Jesus, I trust in You.

Reflection 320: A Zealous Heart

One of the easiest things you can do in life is be lazy. Imagine if you had no responsibilities, had all the wealth you could ever want and could spend your days in luxury and relaxation. This would foster a very lazy heart and it would also foster a very sad heart. Rest is good, but excessive rest can turn into laziness and laziness ultimately becomes very boring. This fact reveals the opposite truth also. Namely, a zealous heart is one that finds great excitement in the activities of the day. Though some may become obsessed with work, becoming a "workaholic," an appropriate balance of rest and work produces the virtue of a zealous heart. Are you zealous? There are many things one can be zealous about in life, and not all of them good or within the Will of God. But zeal for the salvation of souls, and the bringing forth of the Kingdom of God is a zeal we must all strive to foster. In fact, our Lord wants you to have this as the highest priority in life. As you grow in holiness and closeness to our Lord, He will send you forth cultivating the Earth with His Mercy. Doing this with great zeal wins many souls for the Kingdom and produces abundant joy in your heart (See *Diary* #1548).

Do you struggle with a lazy heart or a zealous one? If lazy, look at the effects of this in your life. The boredom and dissatisfaction you experience is a direct result. If, however, you are zealous and diligent in life, what is it you are zealous for? Reflect upon this honestly today and seek to grow in a burning zeal for the building up of the Kingdom of God.

Lord, I offer to You all my work and my talents. Use them for Your glory. Help me to have true zeal for Your Kingdom and to work tirelessly for Your glory. Jesus, I desire to be an instrument of Your perfect Mercy in the world. Use me as You will. Jesus, I trust in You.

Reflection 321: The Seraphic Soul

Everyone is called to holiness and in that holiness is able to obtain complete happiness. But God always chooses some for a special mission of holiness, a higher form of holiness. These souls could be called "Seraphic Souls." The classic example is to compare two glasses of water. One is large and one is small. They are both filled to the brim so they are both full. But one contains more water. So it is with holiness. Some are given a special calling to reach a greater height. All people are to be "full" of the Holy Spirit and, thus, obtain perfect happiness. But some are invited higher in a unique way. This is similar to the Nine Choirs of Angels. The Seraphim are of the highest order and have as their sole purpose the worship and adoration of God. The Guardian Angels are of the lowest order and have as their primary duty the service of man. Each celestial being is perfectly happy and rejoices in the unique calling of each (See *Diary* #1556).

Reflect, today, upon this glorious ordering of holiness for angels and for humanity. At first, it may not seem fair that some are given a special calling to holiness and even a special sharing in the sufferings of Christ. We must all ponder this truth and rejoice in it. And as for those seraphic souls in the world, and those given a special call to share in Christ's sufferings, we should seek them out and seek the wisdom and grace that flows from their lives. God has a good reason for such ordering; it's our duty to embrace it with joy and to benefit from their blessed vocation.

Lord, I thank you for Your perfect wisdom in ordering the holiness of both angels and humanity. Help me to always seek out those seraphic souls, the special saints, who have reached a glorious level of holiness. Thank You for their witness and thank You for their freely embraced suffering. May the world be continually blessed by their lives. Jesus, I trust in You.

Reflection 322: The Obstacle of Pride

The Lord, in His abundant Mercy, comes to you day and night and joyfully enters your soul when it is open to Him. Even the greatest struggles do not deter our Lord from coming to you. But one thing, especially, keeps our Lord away. And that is pride. Pride is the mother of all sins and, simply put, is selfishness. It's a way of turning in on yourself as your primary concern. The problem with this is that you were made, by God, for the purpose of giving yourself away. It's in your very nature to become a gift to others. And only in giving of yourself to God and to others do you discover who you are and, in that act, you become who you were made to be. So pride, in its attempt to become self-concerned, actually has the effect of destroying you. Pride leaves you with yourself and allows no room for another, not even God (See *Diary* #1563).

Reflect upon the sin of pride today. Here is an examination for this sin: Pride is an untrue opinion of ourselves, an untrue idea of what we are not. Have I a superior attitude in thinking, or speaking or acting? Am I snobbish? Have I offensive, haughty ways of acting or carrying myself? Do I hold myself above others? Do I demand recognition? Do I desire to be always first? Am I ready to accept advice? Am I in any sense a "bully" or inclined to be "bossy"? Do I speak ill of others? Have I lied about others? Do I make known the faults of others? Is there anyone to whom I have not spoken for a long time? Am I prone to argue and be offensive in my arguments? Am I self-conscious? Am I sensitive? Am I easily wounded? Reflect honestly on these sins today and seek freedom from them.

Lord, please free me from the self-centeredness that comes from pride. May I seek the good of others with all humility and sincerity. Free me from this sin, dear Lord, and help me to give myself away to You and to others, for in giving of myself I know I will find myself. Jesus, I trust in You.

Reflection 323: Your Unique Mission

God gives to each person a unique mission. Some are called to very public lives; others are called to quiet and simple lives. Some are called to use their minds in powerful ways; others are called to use their hearts in special ways, but each person has a unique mission from God. What is your mission? Seeking to know what the Lord asks of you is essential to your journey of holiness and, therefore, happiness. When fully embraced, this mission will bring abundant fulfillment to your life because of one simple fact: every mission is a mission of Mercy. The struggle many people have is that they embark on selfish endeavors in life, failing to commit all their energies to the work of the Lord. The Lord wants you to work day and night on His mission. This is not too much to ask. In fact, it's what you were made for and the only way to obtain what you truly desire. His mission will certainly include moments of fun and rest, work and struggle, laughter and tears. It will also require a complete death to yourself. But it's worth it! Seek the mission God has given you and embrace it with all your heart. If you do, the Mercy of God will pour forth through your life (See *Diary* #1567).

Reflect, today, upon this simple question: What is my mission in life? It may come to you slowly, over time, taking twists and turns as you go. But never stop seeking to serve our Lord and His perfect plan. This plan will become the delight of your soul. Ponder it and if you are on the wrong path, correct your direction in life.

Lord, I thank You for calling me to a blessed and unique mission in life. I choose, this day, that which You have given to me. I promise to say "Yes" to You throughout my life and to never tire of fulfilling Your Will. I love You, Lord. Help me to love You with my life. Jesus, I trust in You.

Reflection 324: That Longed-for Moment

What do you long for in life? If you could pick one thing that you desire above all else what would it be? Would it be death? Probably not. Surprisingly, the greatest saint would probably desire death over anything else in life. Not an early death or a death of their own choosing; rather, they would see death as the gateway to their true home and anticipate the joy of that encounter with much hope. This may not be something you normally think about but it's worth doing so. When a person has Heaven as their greatest desire it means, in part, that they have come to such a point in life that the things of this world do not matter to them. They long for Heaven and to be with God eternally. This does not undermine their love for family and friends. This love is eternal and will remain with them in Heaven to an even greater degree. The key to this desire is the realization that Heaven will be so glorious and fulfilling that there is much excitement about obtaining it. This may not be your normal way of thinking about death but it is worth pondering and examining your earthly desires in the light of this ultimate goal (See *Diary* #1573).

Spend time today pondering death. But do so in a new way. Look at it not as an end to your life; rather, see it as the beginning of a new and glorious life of perfect fulfillment. Reflecting upon death does not mean you wish for it to come soon. We should only desire to obtain Heaven in accord with God's timing. But, nonetheless, we should desire it and desire it with all our soul. In fact, keeping our eyes on this ultimate prize will help us walk through the hardships we endure here and now.

Lord, of all the many desires and goals I have in life I pray that I may desire Heaven above all else. Please free me from the foolish desires of this life and set my heart solely on You. Jesus, I trust in You.

Reflection 325: Relying on the Saints

Imagine the soul who has lived a life filled with complete abandonment to God. They achieved the heights of holiness and were not deterred by earthly distractions. Throughout their life they sought to serve our Lord and to be a continual instrument of Mercy for others. Many people were saved on account of their sanctity and their total devotion to the Will of God. Now imagine that holy soul entering into the glories of Heaven. What a profound experience of absolute joy! Nothing could be more glorious than that moment. But once in Heaven, is it conceivable that this holy soul will forget about those on Earth? Is it possible that the people who were loved and served so deeply would disappear from their minds as a result of being in Heaven? Most certainly not. In fact, once in Heaven, the holy souls who lived on Earth are even more consumed with a desire to spread the Mercy of God. Seek out these saints. Seek their intercession, ask for their inspiration, follow their example and know that you have a myriad of holy men and women seeking to serve you from the glories of Heaven (See *Diary* #1582).

Ponder the saints this day. Especially ponder their burning love for you and their desire that all people receive the Mercy of God. God uses them from Heaven and continually sends them to distribute His grace. Open your heart to these holy men and women and they will pour forth the Mercy of God into your life.

Oh, holy saints of God! How glorious you are in your Heavenly splendor! I thank you for your love and service on Earth and now I call upon your intercession from Heaven. Please pray for me and for all people that we may imitate your holiness while on Earth and obtain the glory in which you now share. Saints of God, pray for us. Jesus, I trust in You.

Reflection 326: Waiting on the Lord

One common struggle many people have is that of impatience. We tend to want what we want when we want it. In our fast-paced society we are used to instant everything. A full meal can be reheated within minutes, text messages can be sent worldwide in seconds, news travels the moment it happens, and for many people almost anything they could ever want or need is generally only a short drive from their homes at the nearest superstore. All of this fosters a tendency to want what we want when we want it. But the Lord does not work this way. He has His own timing which is always in accord with His perfect wisdom. Very often we can experience a temptation to do what we think is in the best interest of the truth and to do it now. But sometimes God chooses to wait before He acts. When He acts, His ways become clear and convincing and His wisdom is unmistakable (See *Diary* #1587).

Reflect upon your desire to do great things for God or to speak the truth in one situation or another. Is your impulse from the Lord or is it your own impatience prompting you? This is an important question to reflect upon because God's Truth can only come forth at His command, in His time. If we try to push the Hand of God we will be doing so on our own. Yes, God will use even our misguided or impatient works for His glory, but our plans done in our way will never accomplish the glorious works of God as He can only accomplish them. Reflect upon your patience with the Will of God and make an act of surrender this day. Your trust and surrender will open the doors of Mercy in accord with the perfect Will of God.

Lord, I surrender to You and Your perfect Will. Give me patience so that I may set aside my own ideas and plans, submitting only to You. May I learn to wait on You, dear Lord, and act only as You command. I love You, my God. Jesus, I trust in You.

7

Reflections on Notebook Six

We enter, now, the last of the six notebooks that Saint Faustina filled with revelations from our Lord about His unfathomable and perfect Mercy. At this point, the Message of Mercy should be clear and evoking of a deep trust in the incomprehensible love of God. All that has been shared to this point reveals that God is relentless in His pursuit of you, seeking only to love you unconditionally and to draw you into His glorious life for all eternity.

The greatest obstacle to this call to holiness is sin. But it is abundantly clear that sin is no match for the Mercy of God. His Mercy dispels your sin in an instant, disposing of your past errors forever. God's only desire is the present moment, for in this present moment He comes to you, descending from the heights of Heaven, entering into the inner core of your soul so as to form a perfect communion with you, lifting you up to share in His divine life.

This final notebook will be reflected upon as a summary of all that has been reflected upon thus far. Just like the reflections on the first notebook, the reflections for this notebook will be short and to the point. Once you finish this chapter you are invited to return to it often as a way of quickly and easily reminding yourself of the abundant Mercy of God. The Lord's love is perfect in every way. Allow Him to speak this truth to you with clarity and conviction.

Reflection 327: The Hidden Presence of God

God is hiding. But why? He hides under the veil of secrecy and silence so that we will diligently seek Him. He does not choose to compete with the distractions of the world since He wants you to choose Him as your one desire. Desire to seek Him, hidden in your heart, hidden in the holy Sacraments, hidden in the silence and hidden in the people whom you encounter throughout your day. The Lord is there, waiting for you to discover His Heart filled with unfathomable Mercy. Seek Him with all your might (See *Diary* #1591).

Ponder the hidden presence of God today. Be aware of the fact that the presence of God is all around you, constantly calling to you and inviting you into His Heart. If you allow yourself to become disinterested or distracted by the world, you will never discover how close He is. Reflect upon His hidden presence and do not hesitate to seek Him today.

Lord, I love You but at times I fail to live that love fully. I become so very distracted by things that mean little in the end. Help me to regain my focus and to seek You with all my heart. Jesus, I trust in You.

Reflection 328: Heaven

Heaven invites us into a life of glory and fulfillment that is beyond what we could ever comprehend. Not even in Heaven will we fully comprehend the glorious mystery of God and His Mercy. From Heaven, the saints, radiant with glory and grace, look down upon us with love, seeking to lavish us with the Mercy of God. Seek Heaven as your primary and ultimate goal in life. Do all things with this goal in mind and the treasure you will build up for all eternity will be more abundant than you could ever hope for (See *Diary* #1592).

Do you think about Heaven as your one true desire in life? Every act of love offered here on Earth will be remembered and exalted in Heaven. Everything we do on Earth should be but a preparation for the glorious day of our passing from this world into our eternal home. Ponder your desires and if the glories of Heaven is not front and center, be aware of that fact, redirect your focus and seek to place your eyes on this ultimate prize. As you look at the beauty and splendor of Heaven, the Lord will draw you to it with a burning desire.

Lord, please flood my heart with the joyful delight of Heaven. Help me to keep my eyes on this goal and to do all in this life as a preparation for that sweet encounter. I love You, dear Lord, and have great hope in the day of our perfect union. Jesus, I trust in You.

Reflection 329: Confessing with Delight

Why do you fear Confession? This glorious Sacrament is offered to you from the tender Heart of our Lord. Through this glorious gift Jesus lifts the burdens you carry so that you can more fully share in His Mercy. If you understood this, there would be no hesitation in running to Confession on a regular basis. You would desire it not because it reveals your misery, but because it heals it and removes it forever (See *Diary* #1602).

Try to spend time looking at your attitude toward the gift of the Sacrament of Reconciliation. If you see hesitancy within you, examine the reason. Is it fear of facing your sin? Is it fear of facing the priest? Fear should never be a factor. Let go of any fear you have by putting your eyes on the end result. That end result is freedom and union with God. This is a Mercy you need and will never regret receiving.

Lord, please free me from the fear of this glorious Sacrament. Help me to see my sins honestly but only as I also gaze upon Your infinite Mercy.

Give my heart a burning desire for this Mercy and a longing for the freedom it brings. I love You, dear Lord. Jesus, I trust in You.

Reflection 330: Praying for Others

Do not underestimate the power of your prayers. The greater your trust in the Mercy of God, the more powerful will your prayers be for those who need them. The Lord knows all things and He knows who needs what. But He wants to dispense His grace in union with those who ask for it. Your prayers for others are the most powerful way that you can bring the Mercy of God into this world (See *Diary* #1603).

Do you pray for others? If not, resolve to do so. Your prayer may be for a specific need or a struggle that another is enduring. But we should always leave the specific result to the Mercy of God. Offering others to God and trusting that He knows the best outcome for any situation pleases our Lord and wins an abundance of grace for those in need.

Lord, I offer You, this day, all who are troubled and burdened. I offer You the sinner, the confused, the ill, the imprisoned, the weak of faith, the strong of faith, the religious, the laity and all Your priests. Lord, have Mercy on Your people, especially upon those in most need. Jesus, I trust in You.

Reflection 331: Nothing Beyond Your Strength

It's important to know that the Lord will never allow you to carry a cross that is beyond your strength. Do you believe this? If you do, it should help you to set your eyes on the road ahead and plunge forward doing the Will of God. If struggles come your way, even if they are great, know with certainty that the Lord is with you, carrying you if needed, through everything you face in life. Nothing can keep you from His

Mercy and His perfect Will if you keep your eyes on Him (See *Diary* #1607).

Reflect upon the path that you believe the Lord has set before you. What obstacles do you perceive to be too great to overcome? Whatever it is, you must face them with confidence and absolute trust in our Lord. As painful as some things may be, nothing is beyond the Mercy of God. He will transform the rough path before you into a smooth road if you let Him.

Lord, I do believe that You are always with me, leading me and protecting me. When I face some hardship in life, help me to see it as an opportunity to rely more on Your grace. I know that I can do all things You call me to, dear Lord. I commit to walking the road You have laid out for me. Jesus, I trust in You.

Reflection 332: Never Grow Weary of the Cross

The Lord speaks much about sufferings to Saint Faustina. She suffered much through humiliations and through physical illness. And Jesus never tired of reminding her that her sufferings take on great power when united to His Cross. This message must never be forgotten. Though suffering may not be a "happy" topic, it is a joyous one when properly understood. When you realize that your sufferings can act as an instrument of the Mercy of God in the world, you will not hesitate to embrace them and to unite them to Christ. Never doubt this sacred instrument of God's Mercy (See *Diary* #1612).

Sufferings and the talk of sufferings can be wearisome, but only when they are not united to the Cross of our Lord. When they are united to His Cross, the burden becomes light. Reflect upon whether you understand this and live it. If you are living it you will find that your sufferings are no longer a heavy burden, they become a joy. Though it is hard to arrive at this level of surrender, it is your calling and the reward awaits.

Lord, may I never grow weary of offering You every pain and suffering I endure. When serious hardships come my way, help me to give them to You. When small discomforts come my way, help me to give them to You. I unite all things to Your glorious Cross, dear Lord, and trust in Your unfathomable power to transform them. Jesus, I trust in You.

Reflection 333: Simplicity

Life can appear to be complicated at times and so can we. But the truth is that we need to cut through the complexities of life and realize that, from the perspective and Will of God, life is simple. It's simple in that all we need to do is say "Yes" to Him every day, surrendering all to Him and trusting Him every step of the way. We must be diligent in responding to His promptings and grace, but we do not have to enter into the entire complicated world, figure it out and solve it. This is too much and is far better done by God. Seek to be a simple soul who trusts in the perfect wisdom of God and He will sort life out for you (See *Diary* #1617).

Do you find that your life appears complicated at times? Reflect upon this question and if the answer is "Yes" it's probably because you are trying to do more than God is asking and to solve questions that He already knows the answers to. Turn to Him, today, as a simple trusting soul. Be ready and willing to respond to anything He communicates to you and do it with passion and diligence, but do not worry about all the apparent complexities of life. The Lord understands them well and will navigate you through their confusion.

Lord, I pray that I may become a simple soul. I choose to follow this path led by absolute trust in You and Your wisdom. You know all things, dear Lord, and You will guide me every step of the way through the apparent complexities of life if I let You. I do believe this dear Lord. Help me believe it with all my soul. Jesus, I trust in You.

Reflection 334: Serving Souls

One of the greatest blessings we have been given is the ability to serve others. We serve them in many ways, especially in accord with our particular vocation. But the greatest service we could ever render a person is to be a minister of the Mercy of God, leading them to the glories of Heaven. Imagine what Heaven will be like knowing that you have inspired countless souls to grow in their love of God. See this as one of your greatest blessings and privileges in life (See *Diary* #1622).

How eager are you to offer the truth, love and compassion of our God to others? Do you see the great honor this is and the great dignity it bestows? Never doubt how important it is to make this among the greatest priorities in life. Loving God with all your being comes first, but serving others and helping them on the road to salvation is right behind this. Commit yourself to this glorious act of Mercy today and you will be grateful for eternity that you did.

Lord, give me the desire and will to serve others with my whole heart. Help me to love them and to bring Your Mercy and compassion into their lives. May many souls be won for You, dear Lord, on account of the grace that You send them through my life. Jesus, I trust in You.

Reflection 335: Forever Forgiving

One of the hardest things to do in life is to pray for those who persecute you and to treat them with the utmost respect and compassion. But what benefit is there in hating them or lashing out at them? Doing this "harm" to them is far more damaging to your own soul than to theirs. Forgive, forgive, and forgive again. In fact, forgiving another is a form of God's justice in that it reveals that another is in need of forgiveness and dispels the vicious power of their malice in your life. Forgive them, pray for them and entrust them to the Mercy of God. By doing this you will have great peace in your soul (See *Diary* #1628).

Is there anyone in life that you hate? Or anyone that you are at least tempted to have much anger toward? If so, reflect upon this person today and make the conscious choice to forgive them. Though your feelings may not immediately follow this choice, you will begin to find peace in this decision. Forgive them over and over as long as anger remains and the Lord will prune that vice from your life replacing it with His joy.

Lord, in Your great Mercy You have forgiven me for my sins. I am unworthy of such a gift but I thank You for it. Help me to show the same depth of mercy and compassion to others, especially those who have hurt me. I forgive them, dear Lord. I forgive them a thousand times and more. Jesus, I trust in You.

Reflection 336: The Riches of the World...or God?

It's interesting how often we desire earthly possessions. Even if you had every treasure in the world all to yourself, this could not fill the longing in your heart. There is one thing and one thing alone that fills the void within you and that is the Lord and His holy Will. Nothing else suffices, yet we often work so hard at gaining more and more of the things that pass away (See *Diary* #1632).

Spend time today imagining that you obtained a superabundance of wealth. What would this do to your life? Would it make you happy? Perhaps it would be fun, interesting, exciting, and entertaining…at least for a while. But the truth is that nothing can fill the void in your heart except God. Yes, there is a void that needs to be filled. You feel it and are always seeking to fill it. Do so with God and His Mercy. You will find that what you have desired all along is free for the receiving.

Lord, You are my riches and wealth. You must become all that I desire in life. Give me the grace to believe this truth and to choose You as the fulfillment of all my longings. I love You, dear Lord. Help me to love You more. Jesus, I trust in You.

Reflection 337: Helping the Anxiety of Others

In our lives it is almost certain that we will encounter people from time to time who are agitated, upset or worried. They may obsess about this or that and their thinking may even be somewhat irrational. What a graced opportunity this is for Mercy. Anxiety and worry will happen in life and we should not let it draw us in. We must keep our peace, make the situation light, and especially offer prayers for those struggling with this burden (See *Diary* #1636).

How do you react when you encounter the excessive worries or anxieties of another? This is a heavy burden to them and a source of much stress. Reflect upon how you approach people in this situation. Know that the Lord wishes to use you to bring peace to their worried minds and anxious hearts. Commit to this act of Mercy and the Lord will bless them.

Lord, please do make me an instrument of Your peace. When I encounter those who have no peace and are filled with anxiety, help me look at them with compassion and love. Help me to know that these souls need Your Mercy and that I am the one sent to dispense it. Jesus, I trust in You.

Reflection 338: Keeping a Secret

One act of love we can offer another is our confidentiality. We have all had experiences of people coming to us with a problem or confusion and they ask us to keep it to ourselves. Can you keep this form of a sacred secret? Confidentiality is a wonderful act of mercy to others. If you can be truly confidential, others will come to realize this quality in you and they will more readily come to you with their concerns. This act of friendship, given out of love, opens the door to others to open their hearts and let you in. As you enter in, do so with much understanding and care and the Lord will bless them through you (See *Diary* #1638).

Reflect upon the question of confidentiality. When someone shares something in confidence with you, do you immediately think about who else you can tell? Are you tempted to reveal these secrets or, even worse, to spread gossip? The Lord wants many souls who are there for others, to listen to them, to understand them and to love them no matter what they need to share. Be a holy listener and confidant and you will be an instrument of much Mercy.

Lord, I pray that I may become a person of great integrity, offering a compassionate and confidential ear to those who need it. Give me grace to be freed of useless chatter and gossip and to revere every person, respecting their dignity through privacy. May I never push or probe for more but only be a compassionate friend who is always there to show love. Jesus, I trust in You.

Reflection 339: The Pure Soul

It may not be something you immediately conclude, but a soul who has a pure love of God is feared by many. The "fear" that they have is a fear to oppose such a soul. Those with malicious intent will not dare to attack such a person because they know it may backfire on them. It's impossible for anyone to harm you when your heart is perfectly set on the Lord (See *Diary* #1643).

What do you fear? Or perhaps the better question is "Why do you fear?" If your heart is set on Christ's then there is no reason to worry or fear anything. Even if others attack you in some way, if your heart is set on Christ then this will not matter. Reflect the image of fog and see that as the many struggles of life. Then imagine the bright and powerful Sun coming out and burning the fog away. This is what happens when we set our heart on the Lord.

Lord, I want to be a pure soul, setting my heart only on You. My heart is Yours, dear Lord. I entrust it to You with all my might. Jesus, I trust in You.

Reflection 340: Being Tested

It may not be immediately pleasant, but at times we greatly benefit from being tested. The Lord permits this in a variety of ways. Being tested is not a temptation; rather, it's a way that the Lord allows us to endure a trial so as to invite us to more deeply submit to His holy Will. When you feel a trial come your way, the best thing you can do is to get down on your knees and pray, "Lord, may Your Divine Will be done in all things! I submit fully to whatever You desire!" What a perfect prayer, especially when prayed in the context of a trial. This prayer will enable you to pass the test (See *Diary* #1648).

How do you react when you are faced with a trial in life? Do you despair? Or do you get down on your knees and surrender your life to God? Ponder this and resolve to surrender in all things so that you will pass every test in life.

Lord, I do surrender to You my whole being. Take all that I am and all that I hope to be. All is Yours, Lord. Do with me as You will, when You will and how You will. Jesus, I trust in You.

Reflection 341: Adore the Lord My Soul

If you have ever been to a wonder of nature, the moment you behold it is an awe-inspiring moment. Looking at the Grand Canyon, Niagara Falls, or the Swiss Alps for the first time will take your breath away and leave you in a moment of adoration of God's creation. But if the beauty of nature can evoke such a response, then the infinite beauty of God will leave you in awe for eternity. It will be a moment of such "Beholding" that every fiber of your being will be drawn to God the moment you are face-to-face. And that "moment" will become one eternal moment. That moment can begin now if you allow yourself to be drawn into the adoration of God (See *Diary* #1652).

Do you understand the idea of adoring God? There is only one way to understand and that's to do it. For example, someone may tell you all about the Grand Canyon, and it may be interesting, but seeing it with your own eyes completely changes your understanding. Reflect today on whether or not you know what it means to adore God with your whole soul. If you do not, then seek out this supernatural marvel.

Oh Lord, I desire to adore You with all my being. I want to be mesmerized by Your beauty and glory. Draw me in, dear Lord, and allow me to have but a glimpse of the glory I am to behold for all eternity. Jesus, I trust in You.

Reflection 342: The Refreshment of the Passion

Normally we do not put the words "passion" and "refreshment" together. How could the Passion of Christ be refreshing? It is only horrific and sorrowful from an earthly perspective. The Lord suffered greatly and our Blessed Mother suffered with Him with the most sorrowful heart. But they both took great refreshment in this act also. This is because the Passion is pure love. And love refreshes us like nothing other. When you meditate on the Passion of our Lord you also offer joy and refreshment to His suffering soul and your own crosses are transformed as you enter into His (See *Diary* #1657).

Never stop reflecting upon the Passion of our Lord. It must become an image that is imbedded upon your heart. Reflect on how often you do meditate on this act of pure love. Do you understand it? Do you see the love and compassion that brought our Lord to such a gift? Put your eyes on the Passion today and never take them off this refreshing act of perfect Mercy.

Lord, help me to see Your Passion for what it is. Please peel back the veil of Your suffering and pain so that I may see the love that led You to this moment. As I gaze upon this beauty may I bring You delight and be transformed by Your Mercy. Jesus, I trust in You.

Reflection 343: Glorifying the Lord in All Things

It's easy to be grateful only when things go well. But when times are tough we tend to turn in on ourselves in self-pity. But you must learn to glorify the Lord in all things. There are countless blessings and graces that God gives you for which you must experience immense gratitude. Family blessings, spiritual consolations, fulfillment of duties, etc., must all be occasions of gratitude. But gratitude must permeate everything in life, even hardships. Seek to glorify the Lord not only because of the "good things of life," but also throughout the difficult things. Everything can be used by God for His glory and we must rejoice in that fact day and night (See *Diary* #1661-1662).

Reflect upon this "challenge." Can you find joy in all things and offer praise and gratitude to God no matter what? God is worth it and He deserves your continual praise. He never leaves you and when you realize this it will be the source of unending praise and thanksgiving.

Lord, I adore You, worship You, praise You and thank You for all things in my life. Thank You for the blessings and for always being there when life is hard. Help me to grow in my gratitude for You and to rejoice always for Your Mercy. Jesus, I trust in You.

Reflection 344: Stop Worrying About Sin

That may sound like an unusual heading. You should be concerned about sin inasmuch as you should diligently seek to avoid it. But if you were to realize that your understanding of the Mercy of God is but a drop of water compared to the ocean, you would not allow your concerns to turn into worries. To be concerned is to be conscientious and being conscientious is a grace. But when you look at your sin, honestly and thoroughly, in the light of the Mercy of God, you will never worry that your sin is too much for God. His greatest desire is to wipe it away in an instant, forever (See *Diary* #1665).

Reflect upon whether you are comfortable facing your sins with exceptional honesty. If you are not then that is a sign that you do not understand His infinite Mercy. Know that comprehending His Mercy is the best cure for every sin.

Lord, I see my sin but I want to see it more clearly. Give me the grace of knowing Your perfect Mercy so that I can face my sin without worry and without fear. Jesus, I trust in You.

Reflection 345: Drowned in God

Do you ever soak in God? This is a rare and even non-existent experience for most people. Soaking, or drowning in God means that you become immersed so deeply in prayer that it's as if you are lost in His presence. When this happens, the Lord fully takes you over and possesses your soul for that moment. You may not remain this way and you may soon return to your sins, but moments of pure contemplation are treasures in this life beyond anything else. It's a way that God gives you a taste of His glory so that you are left desiring Him all the more (See *Diary* #1669).

Consider the question of whether or not you have ever allowed yourself to be so drawn into the presence of God that you lose track of time and space. It's as if you were transported to the Heart of Christ and rested in His bosom. If you have never entered this depth of prayer know that it awaits you. The Lord's love is so deep and so perfect that, when you experience but a taste, you will be coming back for more as often as you can.

Lord, draw me into Your presence. Help me to know You and Your perfect love. Help me to experience You in perfect adoration and praise. May I receive but a glimpse of Your glory and savor that delight evermore. Jesus, I trust in You.

Reflection 346: The Gifts of Others

One act of Mercy you can offer to others is to perceive the gifts of God in their lives and to rejoice in that fact. Sadly, there can often be a temptation to be jealous or envious of others, especially when you see their natural talents or the grace of God in their lives. But if you can look at them with humility, your heart will be moved to see God at work in them. You will see their natural gifts as gifts from God given at the creation of their souls, and you will see their supernatural gifts as gifts from God given by His grace. Seek to rejoice in the goodness of God alive in all His children and you will add to those gifts in their lives and also in yours (See *Diary* #1671).

What is your first reaction when you see either a natural talent or a supernatural grace in another? Are you jealous or envious? Or do you rejoice that you are blessed to see God at work? Reflect honestly upon this question this day and seek the latter so that the Lord will bring forth even more blessings in your life and theirs.

Lord, I thank You for the way You are at work in all of Your children. As I see Your hand and boundless gifts, give me the grace of a joyful heart so that I may rejoice in the good things You offer to all. Jesus, I trust in You.

Reflection 347: Holy Communion

There is no greater gift in this world than Holy Communion. And yet we so often approach that Sacrament with a distracted and inattentive heart. To overcome such a distraction you must first be convinced, with your entire mind, of the deep truths of the reality of Holy Communion. You must submit, with deep faith, to the reality that God is there, fully, in veiled form, coming to unite Himself with you in the most profound way. Second, as you believe, you must make an act of the will, choosing to receive Him not only into your body, but into every part of your being. Believe and then choose and the

Lord of Mercy will transform your life through your worthy reception of Holy Communion (See *Diary* #1676).

Reflect upon the past several times you have gone forward to receive our Lord in Holy Communion. What was going through your mind at the time? Where was your heart in these moments? Renew your total trust in God as He comes to you through this most Precious Gift and resolve to receive Him more worthily the next time you receive this privilege.

Lord, please do renew my love for You as You come to me in Holy Communion. May I understand You as You come to me in this Precious Gift and may I choose You with my entire will. Jesus, I trust in You.

Reflection 348: God Fulfills what He Reveals

It's amazing to consider two facts side by side. First, consider that Saint Faustina heard Jesus tell her, over and over, that He desired that the Feast of Divine Mercy be promulgated and celebrated on the Second Sunday of Easter every year. How was this lowly cloistered nun to accomplish such a task for the universal Church? Second, when St. John Paul II canonized Saint Faustina on Divine Mercy Sunday, 2000, our Holy Father promulgated that the Feast of Divine Mercy Sunday was to become a universal feast of the Church. God spoke this to the heart of Saint Faustina in silence and solitude over and over from 1931-1938. Just over sixty years later, it came to be (See *Diary* #1680).

Reflect upon the fact that God often calls you to do far more than you could ever imagine doing on your own. If you are attentive to His clear gentle Voice, and if you heed His commands, you will begin to discover that the Lord will do amazing things through your life. They may not be extraordinarily public and noticeable by all, but they will be far more than you ever thought possible. Do not be amazed at

God's Will for your life and do not hesitate to believe what He calls you to do. Say "Yes" and leave the rest to Him.

Lord, to whatever You call me I say "Yes." If Your Will is that I live a quiet hidden life, offering my daily duties as a sacrifice to You, I say "Yes." If it is Your Will that my life become very public and that You use me in this way for the good of the Church, then I say "Yes." Lord, my life is Yours, do with me what You will. Jesus, I trust in You.

Reflection 349: Losing Your Peace of Heart

What is it that has the power to steal away the peace and calm of your heart? What if you were insulted, ridiculed, falsely judged, imprisoned, beaten or even killed? Would any of these rob the peace of God in your heart? Only if you let it. It is essential that you know and believe with firm faith that nothing can steal the peace of your heart unless you let it. Your goal must be to be free from everything in this world. You must be detached from all riches, honors, respect, fear and everything. If you are fully detached then you are free to be fully attached to Christ and no matter what comes your way, no matter what happens to you, your single attachment to our Lord and His Will, can never be taken away from you unless you let it (See *Diary* #1685).

Reflect upon the things that have taken away your peace in the past. Identifying these will help you realize what it is that you are attached to in an unhealthy way. If, for example, public ridicule has stolen your peace, then you are too attached to your reputation. If poverty has left you depressed, then you are too attached to money. If the rejection of a friend or family member has turned you to anger, then you were too attached to this person. This list could go on and on. Though the spiritual goal of total detachment may be very hard to understand and even harder to accept, do not dismiss it too quickly. Reflect upon attachments you have, even to apparent good things. Realize that if the one attachment you have is to God, all good things will follow.

Lord, I choose You and Your Will as my one possession in life. All else is passing and all else can be lost in an instant. But You, oh Lord, are eternal and You can never be taken away if I choose You. I love You, dear Lord, help me to remain firmly attached to You and Your Will. Jesus, I trust in You.

Reflection 350: Beauty in Adoration

The world is beautiful and reveals the beauty of God, but spiritual realities, such as the Holy Eucharist, are far more beautiful. To see the beauty of God, present in the Most Holy Eucharist, you need eyes of faith. One of the best ways to sharpen your vision of this beauty is through adoration. Though receiving Holy Communion must be the ultimate union we experience with our Lord, adoration of Him, present in the Sacred Host, prepares you for this encounter by revealing His beauty. Seek to adore Him exposed in the monstrance on the altar and let the eyes of your soul become enthralled by His beauty (See *Diary* #1692).

Do you ever participate in adoration of the Most Holy Eucharist? If you have adoration regularly at your church, you are blessed. If not, seek it out at a nearby church. Adoration feeds your soul and reveals to you the beauty of God. Reflect upon your experience of Eucharistic adoration and recommit yourself to a wholehearted participation in this glorious act.

Lord, I adore You with the most profound adoration as You are present before me in the Most Holy Eucharist. I love You and seek to know Your hidden beauty and splendor. You are glorious, dear Lord. As I behold Your glory, draw me ever deeper into Your perfect Heart of Mercy. Jesus, I trust in You.

Reflection 351: To Know or Experience God

It must be your constant goal to know God. Study of Scripture, the teachings of the Church, and the lives of the saints all help in this endeavor. But knowing God is not the ultimate goal of life. Knowledge comes from faith and faith is a gift from God. But being fully united to God in charity is of far greater importance. They are not opposed, but they are not the same. In fact, at times the Lord will darken one's mind and not even allow it to understand Him so that He can, instead, transform the will so that this holy soul will choose Him and live a life of charity even in the darkness of faith. This is a deep mystery (See *Diary* #1697).

Are there times when you feel as though you cannot understand God or His ways? Do you experience a cloudy vision and dimmed intellect? If so, this may be a grace of far greater value than you know. It is in these moments, especially, that God invites you to love and to choose His Will despite the fog that appears to have set in. Choose His Will and live charity even when it does not make perfect sense to you and the Lord will bring forth much Mercy through you.

Lord, I thank You for the times of clarity in life. But even when my mind seems darkened and confused, I submit to Your holy Will. Help me to love You and others in those moments so that my life may be a living instrument of Your pure Mercy. Jesus, I trust in You.

Reflection 352: Chastisement and Guilt

It may not be pleasant to consider the chastisement of God. But it must be understood that His chastisements are real and are an act of His abundant Mercy. When souls turn from God and refuse His Mercy, this deeply wounds His Heart. As a result, God becomes more "passionate" so to speak in His tireless pursuit. One way He seeks to open their hearts is through chastisements. Think of the Pharisees, for example. They were filled with pride and egotism and the Lord rebuked them harshly. But He did so to win them back as an act of great Mercy. It worked for some, for others it did not (See *Diary* #1703).

Are you aware of the chastisements of God? For example, have you felt the pain of extreme guilt for your sins? If so, pay attention to this. Know that if you have gone astray, especially through pride, the Lord will pour down judgment upon you. If you persist, He will pour it down with a vengeance. And when a soul remains obstinate, God's Mercy cannot enter. But when these chastisements produce a sense of holy guilt, this means that the conscience is working and is in a position to change. Do not hold onto guilt and do not ignore it. Run to the Mercy of God so that He can free you from your sin and return His peace to your heart.

Lord, please give me the grace I need to turn to You in all things. May I never be in need of the fierce chastisements of Your Mercy. But if I am in need of this grace, please help me to respond with conversion from my sins. Jesus, I trust in You.

Reflection 353: A Hymn of Glory

Music is a discovery and expression of the natural laws of God's creation, relying upon the order and rhythm found in its natural design. Some music uses the natural order of things to glorify earthly realities. Some forms of music even express sin and disorder. But the greatest form of music is that which beautifully and clearly articulates the high order, harmony and symmetry of the life of God. Our lives become like a hymn of glory, offered to God, when we act in perfect harmony with the Will of God. The "music" of your soul must become a hymn of this glory (See *Diary* #1708).

Reflect upon the idea of your life being like a hymn. What does the "hymn of your life" sound like? Is it ordered, beautiful and reflective of the inner life of God? Or does your life better express disorder and interior dysfunction? Be honest and ponder the "music" that comes forth from your life. Allow the Master Musician to take hold of you so as to bring forth a hymn worthy of His glory.

Lord, may my life become a hymn of worship, rising up to Your glorious throne of grace, echoing forth the lovely melody of Your inner life. Take hold of me, dear Lord, and use me as Your instrument of Mercy and Grace in this world. Jesus, I trust in You.

Reflection 354: Untying the Web of Sin

When a person begins to lie, and forms a habit of this sort, they will eventually become entangled in a web of lies. One lie leads to another and pretty soon they do not know how to break free of this web. This is where you must offer mercy. It's very easy to be harsh toward someone who has clearly led themselves down the wrong path. It's easy to point the finger and rub in their sin. But the Lord wants you to look at this person with love and help untangle them from the web they have woven. This is done by being clear and direct about their errors, but also without judgment or harshness. If they perceive you to be offering the truth with mercy, they may just accept your invitation to undo that which they have done. This principle applies to many types of sins (See *Diary* #1712).

Reflect upon anyone in your life who appears to be tangled in a web of sin and cannot get out. Let your heart grow in mercy for this person, refraining from all judgment. Love them, seek to bring them the humbling truth and do so gently but clearly so that they can be set free.

Lord, sin binds us and causes much distress in life. Give me the grace of a merciful heart so that I can be an instrument of freedom to those caught in a life of sin. Give me the grace, dear Lord, to love them with Your perfect Heart of Mercy.

Reflection 355: Idle Talk, a Sign of an Idle Soul

Some people are very good at talking about others. They offer continual opinions and judgments of them and speak freely, as if they have everything figured out. Do not be like one of these people. Those who have their minds and tongues occupied with the activities of others have little time to look into their own souls so as to discover who they are (See *Diary* #1717).

Do you struggle with idle talk? In other words, do you speak regularly and freely about others, issuing opinions and judgments upon them while, at the same time, fail to honestly evaluate your own soul? If you do this it may be hard to admit it. But if this is you, admit it here and now. Tell our Lord you are aware of this struggle and seek His Mercy as your help. He will help you, but only if you are honest with your struggle.

Lord, please free me from the idle chatter and judgments I tend to place upon others. Help me, instead, to become truly recollected and aware of my own life and sin. Help me to also see the abundance of Your Mercy which I must rely upon and offer to others. My Lord, I repent of my sin, please come to my help. Jesus, I trust in You.

Reflection 356: The Beating of Your Heart

When there is excitement in your life, your heart begins to beat faster. This is a natural reaction. For that reason, it is good to ponder whether your heart ever beats for God? Do you allow yourself to become caught up in a holy awe of the presence of

God? Do you become excited about the mission that God has given you? And, if so, do you ever find that your heart beats faster as you ponder the great mysteries of His love and Mercy? Your whole being must react to the majesty and splendor of our glorious God (See *Diary* #1728).

Try this simple examination today. Ponder the last time that you truly became excited over God and His holy Will. Was your excitement something that affected you so much that even your heart began to beat faster? Though this may not be an infallible sign of the presence of God in your life, it may reveal much more than you realize.

Lord, I desire that my heart beat for You every day. May I experience the joy and excitement of Your perfect glory and desire with my mind, spirit and even body, the fulfillment of Your Will. I love You, dear Lord. May my heart beat for You with great intensity and love. Jesus, I trust in You.

Reflection 357: The Promptings of Grace

When someone is troubled, you may shy away from them. It's easy to think that engaging them will impose a heavy burden on your time and energy. But if the Lord is the one directing your conversation, He can do amazing things in a short while. Sure, there are times when love demands many hours of care, but often times a few words, a listening ear, or a gentle smile will do more for a person in need than you could ever imagine (See *Diary* #1736).

Reflect upon the fact that God is able to accomplish amazing things with very little effort on your part. All it takes is a willing response to the gentle promptings of His Heart so as to speak a kind word, listen to a burdened heart, or offer a work of charity. If it's done as a result of the promptings of the Holy Spirit, it will be amazingly simple, delightful and well worth the effort. Ponder how well you listen to the daily inspirations of the Holy Spirit and seek to act the next time you are moved to do so.

Lord, I pray that I will always be ready and willing to act as an instrument of Your Mercy. Please inspire me, dear Lord, to act on the promptings that You send me, and help me to express Your love to others in the simplest of ways. Jesus, I trust in You.

Reflection 358: God's Twofold Gift

Often, when we speak of the Mercy of God, we speak of the forgiveness of sins. This is the first act of God's Mercy. He sees every sin, even the slightest imperfection, and despite the suffering these sins impose upon Our Lord, He lavishly bestows Mercy to forgive. Forgiveness becomes total and permanent. God never brings up sins that have been forgiven. But God doesn't stop there. It's important to understand that God bestows many graces in addition to forgiveness. One such grace is that, when He forgives a particular sin, He actually transforms it in such a way that He is able to use it for our good. Amazingly, God is even able to use sin for His glory in the end (See *Diary* #1745).

Reflect upon two things. First, look at the forgiveness that God has offered you for past sins. This should leave you with humble gratitude. Second, look for ways that God has used even your past sins, once forgiven, for His glory. The Lord's Mercy is overwhelming and awe-inspiring. Allow it to leave you in eternal gratitude.

Lord, I thank You for the forgiveness that You offer me and even more for the infinite grace that You bestow after You forgive. I pray that I will always be aware of these graces and will open my heart to them without hesitation. I love you, dear Lord, and I am eternally grateful to You for all things. Jesus, I trust in You.

Reflection 359: The Love of Eternity

With God there is no time. Time is strictly an earthly phenomenon. In God, all things are, always were and always will be. One effect of this eternal love is that God has loved you for all eternity. He has known you even before the foundation of the world and will know and love you forevermore. This all-encompassing love should give you great comfort. There never was a time that God did not perfectly love you and there never will be a time when His love fails. God's love is eternal, and it is offered before you were created, every second of your life, and for eternity and beyond (See *Diary* #1754).

Ponder eternity today. Though it's possible to understand what eternity means, it's impossible to comprehend its depths. Ponder also the simple fact that God's love is eternal. For that reason, the same truth applies. You can understand that God's love is eternal, but you will never comprehend the depths of God's love. This is very comforting to know.

God of Eternity, I thank You for Your perfect love and for its infinite nature and depth. May I spend my eternity plunging into this love, never growing weary of receiving it and becoming more immersed in its beauty. Jesus, I trust in You.

Reflection 360: Spiritual Battle

The tempter, satan, is real, but he is no one to fear. You should pay no attention to him. You should not engage his ideas. You should not bargain with him. In the face of temptations you should have courage, trust in the Mercy of God, and hope. Do not become curious about the sins of others, do not talk about them, do not be upset when mistreated, and do not complain. Seek wise counsel from others when confused and listen to their advice, as long as it leaves you at peace and is from the Lord. Have strong convictions and do not worry about the battles of this world. Keep your mind and heart on Jesus and let Him defend you (See *Diary* #1760).

When you feel the oppression of the evil one, how do you react? Do you allow your feelings to take over and enter into anger, despair and doubt? When a spiritual battle rages within, there is one defense. Put your eyes on Jesus and not on the temptations or evils. Seek out His peace and remain sheltered in His Mercy. Reflect upon how well you do this. If you struggle, then resolve to pray, pray and pray some more.

Lord, You and You alone can fight off the temptations of the evil one. Give me the grace to keep my eyes on You and to trust in Your abundant Mercy. Give me Your peace in times of adversity and courage to face all that I may endure. Jesus, I trust in You.

Reflection 361: Sacrifice and Prayer

Though this may be hard to understand and to believe, interior sacrifice united with pure prayer does incredible good for the proclamation of the Gospel throughout the world. In fact, if missionaries did not have the power of holy souls who offered daily interior sacrifices and prayers, their efforts would have little effect. The grace of God is what moves people and this grace is especially won through souls whose sacrifices are: silent, hidden, permeated with love and imbued with prayer. (See *Diary* #1767).

Reflect upon the fact that you have so very much to offer for the upbuilding of the Kingdom of God through your personal and interior sacrifices. By choosing those things that are difficult, and even repulsive to your feelings, you are able to offer powerful intercession for the good of the Church. There is an incredible amount of spiritual power in this kind of sacrifice. God chooses some special souls to offer this sacrifice in a profound way, but everyone must strive to do so. Reflect upon the opportunities you have right now to embrace some interior struggle. By embracing it and offering it to God, you transform this suffering into grace that prayer and work alone could never achieve.

Lord, help me to understand the power of my interior sacrifices. Help me to know that choosing You and embracing my sufferings for You becomes a powerful source of grace in this world. When this confuses me, dear Lord, help me to put my eyes on You and to know Your most holy Will. Jesus, I trust in You.

Reflection 362: Two Hearts of Mercy

Jesus' Heart is pure Mercy. It's a fountain of grace pouring out upon the world. This is consoling but there is another heart that must also become a fountain of Mercy, and that is yours. You must become so immersed in the Mercy of the Lord that your heart bursts forth with rivers of grace for others. This is especially how God touches those souls who are lost and do not pray. By you going to them, loving them with great devotion and lavishing the Mercy of God upon them, their hearts meet the Lord's (See *Diary* #1777).

Reflect upon your call to be the very Heart of Christ to others. His Heart must beat in yours and His Mercy must become yours. This takes total surrender and requires much personal sacrifice. But if you can allow our Lord to flood your heart with His Mercy, the overflow from your heart will affect countless others.

Lord, please make my heart Your Heart. I give it to You dear Lord to use in this world to touch many lives. May I so humble myself before You that a flood of Mercy flows through me to touch the lives of many. I love

You dear Lord, help me to love all Your children with a burning love. Jesus, I trust in You.

Reflection 363: Hearing God Speak

Imagine you were in a crowded room with much noise and someone whispered to you from across the room. You may notice them trying to speak but it would be difficult to hear. This is much like the Voice of God. When God speaks, He whispers. He speaks gently and quietly and only those who are truly recollected throughout the day will notice His Voice and hear what He says. The Lord wants us to eliminate the many distractions of our day, the constant noise of the world and all that drowns out His gentle command of love. Seek to be recollected, silencing the noise of the world, and the Lord's gentle Voice will become crystal clear (See *Diary* #1779).

Do you hear God speak to you? If not, what is it that distracts you and competes for your attention? Look into your heart and know that the gentle Voice of God speaks to you day and night. Try to be absolutely attentive to His Voice of perfect love, and follow all that He asks. Ponder His Voice not only today, but always. Build a habit of attentiveness so that you will never miss a word that He says.

Lord, I love You with a burning love and desire to hear You speak to me always. Help me to eliminate the many distractions of life so that nothing will ever compete with Your gentle Voice. Jesus, I trust in You.

Reflection 364: Prayer for the Dying

In regard to your eternal salvation, the hour of your death is so very important. When you pray the "Hail Mary" prayer, you pray specifically for this sacred hour. It is a holy hour. But it is also an hour when the evil one will lash out at you one more time to try to steal your soul for all eternity. It is essential that you spend your life preparing for this sacred hour by your prayers, a life of sacrifice, and a life of charity. But it is also essential that you pray for those who are in their last hour. For some, this is a moment of true spiritual battle. See it as a duty of charity to regularly remember those who are in their last hour in your prayers. They will thank you in Heaven (See *Diary* #1798).

Reflect upon your death this day, and especially try to pray the rosary for this moment. Consider, also, making a commitment to pray for those who are dying. Death brings many temptations, such as fear, and is a time when much grace is needed. Pray that every soul, including your own, will enter this hour with confidence and faith, trusting in the abundant Mercy of God.

Lord, I offer You my last hour in this life and pray for all those who will face this moment today. May it be a sweet hour in which we are surrounded by Your angels and saints. May we especially receive the consolation of knowing the prayers of Your dear Mother at this moment. Mother Mary, pray for us, now and at the hour of our death. Amen. Jesus, I trust in You.

Reflection 365: The Queen of Mercy

This last reflection is dedicated to the Queen of Mercy, the Most Glorious Mother of God. She, more than any other, was and continues to be a perfect instrument of the Mercy of God. She brought forth Mercy Himself into this world by her *fiat,* her "Yes," at the Annunciation. She suffered greatly as she watched her Son suffer such brutality, and offered her motherly love to console His Heart and to win much grace in the world through her sacrifice. She was taken body and soul into Heaven and given the Crown of Glory by her Son, so that from her glorious throne in Heaven, she may continue to lavish Mercy on the world. Seek her prayers, trust in her intercession, consecrate yourself to her motherly care, and know of her perfect love for you. She will never abandon her children and, therefore, she will never abandon you.

Dearest Mother, my Queen, I love you with a profound love and I desire to consecrate myself to your Immaculate Heart. Your heart, dear Mother, is a heart overflowing with the Mercy of Your Son. He has given you all grace and entrusted you with the dispensation of this grace upon the world. May I never doubt your maternal care and intercession. I love you, dear Mother. I give myself entirely to you so that you may bring me to Your Son, Jesus. Mother Mary, my Queen, pray for me. Jesus, I trust in You.

Made in United States
North Haven, CT
01 May 2022

18759418R10209